The Church's Ministry With Families

The Church's Ministry With Families

A Practical Guide

Diana S. Richmond Garland, Ph.D.
Diane L. Pancoast, Ph.D.

WORD PUBLISHING
Dallas·London·Vancouver·Melbourne

THE CHURCH'S MINISTRY WITH FAMILIES

Library of Congress Cataloging-in-Publication Data

The Church's ministry with families : a practical guide / Diana S.
    Richmond Garland, Diane L. Pancoast, editors.
        p. cm.
    Includes bibliographical references.
    ISBN 0-8499-3141-X :
    1. Church work with families.   I. Garland, Diana S. Richmond,
1950-   . II. Pancoast, Diane L.
BV4438.C49   1990
259'.1—dc20
                                                    90-33119
                                                    CIP

Printed in the United States of America
9 8 0 1 2 3 9 AGF 9 8 7 6 5 4 3 2 1

Dedication

To all the churches who have committed themselves to ministry with families and who have given us the opportunity to know and learn from them.

Contents

Acknowledgments

We extend our gratitude to the many persons whose support has made this volume possible:

To the Paul Adkins Institute for Research and Training of the Carver School of Church Social Work, the Continuing Education Department of The Southern Baptist Theological Seminary, and the Sunday School Board of the Southern Baptist Convention, who sponsored the conference "Church and Families: New Directions in Church Social Work and Family Ministry" in October 1987. The purposes of this conference were to (1) explore biblical and theological concepts of the family as they support and expand our cultural focus on the nuclear family; (2) develop models for ministry with families which go beyond current models, focusing on parent-child and marital relationships; (3) describe ways families can be a focus of ministry, both by incorporating persons into family networks, and by developing the family's potential for ministry in its own context; and (4) articulate together a new foundation for church social work with families. This conference enabled many of the contributors to begin the discussion with one another that has culminated in this volume.

To the Lilly Foundation, which has provided travel funds for the editors so that we could bridge the thousands of miles that separate us and thus do our work more effectively.

To the faculty of the Carver School of Church Social Work, Dean Anne Davis, and Provost Willis Bennett, who have been especially supportive and encouraging during the four years it has taken to organize the conference and edit this volume.

To the many students of The Southern Baptist Theological Seminary who have read drafts of several chapters and provided helpful critique and suggestions.

To the Retirement Research Foundation for supporting James Ellor and Sheldon Tobin in their research on the church as service-provider to the elderly.

To Pauletta Dick, David Akers, and other staff in the seminary's office services who have tirelessly typed numerous drafts of several chapters and in other ways assisted us in this project.

To the contributors of this volume, who have worked diligently with us and tolerated and have been responsive to our suggestions for revisions that would weave all our separate efforts into one volume.

To our own families, who have supported us and been patient with the long hours that this project has required.

A most significant benefit of this project, from our perspective, has been the opportunity to develop a working relationship with one another and to nurture a growing informal network of social workers and other helping professionals working in churches and church agencies. To all those who have given us the gifts of their time and encouragement, we express our heartfelt thanks.

Diana S. Richmond Garland, Ph.D.   Diane L. Pancoast, Ph.D.
Louisville, Kentucky   Portland, Oregon

Foreword

The people who make up the families of the early 1990s, with the exception of infants, were born in and thus are heirs of the culture of previous decades who bring their memories to anything they read. To be a bit too neat about decades, the picture goes something like this:

In the fifties "we" overproduced babies, in a setting which overvalued the nuclear family and undervalued the independent career interests of women. Too *much* family. In the sixties, the young rebelled, adults turned to "new morality" to develop a new sexual and family ethic, and everything fell apart. In the seventies, the family suffered because it was the "Me Decade," and families can only survive if people conceive of "We" and not just "Me." Americans did their own thing, their way—and not even "Dad's Way," or "Sister's Way." In the eighties, the Decade of Greed, we turned phony about the family, talking a good line about traditional values while departing from them ever more.

Of course, not everyone conformed to these patterns, and the talk about them was sometimes as much the creation of mass media as it was a signal of reality, accurately depicted. Still, we live with the legacy of past cultural decisions, including the stereotypes people had about the forms of life in which they participated. Any fresh thought about the family, then, appears against the background of such inheritances and pictures. They can be limiting. The family is in trouble: are we free to receive help in addressing the troubles, or are we limited by ideologies and prejudices?

For instance, look at the impact of two poles of thought. Because liberals and moderates were more exposed to the stresses and lures of life in the sixties—they had no defenses, no sects into which to crawl—they seemed to change the most. Extreme individualism, the enemy of the family, afflicted their world immediately. The sexual revolution, the feminist movement, the new morality, came closest to their homes. So the word got out: only cultural traditionalists and fundamentalists care about "family values."

Not so. If homes broke up because of the cultural revolution, there were as many tears on liberal cheeks as there would be on any others; when children rebelled, turned "hippie" and took to drugs or rebelled without a cause, their liberal parents cried. People who might in public participate in efforts to discern new ethical patterns would return to their private spheres and, in confidence, then tell how hard it was for them to endure. They wanted help.

How recover now, when we know the old cultural revolutions are spent; that they failed to deliver on their promises, and offer no hope now? Here is where stereotypes and expectations lead to confusion. Not long ago a very well-reputed Christian ethicist told me that he had grown ever more curious about the family: he had things to discover and to say about the future of the family. But if he made the family a specialty, would he lose his reputation? "After all, in the eyes of many people, families are what fundamentalists fight about; dare anyone else set out to focus on the family?"

As for the other side, the conservatives who camp on family values; how are they doing? The stresses are there, too. They find increasingly less place to hide; their "sects" are porous, and their children are influenced by whatever is out there on television, in the rock music culture, in the high school and young adult world. The parents in these families also feel the impact of the cultural forces and find that their defenses falter, that they have less to say and do about countering them and coming up with positive family values, than they might like to advertise.

One bit of documentation for the hunch that not all is well: one need only look at the seasonal catalogs of publishers who serve evangelicals, pentecostals, fundamentalists, and conservatives, to see that there is a market for books which are realistic about sexuality, marriage, life between the generations, and the family. One will find scores of books, for example, telling conservative Christian adults how to live after divorce. Whereas evangelical books formerly talked only about the *sin* of divorce, now on page 1 they talk about tragedy, sin, inevitability, guilt—and, then, about forgiveness and the need for a new life. The rest of the books offer often helpful prescription, whereas conservative books used to talk about how the devil lured the Other People into abuse, dependency, and hatred, now they tell how to use the power of God to find freedom from abuse and dependency and to recover love when bad things happen to Our Kind of People.

It is time, then, for people of left and right, and particularly of Christian liberal and conservative backgrounds, to admit that they need help and that they need a place of common ground. There they deal frankly with the problems of the family. There they can find resources to deal hopefully with the promises for the family. It is too late to enjoy keeping up appearances, acting as if all is well when it is not, with the family. It is also too late for anyone to wallow in despair, acting as if nothing can be done about the family, when much can be done, not least in the spheres shaped by Christian faith and hope.

I thought of this new common ground, this possibility of new approaches— once we get past accusing ourselves and others, claiming virtues we do not have or ruing vices not unique to "our kind"—as I read the galleys for the book you hold in your hand. Its authors are expert. They know their limits: no one has easy solutions. But they draw on their research and experience to present a "state of the art" approach. One learns here of the power of ritual in family life; of the networks one needs to reinforce the family; of the need for new definitions even as we draw upon the past. This is not one more literary gripe session or finger-pointing episode. It is a miniature encyclopedia of resources. Instead of an exercise in the pointing of fingers, it is an invitation to use the fingers for turning pages, an activity from which the writer of a Foreword should keep you no longer. Identify, enjoy, profit, and help rebuild, one is tempted to say, in the spirit of the authors of these pages.

Martin E. Marty
The University of Chicago

PART ONE
A Theoretical and Theological Overview

1

The Church's Ministry with Families: An Introduction

Diana S. Richmond Garland

Churches are concerned about families. Church leaders publicly worry about national divorce statistics and privately express dismay that families in their own congregations are troubled. Churches invest major portions of their resources in services and programs for families in crisis and for preventing family troubles and strengthening family relationships. These services and programs, along with everything from aerobics classes to emergency financial assistance for persons in need, are called *family ministry*.

To help churches channel their concern for families into effective ministry, this book defines family ministry, presents theoretical and biblical frameworks for this field of church leadership, and describes models which church leaders can use for family ministry in their own congregations and communities. Additionally, social workers and community planners interested in the potential of churches for contributing to the social welfare of the community will find this book useful. In this chapter, we offer a definition of family ministry intended both to limit and to sharpen this ministry emphasis. We begin by looking at some actual examples of family ministry:

A Sunday School class of young married couples spends a weekend in a state park lodge on a marriage enrichment retreat. Their church has provided financial resources to enable them to have professional leaders for sessions focusing on conflict management, changing sex roles, intimacy, and Christian marriage.

A large inner-city church hires a director of family ministry to administer and develop programs for the church's recreational complex which includes basketball and handball

---

DIANA S. RICHMOND GARLAND, M.S.S.W., Ph.D., is associate professor of social work in the Carver School of Church Social Work at The Southern Baptist Theological Seminary. An author of books and articles on family issues, Dr. Garland has served as a social worker and director in a community mental health center and pastoral counseling agency.

courts, a skating rink, and a swimming pool. The facility is made available to the families in the surrounding community as well as to the church membership. Meeting rooms are available for a wide variety of groups, including chapters of Alcoholics Anonymous and Al-Anon, Adults Molested as Children, Recovery, Girl Scouts, and Boy Scouts. Seminars are offered for the recently divorced, the recently widowed, those facing retirement, and parents of children in differing age groups.

A denominational publishing house employs eighteen professional personnel, nine secretaries, and a host of contract writers to prepare resources for family ministry in churches throughout the denomination. These include periodicals on family life, raising children, single life, and aging; courses and leader's guides for married couples and parents; guides for developing family ministry programs in local churches; and cable television programs and videotapes on ministering with families. Many of the users of these materials, including family life course leaders, are persons in churches who have no formal education in family issues or professional helping but have a desire to strengthen family relationships in their congregations.

A social worker employed by a denominational child welfare agency provides family counseling, family crisis intervention, and prevention services through a newly-opened Family Resource Center. The social worker speaks often to local church congregations about her work and encourages persons to volunteer to help in various programs of the Family Resource Center which include a foster grandparent program, a drop-in center for families at risk for child abuse, and a parent warmline.

Family ministry includes *any services provided by a church or church agency, whether by a helping professional or a nonprofessional volunteer, which aim to strengthen the relationships between family members.* Family ministry can be offered by any number of persons—(1) professional church leaders in traditional church staff positions such as pastor and Christian educator; (2) professional social workers, pastoral counselors, and psychologists who are hired by the church or a group of churches because of their particular expertise in working with families; or (3) church members who are neither paid staff of the church nor family service professionals but who have a commitment to ministering with families. Family ministry is not defined by the person offering service but by the context in which services are offered—the church. It is, in fact, the ministry of the church, offered through a variety of professionals and nonprofessionals, in response to the needs of families both within and outside the church membership.

The term *ministry* creates confusion; it has unfortunately been used interchangeably with those who are *pastors,* even though these terms are not equivalents. "Minister" is synonymous with *Christian;* every Christian is a minister, expected to help others, whether that help takes the form of personal care or concern, social services, or social change efforts (Cox 1967; Delamarter 1970; Pinson 1971; Stagg 1981). The role of minister therefore transcends professional identity; it is an approach to all the roles in which Christians find themselves. According to this perspective, church members cannot pay persons to be the *minister* and by so doing escape the personal responsibility for living lives of service to others. Even so, the ministers of the church need leaders, who are often professionals employed by the church, to guide them in ministry. Churches therefore turn to professionals to provide leadership, direction, and education of lay persons—the ministers—for family ministry.

Professional Leadership in Family Ministry

Family ministry does not belong to any one of the professions which provide leadership in the church (pastor, educator, social worker, psychologist), and it includes, consequently, widespread interdisciplinary involvement of church leadership. Some churches, as in one of the examples, have created staff positions specifically titled *Director of Family Ministry* or have added this specialty to other traditional church leadership roles.

The evolution of family ministry as a specialty for clergy parallels what has been happening in all of the helping professions. Physicians have been embracing the *family medicine* specialization with enthusiasm; since its introduction as a specialization fifteen years ago, it has become a strong trend in medical care worldwide (Geyman 1985). Systems theory, developed in the sixties, has identified the family as a key focus for intervention in the lives of individuals for a variety of problems, even problems which appear on the surface to be individual rather than family troubles. Consequently, increasing numbers of students wanting to become helping professionals have abandoned educational programs which follow the traditional professional lines of social work, psychology, psychiatry, and the clergy to enter programs in family therapy and family studies.

Among helping professionals, the push for a new name and new professional designation continues. *Family science* is now appearing in the names of educational programs (i.e., Masters of Family Science) and in research and professional practice journals. Helping professionals are joining family organizations such as the American Association of Marriage and Family Therapists in addition to or in place of membership in professional organizations defined along traditional professional boundaries.

The shift in emphasis toward family is hardly occurring in the professions only; politicians are rushing in to support the American family. Rapid social changes in the industrialized countries, such as the changing roles of women, family mobility, urbanization, decreasing birth rates, and increases in expectations for the quality of life, have contributed to significant changes in family life. Americans are waiting longer to marry; the average couple marries two years later than they did fifteen years ago. Almost one out of two marriages ends in divorce, and more people are deciding not to marry at all. The result is that 20.6 million Americans live alone, a jump of 90 percent since 1970 (Around the Network 1986). To many Americans, the very institution of the family appears threatened. The popularity of family ministry among budding church leaders and as focus for church programs, then, reflects cultural as well as professional concerns.

Various professions that provide leadership to churches want to provide guidance, so there is inevitably some scrambling to stake out professional territories (Garland 1983). There is also the opportunity for cross-disciplinary sharing and the consequent enrichment of family ministry as it draws from several professional roots. It is in the spirit of such cross-disciplinary sharing that this book is written. In *The Church's Ministry with Families*, we present a social work perspective on the issues, possibilities, and practice of family ministry. We hope that social workers working in and with churches will find it useful and that it will also be useful to pastors, pastoral counselors, Christian educators, and others who are leading family ministry, as well as community human-service professionals who want to work with churches.

Social work has the purpose of maintaining and enhancing the psychosocial functioning of individuals, families, and small groups "by maximizing the availability of needed intrapersonal, interpersonal, and societal resources" (Cohen 1979, 30). Social work begins with the person-in-situation, concentrating on the interaction between the individual and the individual's environment. The most immediate social environment for most persons is the family. Historically, social workers "have always thought of themselves and have been seen by others as professionals who 'work with families'" (Hartman and Laird 1983, 11). Even though social workers are only recently being added to staffs of local church congregations in any significant numbers (Garland 1987b), social workers have long been involved in the social ministries of the church as employees of the agencies and institutions of the church which serve families. And historically, social work's roots are in the church (Brackney and Watkins 1983; Leonard 1988; Marty 1980; Reid and Stimpson 1987). Many of the first social workers were clergy who were educated for their vocation in seminary.

This book looks at family ministry, then, from the interactional perspective of the social work profession. As we seek to describe family ministry, however, we see that the confusion over definitions reflects a generalized confusion of professional boundaries and a variety of perspectives in the whole area of family studies and family services.

Family Ministry as Program or Perspective

Despite the recent flurry of activity in the name of family ministry, there appears to be no common agreement on what family ministry is and what it is not. One denominational agency defines it as ministry to the needs of persons as they relate to one another in families, to themselves, and to God (Family Ministry Department 1986). It is difficult to think of a ministry that would not fall under this definition. What, then, is unique about family ministry?

Without identifiable boundaries, family ministry is simply another name for ministry. Sell argues that family ministry "needs to be integrated into the life of the church rather than being one more program among many others" (Sell 1981, 5). Although few would argue with that statement, without clearer definitions of family ministry, there is little choice but to focus on programs and products to define family ministry. Since there is no clear conceptual definition of what is and is not family ministry, it becomes pragmatically defined as any program under family ministry leadership.

The gaps between family ministry programs, however, create a major difficulty. There must be an overarching conceptual definition of family ministry against which to evaluate programs. Since family ministry is defined programatically rather than conceptually, family ministry becomes whatever programs the church provides for families. For example, church family ministry staff often

- provide family life education programing and other preventive services for church and community families,
- spearhead special emphases on family issues in all church programs, and
- provide or oversee counseling services for individuals and families both within the church and in the larger community.

Some churches are now operating multistaff counseling centers which use sliding fee scales as part of their ministry to families. Family ministry is thus defined as family life education and family counseling.

In one such church, family ministry has the dual focus of prevention and services to troubled families. Professional staff equip lay teams to provide services such as marriage enrichment, grief ministry, parenting groups, and support services for those experiencing job transitions. Specialists in play therapy, couples and family therapy, counseling with adolescents, drug and alcohol counseling, financial counseling, and crisis intervention are available in the church's counseling center. Although the church is also engaged in social action which relates to the family, such as community task forces on pornography and on drug abuse, these activities are not conceptualized as part of family ministry per se—they are not family life education or counseling.

Certainly, churches cannot be criticized for providing much-needed educational and support programs and counseling services. A definition of family ministry which simply reflects current practice, however, assumes that, since this is what churches are doing, this is what family ministry is and should be. This creates two problems. First, the description of current programs becomes the prescription for future programs. There is no conceptual framework which generates innovative programs responsive to the changing needs and structures of families.

Second, if family-ministry programs are limited to education and counseling, churches imply that the problems families experience are largely the result of ignorance (thus the need for education) or inadequacy (thus the need for counseling). So conceived, family-ministry programs inadvertently suggest that crises brought on by outside forces (e.g., unemployment, inadequate child care, neighborhood change) are best dealt with by teaching individuals and families how to cope, not by challenging other social systems or developing alternative cultural norms for family living. Strengthening the social networks of the family, family advocacy, and intervention in social structures and communities have received little attention from family ministry. This is not the fault of churches and church agencies; it indicates the lack of an adequate conceptual framework to aid them in their ministry.

We would suggest that family ministry may need to include family life education and counseling, but it needs to be conceptualized more broadly than any particular configuration of programs, methods, or intervention strategies. *We would define family ministry as any activity on the part of the church and its representatives designed to strengthen the relationships among family members.* This activity may be education, enrichment, therapy, and/or intervention in other social systems that have impact on families. The focus is not on individuals but on the actual or targeted interaction between individuals. This definition of family ministry involves both perspective and programs.

Perspective and Programs

With this definition, family ministry is a perspective from which to evaluate and intervene in all the programs and structures of the church, both formal and informal, as well as other social systems that affect families. As important as programs may be, too much is ignored when a particular set of programs is considered the centerpiece of family ministry. Instead, family ministry can provide a framework for thinking about the impact of all church ministries on family relationships. At the governmental level, Kamerman and Kahn (1978) have suggested that family ministry should serve a monitoring function, advocating for families and initiating or monitoring programs which are designed for families instead of being limited to a set of particular family programs.

In the same way, family ministry can serve as a perspective for guiding the integration and evaluation of programs and policies of the church as they affect family members and can point to needs for intervention in other social systems and in the church itself on behalf of family relationships. For example, the norm of segregating religious education programs and worship services by age often has an inadvertent impact on family life. Dual-career parents may be ambivalent about placing preschool children in the church nursery for yet another half day of group child care on Sunday in addition to the long hours their children spend in a day care center during the week. Theological positions often have direct impact on family relationships (e.g., the role of women, the use of birth control, the function of the church as an advocate for children) and need to be foci of family ministry.

This does not mean that family ministry is exclusively a perspective on the policies, processes, and ministries of the church, but that it must include both programs and perspective. So conceived, family ministry has two major tasks: (1) providing programs and (2) critically evaluating its own as well as other ministries of the church in light of their impact on family relationships. Perspective without program is empty; program without perspective is purposeless.

Family ministry thus provides the framework for programs and structures designed to strengthen family relationships. These are not limited to marriage and parenting programs, however, but address the vast array of family forms and relational needs. These include single-parent families (widows and parents who have never been married); single-parent households (parents who are divorced or separated); parents and their adult children; single adults and their roommates, close friends, and extended family; blended families; and persons who live in family-like groups (communes, residential child-care facilities, senior-citizen residences, etc.).

Boundaries

Finally, family ministry has boundaries. If family ministry focuses on developing and strengthening the relationships between persons in families, then by definition, individuals and communities and social institutions may be targets for intervention as they influence these relationships, but they are not the primary focus of concern. Family ministry involves the individual needs of persons as well as communities and social institutions. Part of the current interest in family ministry no doubt stems from increasing awareness of the problems created by the individualism which permeates our society (Bellah et al. 1985). Our culture accentuates self-actualization, the autonomy of persons, and selfhood; and family ministry appears to be an appealing antidote. A healthy balance must be maintained among the ministry foci of relationships, individuals, and communities and social institutions. To allow the pendulum to swing to an exclusive emphasis on relationships and disregard either individuals (individual autonomy, responsibilities, and spiritual development) or the larger community and social issues (concerns for world peace, social justice, and the impact of humanity on the world's ecology) unbalances the overall ministry of the church.

Although such a definition of the target of family ministry begins to offer conceptual clarity, there is still an area of significant confusion: We have yet to define family.

What Is "Family"?

Definitions of family ministry, even the one offered above, have elements of circularity: family ministry is ministry which strengthens family relationships. We do not think to define family; we assume that we all know what we are talking about. The dictionary defines *family* as "parents and their children" or "persons related by blood or marriage" (*American Heritage Dictionary*). Current family ministry embraces this definition in its targets of ministry—marital couples, parents and children, single-parent families, senior-adult families, and single adults. The nuclear family—married couple and their children—is assumed to be the norm. Target groups vary from this norm because they do not include either the parent-child relationship or the spouse-spouse relationship: *marital couples* means couples without children present; *parents and children* implies that both parents may not necessarily be involved and that the marital relationship is peripheral to the tasks of the program; *single* is the qualifier added to the parent role, not *married*, since marriage is assumed as the norm unless stated otherwise; even *senior-adult families* implies that these are families which do not contain children. By assuming that family ministry is ministry with nuclear family relationships or relationships between fragments of the nuclear family, the church implicitly endorses the nuclear family as what a family not only is but ought to be. Therefore, churches have taken the sociological definition of what a family is in our culture and have transformed that definition into what the ideal family should be. In essence, *description* has become *prescription* (Garland 1987a).

This definition creates problems for the church. First, those not living in nuclear families do not fit. If the church tries to spread the definition of family ministry to be inclusive of all people, singles have to be considered *one-person families*, those who are not living with either a spouse or a child. Family, therefore, becomes equated in many cases with *individual people* and family ministry becomes ministry to people. What distinguishes family ministry, then, from any other ministry specialization, since the basic focus of all ministry is people?

A second problem with using a nuclear definition of the family is that the Bible, the church's statement of values, offers little support for defining a strong nuclear family as the goal of Christian relationships. Nuclear family terms—parent, child, brother, and sister—are common in Scripture, but they are not used to limit family to nuclear relationships. Instead, they prescribe how God's people are to relate to one another *across* the sociological boundaries of family units. Jesus said that his family was defined not by biological ties but by the community of faith (Mark 3:33–35). The writer of 1 Timothy speaks of the church community as "the household of God" (1 Tim. 3:15). Christians are exhorted to practice hospitality, opening their homes to the community of faith and also to strangers (Rom. 12:13; 1 Tim. 3:2; Titus 1:8; Heb. 13:2; 1 Pet. 4:9; and 3 John 5–6). The focus of the Bible is the communal nature of the church. Nuclear family boundaries are to be opened and Christians encouraged to invite others into their personal networks and families, not shut them out. David Garland describes the biblical base for family ministry more fully in the next chapter.

The focus of Christian faith on families created among community members that transcend biological and marital bonds fits perspectives in social work practice which define the family as follows:

A family becomes a family when two or more individuals have decided they are a family, that in the intimate, here-and-now environment in which they gather, there is a sharing of emotional needs for closeness, of living space which is deemed "home," and of those roles and tasks necessary for meeting the biological, social, and psychological requirements of the individuals involved (Hartman and Laird 1983, 30).

This has been called an "ecological" definition of the family (Hartman and Laird 1983), based as it is on the functional relationships between persons in a particular social-physical environment. Although we are in basic agreement with this definition, the physical boundaries of living space may artificially delimit family. After all, while most families have a home base (except the tragic examples of homeless families), many persons consider as family extended kin relationships, young-adult children living separate from their parents, and spouses living in different cities because of their careers who may share a household only on alternate weekends. Similarly, close friends may meet the need for family, even though they live separately. We would suggest, therefore, that, for the purposes of family ministry, family is more usefully defined as *the relationships through which persons meet their needs for intimacy, sharing of resources, tangible and intangible help, commitment, responsibility, and meaningfulness over time and contexts.* In order to distinguish what we mean by family from the nuclear family, we have called families defined in this way *ecological families.* Such families may be composed of *fictive kin* ("aunts" and "uncles" who are not related by blood or marriage but have been informally adopted), workplace "families" (including the close friends and neighbors who share the workday of homemakers), roommates, army buddies, communal groups, and friends, as well as blood kin (Lindsey 1981).

Cohesion

The critical variable in describing ecological families is cohesion. Families vary in the degree of cohesion, or the "emotional bonding that family members have toward one another" (Olson, Russell, and Sprenkle 1983, 70). In their model of family systems, Olson and his colleagues have determined that families vary on a continuum of cohesion from disengaged relationships, in which members have limited attachment and commitment to the family, to enmeshed relationships, in which members have such a high level of identification with and loyalty to the family that developing an individual identity is difficult. In disengaged families, members "do their own thing." They may talk with each other about their individual activities and interests, but they do not engage in these together. In contrast, enmeshed family members may not feel comfortable doing anything without involving other family members. They think in terms of "we" rather than "I." Olson and his colleagues suggest that healthy families tend to fall in the middle between these two extremes.

Families may vary all along this continuum from disengagement to enmeshment, however, and still be considered healthy. For example, Watson and Protinsky's (1988) research suggests that healthy black families tend more toward the enmeshment extreme of the continuum. This intuitively makes sense in a society which these families experience as oppressive—they pull themselves together tightly for protection (see also McCubbin and McCubbin 1988; Vega et al. 1986). In contrast, Pill (1988) has reported that healthy stepfamilies tend to be much less cohesive than other family types, and that higher levels of cohesion may actually indicate dysfunction for stepfamilies. These families must have more openness as children move from the household of one biological parent to another, as parents negotiate with ex-spouses about child rearing issues, and as multiple grandparents play varying roles in these families' lives.

Although their study of family systems has been limited almost exclusively to nuclear families, there is nothing inherent in the model of Olson and his colleagues that suggests that it cannot be applied also to other forms of family. Certainly, it suggests some interesting hypotheses about ecological families. Nuclear families, if theories of family therapy are any indication, appear to have more difficulty with enmeshment than with disengagement. This reflects, in all probability, our cultural norms that encourage individual achievement and autonomy and deemphasize family obligations that require the sacrifice of individuality. Bowen, Satir, and Minuchin, three of the primary shapers of family therapy, have emphasized helping families to accept difference among members, to develop the autonomy of individual members, and to establish appropriate boundaries—all moves away from enmeshment (e.g., Bowen 1978; Minuchin 1974; Satir 1983).

In contrast, we would suggest that the ecological family, having no societal sanction and identity as a family unit, will more likely struggle with disengagement. It is easier for roommates or friends to end a relationship than marital partners or biological parents and their children. There is no legal process to be undertaken and paid for, no names to change, and far less upheaval in extended family relationships. Conflict may sooner end a relationship between neighbors or good friends than between nuclear family members. They may simply drift into a less involved relationship by some nonverbal but mutually understood process, seeking others to fill their needs for intimacy and mutual support. Although similar processes occur in nuclear families (extramarital affairs or children going to live with relatives), they create far more upheaval and negative social response than do such processes in ecological families.

Just as nuclear families vary all along the cohesion continuum from disengagement to enmeshment, however, so may the ecological family. Three components of cohesion must be understood:
- the degree of difference tolerated among members,
- the degree of boundary definition, and
- the degree of commitment members feel toward the family.

The Degree of Difference Tolerated Among Members. Olson and his colleagues have used the concept of cohesion to refer primarily to the degree to which a family unit will tolerate difference among members. Enmeshed families are highly intolerant of difference and "prevent individuation of family members." Disengaged families, by contrast, encourage family members to act independently of one another (Olson, Russell, and Sprenkle 1983, 70). Difference—or rather the lack of it—is a primary factor in the formation and development of cohesion in an ecological family. Ecological families often exercise a greater degree of choice in their formation than nuclear families. Although spouses exercise considerable choice in establishing the nuclear family unit, other nuclear family relationships involve considerably less volition. Parents may choose to become parents; but except in the case of adoption, there is no actual choice as to the child's personality or the degree to which the child fits their expectations. In contrast, ecological families are likely to be more intentional in their formation because they include more nonkin and because they are formed often on a basis of shared values and interests. Consequently, racism, classism, and other indicators of intolerance are significant challenges for family ministry.

Ecological families are also less subject to social pressures to maintain the family unit than nuclear families and thus may more easily withdraw membership status from one whose difference becomes intolerable to the others.

Degree of Boundary Definition. The boundary of a family is the family members' perceptions of who is and who is not a member of the family unit. A diffuse boundary is one so open that there may not be consensus even about who is inside and who is outside the family unit. A rigid boundary is one so closed that it is difficult for persons to have relationships with others outside the family system.

Boundaries differentiate the family unit from the individual's social network. If one asks each person in a family unit "who is in your family?" consensus is expected. By contrast, if one asks each person in a family "who are the people that you confide in, that you care the most for, that meet your needs?" consensus is less likely. This kind of question taps the social network, which is likely to vary, as family members include friends, work colleagues, and others with whom they associate. The more disengaged family members are from one another, the more variance in members' social networks (Bott 1971).

There appears to be a continuum of difference rather than a categorical difference on the variable of family boundaries. Even in a rigidly bound nuclear family, some members may consider a nonresident grandparent or aunt or close neighbor within the boundaries of the family while others may not. Blended families certainly may vary in the extent to which steprelatives, including a spouse's children, are included or not included in members' perceptions of *our family*. This ambiguity about boundaries is not related to the marital adjustment of the spouse or even the health of the family (Pasley and Ihinger-Tallman 1989). Families may also choose to include certain relatives to whom they have physical and/or emotional closeness in their family and omit others who would be considered equally close if blood and marital relationships were the sole criterion for defining the family.

> Uncle Joe lives fifty miles away. He has dinner with the family every Sunday and spends the afternoon taking the children on outings; he is considered by others in the family to be a family member. He is the divorced spouse of Aunt Sue, Dad's sister. Aunt Sue, who lives in the same town, is rarely included in the family circle and is inadvertently omitted when the children are asked to "draw your family." In the same drawing, Uncle Joe is quite prominent.

Because ecological families are more likely to be disengaged, and because they do not usually have either forming rituals or social recognition, the boundaries of the ecological family are more likely to be diffuse than those of nuclear families. Ecological families often begin, in fact, as a social network. They may be generated from a nuclear family unit and others who, over time, cluster around this unit (close friends, a neighbor, an *adopted* child of a relative, etc.). They are less likely than the nuclear family to be defined by a household, although even nuclear households may differ in the extent to which they include a nonresident grandparent in the concept of family.

Degree of Commitment. Although cohesion implies a commitment of members to one another, members may be highly committed to one another at the same time that they are highly tolerant of difference, and to persons who may or may not be considered by others in the family unit to be a family member. Commitment implies obligation to care for and act in behalf of the other, regardless of the other's ability or even willingness to reciprocate.

Commitment is a continuum. At one extreme is the contractual relationship, in which the reciprocity of the relationship is explicit and often time-limited: "If you do this for me, then I will do that for you." Some marriages are contractual by nature, with the expectations of each for the other implicitly or explicitly known, and perhaps even with agreements about what will constitute just cause for ending the relationship and how property will be divided. At the other extreme is the covenant, a relationship in which the members commit themselves unconditionally to stay permanently in relationship with the other ("for richer, for poorer, in sickness and in health, till death us do part").

Family relationships move on this continuum, often beginning with contractual relating and moving toward covenantal relating. For example, the courting process often begins with some kind of mutually rewarding or contractual exchange, such as enjoyment of one another's company and shared interests. As the relationship develops, reciprocity may become less immediate and more long term; there are periods of time when the relationship may appear to be one-sided, achieving balance only over time. The sense that "I love you no matter what happens" begins to take root alongside the need for reciprocity, and may eventually become dominant. This courtship process occurs not only between spouses, but in the adoption process, in the process of blending the families of previously married spouses and, to a lesser extent, in friendship formation. Chapter 3 will examine these processes of family development more closely.

Ministry with Families

With this definition of families, then, the tasks for ministry with families become identifiable as:
1. Strengthening the relationships among ecological family members;
2. Providing a catalyst for the development of new family relationships and the successful navigation of family developmental stages; and
3. Advocating in behalf of ecological families and social networks in church structures, in the development and assessment of church programs, and in other structures and institutions of society.

Strengthening the Relationships among Family Members

Up to this point, as described earlier, strengthening family relationships has been the primary goal of family ministry activities in the church. These activities need to be expanded, however, to focus not only on strengthening nuclear family relationships, but *all* family relationships. Roommates, neighbors, friends, and others who are ecological family for one another need skills in conflict management and decision making just as much as marital couples do. Perhaps even more than married couples and parents and children, they need opportunities and rituals for recognizing and celebrating their ties to one another. They need resources for facing the crises in their relationships, and they may need professional intervention to change dysfunctional relational patterns and structures.

Providing a Catalyst

This task is providing a catalyst for the development of new family relationships and the successful navigation of family developmental stages. For the most part, nuclear families appear to form without much programatic or structural intervention and are overtly encouraged by our societal norms. We do not spend much time in the church matching prospective marital partners with one another! Some ecological families also form without programatic or structural intervention. Recent research, however, has found that isolation of individuals and nuclear families is correlated with a whole array of problems, including physical illness, suicide, psychiatric hospitalization, alcoholism, accident proneness, difficult pregnancies, depression, anxiety, child abuse, and family violence (Cobb 1976; Garbarino 1979; Hurd, Pattison, and Llamas 1981; Pilisuk and Parks 1983; Scheinfeld et al. 1970). This research indicates that nuclear families as well as individuals need to be a part of larger ecological units and that many persons and nuclear family units are not able to form these key relationships on their own.

In response, church programs and structures can provide opportunities for family-like relationships to be initiated. We have a glimpse of the potential of ecological families already in current practices in many churches: baby dedications and baptisms in which the church community pledges shared support and involvement in the tasks of parenting; Wednesday night church suppers where generations and nuclear families mix, share concerns, pray for one another, and make provision to care for one another in times of need. These are only beginnings, however, and do not touch isolated persons and nuclear families uninvolved in such a supportive community. Several chapters in the second part of the book will show how churches can encourage the development of ecological families.

Church structures and programs can also help relationships which already exist—friendships and other social network connections—to develop into ecological families. In other words, church programs cannot choose people to be family for one another, but they provide contexts in which such choices can be made and nurtured. Of course, people need social networks just as they need family relationships, and certainly all social networks do not need or should not become ecological families. Both ecological families and social networks serve vital and differing functions. Developing and strengthening both social networks and ecological families, however, can be the focus of family ministry.

Advocacy in Behalf of Ecological Families

This task is advocating in behalf of ecological families in church structures and in other structures and institutions of society. Family ministry needs to be involved with more than the developing and strengthening of family relationships within the church community. If the church fulfills its responsibility to be a voice for social justice in society, it will point out that families need more than education and crisis intervention for dealing with the stresses they face. Even though family life education and counseling programs may effectively alleviate some of the problems families face, such programs cannot be the church's sole response to the needs of families. Since family life education and counseling sometimes alleviate the stresses and strains that many families experience, it is erroneously assumed that the lack of such services is the cause of their problems. This is much like people who get frequent headaches learning that if they take aspirin at the first sign of a headache they can *prevent* the headache from developing. It is not lack of aspirin, however, that causes headaches (Markman, Floyd and Dickson-Markman 1982). This does not mean that we should do away with family services any more than we should do away with aspirin. It *does* mean, however, that family ministry needs to be concerned with the social issues that create the stresses and strains that cause the headaches of family troubles.

An Overview

This book grew out of a conference entitled "Church and Families: New Directions in Church Social Work and Family Ministry," which was hosted in October 1987 by The Carver School of Church Social Work of The Southern Baptist Theological Seminary in Louisville, Kentucky. The conference pulled together seminal thinkers and creative practitioners in social work and family ministry in the United States to share their work with one another and to develop practical applications of ecological approaches to family ministry. Some of the contributors to this volume participated in that conference. In the time since the conference, others have been invited to write in this volume because of the significant contribution they are making to family ministry.

The Church's Ministry with Families addresses the work of the family professional in a church context, whether that professional be pastor, social worker, educator, pastoral counselor, or psychologist, and whether that professional is employed in a small local congregation, large parish church, or in a church-related social services agency. The book deliberately draws the boundaries of its attention around Christian denominations in order to stay focused and because a religious value base is considered essential in defining the unique rationale and methodology of family services in a religious context.

Even so, those working with families in other religious traditions and communities should find value in this book. We also hope that family-service professionals in public and private nonsectarian agencies will find this book useful in their work as consultants, both formally and informally, with churches in their communities. Several of the writers are not church or denominational employees but work with churches as key resources and influences in family and community life. Family ministry as defined in this volume offers a beneficial interface for the church and community social service agencies.

We have tried to address churches and church agencies in a variety of denominational, cultural, and ethnic contexts and to acknowledge the continuum from the very small church with few resources to the mega-church which can sponsor its own family service agency. We also recognize the wide variety of theological and professional stances that can be and are taken on family-related issues. In doing so, we know that some of the ideas presented in this volume will not fit comfortably in some faith traditions or will be impractical in some church contexts. It is our hope that in sifting through what will and will not work in their own context, the readers' imaginations will take the next step concerning what *will* work and what will carry us further toward effective family ministry.

The book is divided into two parts. The first part presents a theoretical and value base for an ecological approach to family ministry. This first chapter has introduced an ecological perspective on family. This concept, derived from the social sciences and a theological understanding of family, provides a new direction for family ministry. In chapter 2, David Garland explores the key biblical texts which provide the value base and impetus for family-ministry programs. He concludes that Jesus' teaching redefines the family, moving away from the limitation of nuclear-family boundaries and moving toward family networks formed by shared commitments.

In chapter 3, I describe development in families. Family-development models based on the stages of the nuclear family life cycle do not fit the experiences of many ecological families and thus are inadequate as a framework for family ministry programing. The model in chapter 3 describes the process of relationship development which occurs in families regardless of varying structures or composition.

Diane Pancoast in chapter 4 explores social network research as a useful tool for family ministry. She describes the use of social networks and problem-anchored helping networks in assessing and intervening in relationships in a church community. She suggests ways in which churches can strengthen their capacities to provide healthy social environments.

Chapter 5 describes the church as a context for professional practice. From our differing church traditions (Roman Catholic and Southern Baptist), Sister Ann Patrick Conrad and I describe the church context which functions both as constraints and resources for work with families in churches and denominational agencies.

Part 2 provides examples of the directions in which an ecological definition of the family can lead family ministry. By looking at actual family ministry programs and the characteristics of varying church communities, this part describes family services and programs, practice principles, and additional resources to apply or adapt. These chapters in no way provide a comprehensive or even representative sample of the myriad forms which family ministry can take. They are meant, however, to provide the reader with examples of the ways an ecological perspective can take to work in some selected contexts.

Both professional practice and Christian ministry begin with a clear articulation of the values and belief systems on which they are based and which provide the continuing motivation for action. We begin, therefore, with a chapter that examines biblical texts as the basis for family ministry.

References

Around the network. 1986. *The Family Therapy Networker* 10 (March–April), 16–17.

Bellah, Robert N., et al. 1985. *Habits of the heart: Individualism and commitment in American life.* New York: Harper and Row.

Bott, Elizabeth. 1971. *Family and social network: Roles, norms, and external relationships in ordinary urban families.* London: Tavistock Publications.

Bowen, Murray. 1978. *Family therapy in clinical practice.* New York: Jason Aronson.

Brackney, R., and D. Watkins. 1983. An analysis of Christian values and social work practice. *Social Work and Christianity* 10:5–20.

Cobb, Sidney. 1976. Social support as a moderator of life stress. *Psychosomatic Medicine* 38:300–14.

Cohen, J. 1979. Nature of clinical social work. In *NASW conference proceedings: Toward a definition of clinical social work*, ed. P. L. Ewalt. Washington, D.C.: NASW.

Cox, H. G. 1967. *The church amid revolution.* New York: Association Press.

Delamarter, W. 1970. *The Diakonic task.* Atlanta: Home Mission Board of the Southern Baptist Convention.

Family Ministry Department of the Baptist Sunday School Board of the Southern Baptist Convention. 1986. *Keys to effective family ministry.* Nashville: Sunday School Board.

Garbarino, James. 1979. Using natural-helping networks to meet the problem of child maltreatment. In *Schools and the problem of child abuse*, eds. R. Volpe, M. Breton, and J. Mitton, 129–36. Toronto: University of Toronto.

Garland, Diana S. R. 1987a. Myths about marriage enrichment and implications for family ministry. In *Family Strengths*, eds. H. G. Lingren et al., 8–9. Lincoln: University of Nebraska.

————. 1983. The social worker and the pastoral counselor: Strangers or collaborators? *Social Work and Christianity* 10:22–41.

————. 1987b. *Social workers on church staffs.* Louisville: The National Institute for Research and Training in Church Social Work, The Southern Baptist Theological Seminary.

Geyman, John P. 1985. International renaissance of primary care and family practice. *The Journal of Family Practice* 20:17–18.

Hartman, A., and J. Laird. 1983. *Family-centered social work practice.* New York: Free Press.

Hurd, Gary S., E. Mansell Pattison, and Robert Llamas. 1981. Models of social network intervention. *International Journal of Family Therapy* 3:246–57.

Kamerman, Sheila B., and Alfred J. Kahn. 1978. *Family policy: Government and families in fourteen countries.* New York: Columbia University Press.

Leonard, Bill. 1988. The modern church and social action. *Review and Expositor* 85:243–53.

Lindsey, Karen. 1981. *Friends as family.* Boston: Beacon Press.

Markman, H. J., F. Floyd, and F. Dickson-Markman. 1982. Towards a model for the prediction and primary prevention of marital and family distress and dissolution. In *Personal relationships 4: Dissolving personal relationships,* ed. S. Dick. London: Academic Press.

Marty, M. E. 1980. Social service: Godly and godless. *Social Service Review* 54:457–81.

McCubbin, Hamilton I., and Marilyn A. McCubbin. 1988. Typologies of resilient families: Emerging roles of social class and ethnicity. *Family Relations* 37:247–59.

Minuchin, Salvador. 1974. *Families and family therapy.* Cambridge, Mass.: Harvard University Press.

NASW conference proceedings: Toward a definition of clinical social work, ed. P. L. Ewalt. Washington, D.C.: NASW.

Olson, D. H., C. S. Russell, and D. H. Sprenkle. 1983. Circumplex model of marital and family systems: VI. Theoretical update. *Family Process* 22:69–83.

Pasley, Kay, and Marilyn Ihinger-Tallman. 1989. Boundary ambiguity in remarriage: Does ambiguity differentiate degree of marital adjustment and integration? *Family Relations* 38:46–52.

Pilisuk, Marc, and Susan H. Parks. 1983. Social support and family stress. *Marriage and Family Review* 6:137–56.

Pill, Cynthia J. 1988. Are stepfamilies more adaptable? *Stepfamily Bulletin* 8:14–15.

Pinson, W. M. 1971. *Applying the Gospel: Suggestions for Christian social action in a local church.* Nashville: Broadman Press.

Reid, W. J., and P. K. Stimpson. 1987. Sectarian agencies. In *Encyclopedia of Social Work,* ed. A. Minahan. Silver Spring, Md.: NASW.

Satir, Virginia. 1983. *Conjoint family therapy.* 3d ed. Palo Alto, Calif.: Science and Behavior Books.

Scheinfeld, D., et al. 1970. Parents' values, family networks and family development: Working with disadvantaged families. *American Journal of Orthopsychiatry* 40:413–25.

Sell, Charles M. 1981. *Family ministry: The enrichment of family life through the church.* Grand Rapids: Zondervan.

Stagg, F. 1981. Understanding call to ministry. In *Formation for Christian ministry,* eds. A. Davis and W. Rowatt. Louisville: Review and Expositor.

The Sunday School Board of the Southern Baptist Convention. 1981. *The church family life committee.* Nashville: Sunday School Board.

Vega, William A., et al. 1986. Cohesion and adaptability in Mexican-American and Anglo families. *Journal of Marriage and the Family* 48:857–67.

Watson, Marlene F., and Howard O. Protinsky. 1988. Black adolescent identity development: Effects of perceived family structure. *Family Relations* 37:288–92.

2

A Biblical Foundation
for Family Ministry

David E. Garland

An understanding of biblical texts is vital for any useful formulation of services with families in a church for two reasons. First, though Christian denominations may vary dramatically in their organizational structures and processes, and individual churches may come in all sizes and with varying cultural contexts, there is a shared belief in the Bible. In particular, the New Testament stands as a sourcebook for the values and life strategies by which the church's common life ought to be structured. An understanding of the Scripture gives the stranger to a particular church community or to a particular strain of Christian tradition a beginning for understanding the beliefs of that social system.

Second, the Bible is used to intervene in the ongoing life of a church community. For centuries, social activists have used Scripture as the foundation for their causes. Christians' understanding of the intention of their Scriptures has motivated them to found alternative communities, from monasteries to communes, challenge oppressive social structures such as racism and child labor, and strive to meet the needs of persons in their own communities and in faraway places with social and medical services (Leonard 1988). It is essential that an approach to family services be firmly rooted in Scripture.

Family ministry therefore needs to be firmly rooted in a biblical definition of what families are and ought to be. Unfortunately, too many times church leaders develop church programs or models for ministry and then muster scriptural texts to support their validity. In this way, positions based on scriptural proof texts are sometimes established that are in direct opposition to one another. A current example is the raging debate among Christian groups about how husbands and wives are to relate to one another—hierarchically or as equals (Garland and

DAVID E. GARLAND, M.Div., Ph.D., is professor of New Testament interpretation at Southern Baptist Theological Seminary. His publications include *The Intention of Matthew 23* and several books coauthored on family living and New Testament interpretation.

Garland 1986)—and the array of marriage education programs that have sprung from these opposing camps.

This book, therefore, has taken the opposite tack. It first asks the question, "What does the Bible say about what families ought to be?" From this base, an approach to family ministry can be built that is congruent with the church's value base. We can then use what we know from the social sciences to work toward objectives for the church's family ministry.

Family in the Old Testament

The Bible does not dictate any single sociological definition of the family. One finds in the Bible family structures that would be not only unusual but also illegal in modern industrialized nations. Abraham married his half sister (Gen. 20:12). Amram, Moses' father, married his paternal aunt (Exod. 6:20). Levirate marriage, a kind of ancient insurance plan in which if a husband dies childless, a surviving brother is required to cohabit with the widow to provide offspring for his brother's name and keep wealth within the family, was enjoined (Deut. 25:5–10). Concubinage was not unfamiliar, and many notable biblical heroes, David and Solomon, to name two, practiced polygamy. Joseph Heller in his novel, *God Knows*, parodies David's situation with seven wives and a budding relationship with Bathsheba who complains, "You never say you love me except when we're alone." David exclaims at this suggestion, "Are you crazy? . . . I'm a married man! I don't want Michal, Abigail, Ahinoam, Maccah, Haggith, Abital, or Eglah to find out about us" (Heller 1984, 276).

Descriptions of family in the Old Testament indicate that family life was geared primarily for survival, the preservation of a family's wealth, and conformity to ancient cultural norms to preserve the family's honor. There are no divinely prescribed patterns of how a family is to be structured or to operate. The story of Jephthah and the sacrifice of his daughter (Judg. 11:29–40) and the story of the host who offered a mob his virgin daughter and a concubine to prevent them from doing harm to a stranger who was his guest (Judg. 19:16–30) hardly serve as models for father-daughter relationships.

But the Old Testament, as might be expected, does contain affirmations of family life. The climax of the creation account in Genesis 1:27–28 is the statement, "Male and female he created them," and the command for them to "be fruitful and multiply." It is assumed that God's intention in creation was for the male and female to enter into a family relationship, to become one flesh. The highlight of the account in Genesis 2 is God's concern that it is not good for the man to be alone and God's decision to provide a partner "fit" for him, that is, a soul mate (Gen. 2:18). Family was designed to assuage the aloneness of the man. The Psalmist echoes this affirmation, "God sets the lonely in families" (Ps. 68:6, NIV).

A major part of the story in Genesis concerns Abraham and his family. Abraham was first called by God; and, when he responded with belief (Gen. 12:1–3), he was then given his family, an only son by Sarah. This son was the beginning of a clan that God promised would eventually number as the stars. God also promised that through Abraham all the families of the earth would be blessed (Gen. 28:14). The Old Testament Wisdom Literature praises the family virtues of chastity, industry, temperance, and self-control. The family was not only viewed as the basis of social and economic life, but having one was considered obligatory to the fulfilment of the divine command to be fruitful and multiply.

The primary goal of life, then, was to perpetuate the family line. The advice found in Sirach 26:19–21 sums it up:

My son, keep sound the bloom of your youth, and do not give yourself to strangers. Seek a fertile field within the whole plain, and sow it with your own seed, trusting in your fine stock. So your offspring will survive and, having confidence in their good descent, will grow great.

The Difficult Sayings of Jesus Regarding the Family

We encounter something quite different in the perplexing sayings of Jesus concerning the family. One writer on the family recalls the shock when as a child he first came across these texts of Jesus: "The tone is so fierce, so unyielding" (Mount 1982, 15). We will first identify these disturbing sayings and then briefly note some negative attitudes toward the family in the early church. Then we will examine Jesus' sayings more carefully to understand better Jesus' view of the family.

The Gospel of Mark reports that when Jesus' family heard that the story going around the countryside was that he was "beside himself," they went out to try to bring him home (Mark 3:21). Jesus, being informed that his mother and brothers were outside, looked at the crowd around him and said, "'Here are my mother and my brothers! Whoever does the will of God is my brother, and sister, and mother'" (Mark 3:34–35; compare Matt. 12:46–50 and Luke 8:19–21). Jesus' mother is left with her other sons outside the circle of Jesus' intimates.

Similar teaching can be found in Luke 11:27–28. Jesus had been addressing the crowds when a woman exuberantly burst forth with lyrical praise, "'Blessed is the womb that bore you, and the breasts that you sucked!'" Jesus responded to this outburst, "'Blessed rather are those who hear the word of God and keep it!'"

The Gospels record two other less than affectionate encounters of Jesus with his mother as he responded to her with seeming exasperation when she protested something he had done or implored him to do something. When Jesus was still a youth, he failed to return with the caravan to Galilee after his family had made a pilgrimage to the temple in Jerusalem. A desperate mother chastised him when she found him: "'Son, why have you treated us so? Behold, your father and I have been looking for you anxiously.'" Jesus replied, "'How is it that you sought me? Did you not know that I must be in my Father's house?'" (Luke 2:48–49). The implication is clear that he must serve a greater Father than his earthly father.

The other occasion is found in John's Gospel. Jesus and his disciples arrived for a wedding celebration at Cana. When the host ran out of wine, Jesus' mother attempted to intercede by telling Jesus they had no wine. Jesus responded "'O woman, what have you to do with me?'" (John 2:4). While there is no lack of affection or disrespect in calling his mother "Woman" as might seem to be the case, Jesus' answer does imply that he and his mother are on completely different wave-lengths. She was concerned about the world of mundane amusement, a wedding party; Jesus was concerned about his vocational destiny ("'My hour has not yet come'"). The two are worlds apart.

Jesus also had some rather startling things to say regarding the families of others. When Jesus called one to follow him, the would-be disciple replied, "'Lord, let me first go and bury my father.'" It seems a reasonable request; but Jesus responded, "'Leave the dead to bury their own dead; but as for you, go and proclaim the kingdom of God'" (Luke 9:59–60; compare Matt. 8:21–22). To another who offered to follow him after he had first said farewell to his family, Jesus said, "'No one who puts his hand to the plow and looks back is fit for the kingdom of God'" (Luke 9:61–62).

At another time, Jesus warned his disciples that he did not come to bring peace but a sword:

> For I have come to set a man against his father, and a daughter against her mother, and a daughter-in-law against her mother-in-law; and a man's foes will be those of his own household. He who loves father or mother more than me is not worthy of me; and he who loves son or daughter more than me is not worthy of me; and he who does not take his cross and follow me is not worthy of me. He who finds his life will lose it, and he who loses his life for my sake will find it (Matt. 10:35–39; compare Luke 12:51–53).

In Luke 14:26, Jesus told the great multitudes that accompanied him, "'If any one comes to me and does not hate his own father and mother and wife and children and brothers and sisters, yes, and even his own life, he cannot be my disciple.'" We are hardly surprised at the report in the Fourth Gospel that many disciples drew back and no longer went around with him (John 6:66); the cost was too high, if not totally unreasonable. But apparently some took Jesus at his word and became loyal disciples. Peter informed Jesus, "'Lo, we have left our homes and followed you.'" Jesus attempted to reassure him by saying, "'There is no man who has left house or wife or bothers or parents or children, for the sake of the kingdom of God, who will not receive manifold more in this time, and in the age to come eternal life'" (Luke 18:29–30; compare Matt. 19:27–29; Mark 10:28–30).

These texts are hardly prized as great ones for Mother's Day sermons or *Family Enrichment Sunday*; they do not even seem to be very helpful texts on which to build a biblical view of the family. In fact, many have considered Jesus' views as subversive to family life. Ieuan Ellis (1985) cited the view of the noted nineteenth-century *Life of Christ* by Ernest Renan wherein Renan asserted that Jesus "cared little for the relations of kinship." They were rather petty loyalties and a hindrance. In what he describes as a "bold revolt against nature," Renan claimed that Jesus trampled "under foot everything that is human, blood, love, and country" (Renan 1897, 97–98).

Developments in the Early Church

In the development of early Christianity, various groups arose who discredited marriage and family ties. Some of these sayings of Jesus must have been very congenial to those groups opposing marriage, if the sayings were not in fact responsible for spawning antimarriage attitudes. From Paul's reactions (see 1 Corinthians 7) to misconceptions we can see that aberrant views concerning marriage arose early. When one reads between the lines and tries to establish what the opponents argued from Paul's counterarguments, it seems that some at Corinth considered sexuality and marriage hindrances to salvation. They therefore dissuaded the unmarried from marrying and encouraged sexual abstinence for married partners. Apparently, they believed that sexuality defiled one in some way and that renunciation of it would elevate the Christian to a higher spiritual plateau. Celibacy was a badge of an exalted spiritual state. Jesus himself said:

> The sons of this age marry and are given in marriage; but those who are accounted worthy to attain to that age and to the resurrection from the dead neither marry nor are given in marriage, for they cannot die any more, because they are equal to angels and are sons of God, being sons of the resurrection (Luke 20:34-36).

This kind of saying, if separated from its immediate context, could have easily and erroneously fueled an ascetic view that opposed nuclear family relationships. That would be particularly true if some believed, as seems to have been the case in Corinth, that they were already on the level of angels.

One finds other evidence in the New Testament that a negative attitude toward the family seems to have been a problem in the early church. Some apparently forbade marriage (1 Tim. 4:1-3). The fact that the writer of Hebrews felt obligated to enjoin that marriage should be held in honor by all (Heb. 13:4) suggests that some held it in dishonor. That the writer of the Pastoral Epistles needs to affirm the goodness of childbearing—"a woman is saved through bearing children" (1 Tim. 2:15); "I would have younger widows marry, bear children, rule their households" (1 Tim. 5:14)—indicates that some must have disparaged this role for women.

In fact, that is exactly the attitude that is found in New Testament apocryphal works such as the *Acts of Paul and Thecla*, the *Acts of Thomas*, the *Acts of Peter*, and the *Acts of Andrew*. These works give the impression that the central teaching of Christianity is that virginity is the supreme good. In these stories, a Christian heroine typically renounces marriage and/or family responsibilities, including caring for an infant, to obey what she considers to be a higher calling. We also find in the second century that the Marcionites would baptize only virgins or married partners who vowed sexual abstinence, and some Christians considered celibacy obligatory for all.

This perspective was later judged heretical and prompted reactions from later church fathers. For example, Clement of Alexandria interpreted the saying in

Matthew 18:20, "Where two or three are gathered in my name, there am I in the midst of them," to mean that the two or three are husband, wife and child because the husband and wife are joined by God (*Stromateis* 3:10). The only reason that he would adopt such an unlikely interpretation of this saying is because he was countering those who devalued the family.

The Sayings of Jesus Reconsidered

An antifamily current has been present in church history; at times, it has been the mainstream. And one can see how it might have developed from the teaching of Jesus. Rather than choose the bits from the Bible to suit the case for a positive view of the family, the hard sayings of Jesus need to be explored in greater depth to see what his view of the family was.

"Leave the Dead to Bury the Dead"

One can hardly conceive of a more valid excuse to postpone following Jesus than the disciple's request to bury one's father. This was particularly the case in the time of Jesus. For a Jew, burying a parent took precedence over all other duties and was considered a chief responsibility of a son (see Gen. 49:29; 50:5, 25; even the apocryphal Tobit contains examples—Tobit 4:3; 6:14; 14:11).

Jacob, for example, was promised by God that the hand of his lost son, Joseph, would one day close his eyes (Gen. 46:4). Closing the eyes was the first act done for a dead person, and it normally fell to the son.

It may not have been that the father of this would-be disciple had just died and that he was requesting time to proceed with the funeral preparations which normally took place on the same day as the death. It is possible that the father was elderly and nearing death, and the son was asking permission to care for his father until he died. Having fulfilled that duty, he would then be free to commit himself to the cause of Jesus. Whatever was the case, to forbid a son to bury his father or to care for him until he died was unparalleled and seemingly unconscionable. It ran counter to the law, which commanded one to honor parents. It ran counter to piety, which had so exalted burying the dead that it was one of the highest of all good works (see *Mishnah Peah* 1:1; Mark 14:5–9). It ran counter to custom, which in both the Greek and Hebrew world considered the refusal to bury someone the greatest impiety.

Scholars have duly noted that this saying was uniquely offensive by calling it, "completely unthinkable to Jewish sensitivities, a purely sacrilegious act of impiety" (Hengel 1981, 14). In the Old Testament, when Elijah placed his prophetic mantle on Elisha, Elisha requested, "Let me kiss my father and my mother, and then I will follow you" (1 Kings 19:20). Elijah naturally consented to this; and Elisha went to his home, bade farewell to his parents, and even threw a going away banquet for his friends. What Jesus said, then, was shocking. No other rabbi would have ever said or would have even thought of saying this to a disciple. Jesus' saying appears to be antifamily.

But some precedent for this kind of absolute demand can be found in the Old Testament. Yahweh is the one who makes such demands. For example, God forbade the prophet Ezekiel to lament his dead wife or to carry out a mourning ritual for her (Ezek. 24:15–24). The purpose of this unsocial, unthinkable behavior was to convey God's judgment against the people. God also forbade Jeremiah from lamenting the dead or comforting the mourner, again, to show God's displeasure with the people (Jer. 16:5–7).

Therefore, when Jesus insisted that this favorably-minded follower disregard the Fourth Commandment and common decency, he was demanding what only God had enjoined on the prophets. Jesus was not antifamily but was proclaiming the impending judgment that was to befall the people (Hengel 1981). Jesus believed that his ministry was in complete accord with the will of God, that he could act with the authority of God, and that the time was urgent.

Disciples of Jesus learn that there are no excused absences from the kingdom of God, whether they be business commitments, social obligations, or family duties. Jesus labels those who do not follow him the spiritually dead, and plenty of them will be around to take care of the task of burying the physically dead. This incredible statement makes it quite clear that discipleship for Jesus, as Tannehill puts it, "is not merely another commitment which we add to the long list of our other commitments, but it is the commitment—demanding a reordering of our lives from the bottom up" (Tannehill 1975, 159).

Jesus' saying, then, is not an expression of his attitude toward filial responsibility. It was intended to be a dramatic pronouncement clarifying the seriousness and urgency of his mission, not declaring the irrelevance of family commitments.

Jesus believed that the call of God surpassed the call of family, but one should not conclude that Jesus depreciated the value of family or the need for family members to care for one another. For example, when Jesus happened on a funeral procession as they carried the body of the only son of a widow out of the gates of Nain, he did not tell her to leave the dead to bury the dead (Luke 7:11–17). Instead, he showed compassion on the widow by raising the son from the dead. Jesus, touched by her bereavement, recognized that she would be all alone in the world with no male family member to care for her in her old age and no son to close her eyes at death. Jesus moved to rectify the tragic circumstance and restore her only son to life. Jesus' compassion is further seen in his words on the cross to his mother. He made arrangements for the care of his mother by commending her to the beloved disciple and him to her. From that hour, the text says, that disciple took her to his own home (John 19:26–27).

Jesus also condemned the casuistry that found a loophole in the law which enabled a son to avoid providing financial support for parents. In Mark 7:9–13 (see also Matt. 15:3–7), we read of Jesus' attack on the legal tradition that sanctioned a man notifying his father or mother, "'What you would have gained from me is Corban' (that is, given to God)." A son could take a vow that something that normally could be used to assist in the support of his parents was now dedicated to God and could not be used for support of the parents. The catch was that it need not be actually offered to God by being donated to the temple. It was destined for God eventually, but for now it was no longer something that the parents could claim or use. Jesus' anger was directed at the rigid legalism that would condone this type of action and permit a vow to override helping one's aged parents. In countering this kind of pettifogging, Jesus cited the familiar words of Moses, "Honor your father and your mother," and "He who speaks evil of father or mother, let him surely die" (Mark 7:10).

In this passage, Jesus assumed that the duty to father and mother was not to be negated even by holy vows. Jesus labeled as a willful perversion of the law of God any attempt, however legal, to evade this responsibility. In fact, the well-known parable of the prodigal son turns on this assumption. The original listeners, including the teller of the parable, would have assumed that it was the duty of the son to stay home with his father, to labor in the fields, and to obey. The younger son becomes the "prodigal" by abandoning his duty to his father for foolish and selfish reasons. The younger son becomes the hero, we know from sermons and hymns, when he penitently returned to his father, presumably to finish his days laboring in the fields and obeying his father.

The weight of scriptural evidence, then, suggests the seriousness with which Jesus viewed filial responsibility. Only one's obligation to God superseded it in his teaching.

"Who Is My Mother?"

The second saying is Jesus' reaction to the news that his mother and brothers had come to see him. Jesus said, "My mother and brothers and sisters are those who do the will of God." This response reveals Jesus' understanding of the family and the reign of God. First, nepotism will have no place in the reign of God. In Hebrew society, the advance of one member of a family meant the advance of all other members of that family. For Jesus, however, biological descent has nothing to do with participation or priority in the reign of God. This differed dramatically from the way earthly kingdoms normally operated in the ancient world.

For example, if the mother of James and John could have had her way, appointments to the high positions in God's kingdom would be attained the way political appointments are made. She came and knelt before Jesus saying, "'Command that these two sons of mine may sit, one at your right hand and one at your left, in your kingdom'" (Matt. 20:21). Domestic selfishness is the guiding principle behind this request. But Jesus taught that the reign of God is the only consideration, and family ties are irrelevant.

Second, it should be noted that the family of Jesus was not making a friendly visit but had come to seize him. They were worried that his continuing asocial behavior endangered his life and would bring shame to the family name. They assumed that Jesus would accede to the authority of his family, and that family obligations took precedence over all else; the brothers of Jesus acted to try to preserve family honor by bringing him under their control. Jesus challenged their assumptions about the traditional authority of the family, particularly in the face of the greater responsibility of giving obedience to God. God ranks above family and family honor.

Third, the saying assumes a central tenet in the preaching of Jesus, namely, that God is the Father of all. This can be seen in Jesus' uniquely familiar address to God as *Abba*, "Daddy." Jesus prayed and taught his disciples to pray, "our Father," and *Abba* became a confession of the early Christians (Rom. 8:15; Gal. 4:6). Jesus preached that a new and intimate relationship with God as *Abba* was available to all. But the saying assumes that God is the Father of those who *behave* as God's children and those who give God their ultimate allegiance.

Fourth, this saying redefines family. When Jesus asked, "Who is my mother?" the answer seemed obvious. The obvious answer, however, was wrong. Jesus' family consisted of those who chose to obey God and follow him. Nuclear family relationships are not based on choice but on birth. Belonging to the family of God, however, *is* a matter of choice. One can choose to be obedient to God's will and thereby be joined to others in a family comprised of those who accept God's rule. In the family of God, obedience and membership are completely voluntary.

Those who are deprived of traditional family relationships can therefore become members of a greater family, as is illustrated in the story of the Ethiopian eunuch found in Acts 8:26–40. Philip happens upon a eunuch reading the book of Isaiah. He was reading the Bible, even though the Bible clearly states the eunuch is to be excluded: "He whose testicles are crushed or whose male member is cut off shall not enter the assembly of the Lord" (Deut. 23:1). Why, then, was he reading the Bible that would seem to offer him no hope? Perhaps he was reading it in hope against hope. Hope is extended in Isaiah 56:3–5 for even the eunuch: "Let not the eunuch say, 'Behold, I am a dry tree'" and it promises, "I will give them an everlasting name which shall not be cut off." There was his name—dry tree, cut off, no possibility of family! After reading Isaiah 53, he asked Philip about whom this Scripture was speaking. Philip told him about Jesus Christ, and that one without a family can now be a part of Jesus' family. This family is open to all and especially those who are normally cut off from family relationships.

Other sayings of Jesus show that membership in the family of God transcended this life. The Sadducees, who did not believe in a resurrection, regarded the family as the only part of a person that lived on. This is the assumption behind the riddle that they put to Jesus to make the belief in the resurrection seem ridiculous. They confronted him with the conundrum of seven brothers. The first brother died with no children to carry on his name. Each of the other brothers married the widow according to the custom of the Levirate marriage and died childless, until finally the widow died. Hardly concealing their glee, the Sadducees asked Jesus, "'In the resurrection, whose wife will she be?'" (Matt. 22:28). They mistakenly assumed that family is all there is to life. Their faith was placed in the family.

Jesus responded to the riddle that in the resurrection there will be no marriage, and that God "'is not God of the dead, but of the living'" (Matt. 22:32). This answer assumes that, first, one does not need an heir to thwart death. Second, family relationships in the life to come will be transcended. In this world, family relationships are time-limited. How long is one a husband or a wife? The answer is, till death do us part. Earthly families live on only in memories and photographs that soon fade away. The family of God lives on in God's heart and never fades. For Jesus, the life here and now was to be governed by the values of life to come. Therefore, life could not be totally centered around the biological family.

In the Old Testament, "life" is used almost interchangeably with family (*mish-paha*). We can see this reflected in Jesus' saying, "'If any one comes to me and does not hate his own father and mother and wife and children and brothers and sisters, yes, and even his own life . . .'" (Luke 14:26). One's family was one's life, and to reject family or to be cast out of one's family was to lose one's life. But from Jesus' perspective, life under God was no longer to be defined by relationships in a biological family. Therefore, one's ultimate allegiance is owed to God as the head of a new divine family.

When the disciples also expressed their concern about what they would receive for having left everything including their families, their very lives, to follow him, Jesus responded by saying,

"There is no one who has left house or brothers or sisters or mother or father or children or lands, for my sake and for the gospel, who will not receive a hundredfold now in this time, houses and brothers and sisters and mothers and children and lands, with persecutions, and in the age to come eternal life." (Mark 10:29-30)

This is not an antifamily response; but, again, it teaches that the family of God extends beyond traditional clans. The saying implies that the new family will consist of the caring fellowship to be found in a group of mutually committed believers. This was echoed in the sharing of goods and meals that marked the fellowship of the early Jerusalem church, according to Acts 2:44-45; 4:32-37. Family was not depreciated by Jesus; it was enhanced.

On the cross, Jesus brings to fruition the promise of family. John reports that Jesus' mother and the beloved disciple were standing close by when Jesus was being crucified. Jesus spoke to his mother, saying, "'Woman, behold, your son!'" To the disciple, he said, "'Behold, your mother!'" (John 19:26-27). This new relationship between his mother and the beloved disciple is the fruit of the completed work of Christ (Bampfylde 1969). Jesus' death enables people to become family to one another in a new and different way.

The new relationship also involves Jesus' Father. Jesus referred to God as "my Father" throughout the Gospel of John. After his death and resurrection, a change occurs. In Mary Magdalene's encounter with Jesus at the tomb, he instructed her to inform "my brethren" that he was ascending "'to my Father and your Father, to my God and your God'" (John 20:17). This is the first time in the Gospel that Jesus identified his disciples as his brothers (in 15:15, they are "friends"), and the first time that he referred to God as their Father as well as his own. Jesus' death and resurrection, then, had repercussions on the nature of the family.

Jesus said that he had come not to abolish the law but to fulfill it (Matt. 5:17). We may also say that Jesus had come not to destroy the family but to fulfill God's intention for the family. No longer is it to be a self-serving kin group; instead, it is to be the source of nurture and the channel of God's love for all of God's children. Those who for various reasons have been deprived of traditional family relationships now can belong to a family (Garland and Garland, n.d.).

"To Bring a Sword"

Jesus says that he has come to divide families with a sword. This flies in the face of the expectation of some that the messianic age would be a time of unparalleled peace (Isa. 11:6-9; 65:25; 2 Apoc. Bar. 73:6). The reference to the division within families is a quotation from Micah 7:6 (compare Jub. 23:16; 1 En. 99:5; 100:12; 2 Esd. 6:24; m. Sota 9:15)[1] that suggests that the time before the end would be marked by unusual discord. The division between loved ones is not to be understood as the result of Jesus' desire to drive a wedge into family loyalties. Allegiance to God can and will cause conflict and division in the families of some of Jesus' followers, which cannot be avoided as long as there are some "who loved the darkness rather than light" (John 3:19). But when considered in the light of the saying about "who is my mother?" it is clear that those who might lose family because of their loyalty to God are not familyless. They are a part of the new family of faith.

Jesus did not intend deliberately to create strife in families. The opposite was true, if we consider what precipitated his parable of the rich fool (Luke 12:13-21). A brother, presumably a younger brother, interrupted Jesus' teaching with a demand that Jesus force his elder brother to share his inheritance. Jesus responded, "'Man, who made me a judge or divider over you?'" Jesus was obliquely saying to this man that he should feel shame for wrangling with his brother over a few shekels. Jesus was not a third-party arbitrator over legal disputes, but he was instead a peacemaker, a healer. He says through the parable that there is something greater to be gained than getting an inheritance and something greater to be lost than losing an inheritance (Bailey 1980). To drop the dispute might mean that this brother would lose out on some money; but he might regain a brother, which for Jesus was more important.

"Hate Your Family"

One last hard saying of Jesus concerning the family is his insistence that his followers must hate their families. This saying, phrased for dramatic effect, is found in a series of warnings that discipleship should not be entered into lightly.

---

[1] The 2 Apocalypse of Baruch is the title of a late first or early second century A.D. Jewish writing that attempted to explain the catastrophe of the destruction of the temple in A.D. 70. Jubilees is a retelling of the story of Israel's history found in Genesis and Exodus and was written in the second century B.C. 1 Enoch is an apocalyptic vision attributed to Enoch and written in the second century B.C. with revisions from the first century A.D. The Mishnah is the rabbinic compilation of oral law. Tractate Sotah has to do with the laws concerning the suspected adulteress in Numbers 5.

He did not wish to scare away potential disciples but to make sure that disciples enlisted were carefully willing to stake everything.

Jesus insisted that one's commitment to God was to be even greater than commitment to family, the greatest human bond. His statement that to be a disciple you are to hate your family is a Semitic idiom that means essentially *to love less*. When one said, "I love this and I hate that," one was saying, "I prefer this to that." For example, in the Old Testament it says that Jacob loved Rachel and hated Leah (Gen. 29:30–31; compare Deut. 21:15–17); and that God loved Jacob and hated Esau (Mal. 1:2–3). This does not mean that Jacob actually hated Leah or that God literally hated Esau, but that Jacob preferred Rachel over Leah and God preferred Jacob over Esau. Jesus, then, was simply saying that families were not to be preferred over God. One is to love one's family, but one is to love God more.

Jesus was not intent on undermining family bonds and, for example, exalted the sanctity of marriage. Wives were not to be discarded as if they were a useless appendage. Marriage makes a man and woman one flesh, and therefore Jesus rejected divorce entirely. Even though we have a saying in the Gospels that the disciples left everything to follow Jesus (Matt. 19:27), Paul later reminded the Corinthians that Peter and the other disciples are accompanied by their wives on their mission trips (1 Cor. 9:5). Apparently, these disciples did not leave their wives or families for good.

The analysis of these hard sayings leads to the conclusion that we must be cautious in reading Jesus' statements about the family in the Gospels. They should be carefully interpreted before using them to make pronouncements about models of family relationships. Jesus was responding to concrete situations; he never laid out a systematic theology of the family. To one he says leave your family (Matt. 8:22); to another he says, in effect, stay with your brother (Luke 12:13–21). To one he says, "Follow me" (Mark 1:17–20); to another he says, "'Go home to your friends, and tell them how much the Lord has done for you . . .'" (Mark 5:19).

Conclusions

While it is difficult to systematize biblical teaching about the family, the following observations can be made.

First, one cannot conclude that Jesus' view of the family is subversive, or that Jesus considered family relationship to be either a petty concern or an impediment to commitment to God. But it should also be clear that Jesus did not share the traditional view of the family prevalent in his world.

The context for much of what Jesus said about the family was his vision of the coming crisis of God's reign which would turn ordinary life on its head. He perceived the coming of the kingdom to be a revolutionary event; the family could no longer provide true security nor absolute trust. The advent of the kingdom of God required a change in one's basic orientation. One must be prepared to abandon the security that a family provides, the duties that a family might expect, and the affection that a family offers for what one considers to be a greater good.

Supreme loyalty to God puts all other loyalties in perspective, and circumstances might arise for some that would force them to reject family attachments. For this reason, family ministry should be cautious not to elevate the significance of family relationships over the relationship between the individual and God. Intimate, satisfying family relationships, as valuable as they may be, must not be allowed to substitute for an intimate relationship with *Abba*.

Second, the will of God can be done within the structure of the biological family; it can also be done without the structure of the family. The common pursuit of the will of God produces a higher bond than family bonds. This leaves the circle open to others who may not be one's family, and this is precisely the emphasis that is to be found in the rest of the New Testament. Paul said that all who are called to God's household become children of God, heirs, and fellow heirs (Rom. 8:17). Therefore, one is in Christ rather than simply in a biological family. That is why, as a Christian, Paul no longer identified himself in terms of race or tribe as he once did. He once boasted that he was of the race of Israel, of the tribe of Benjamin, and a Hebrew of Hebrews (Phil. 3:5). Now he identified himself through his faith in Christ (Phil. 3:7–9). This allows others who believe in Christ to be accepted as fellow heirs, as brothers and sisters. According to Paul, all, Gentiles and even Jews, receive adoption as children into the spiritual family of Abraham (Gal. 4:4–6). This is why Paul urged Philemon to regard his runaway slave, Onesimus, in a different light. He was no longer to be considered a slave but a beloved brother (Philem. 16; see also Matt. 23:8). This basic premise is the reason why Christians identified themselves not as Christians but as brothers (1 Cor. 8:11). They extended kinship beyond racial lines, tribal loyalties, national boundaries, and the biological family. When we celebrate family in the church, we first need to celebrate the family of faith.

Third, the function of the family household is distinctive for the Christian. In our culture, most consider the home a place of retreat where one can shut the doors against the needs and demands of others; this retreat is secure and en-riched. The New Testament presents a different perception of the home, for family is not regarded as a retreat from the world but as a place where service can be rendered to the world. Indeed, hospitality is one of the chief virtues found in the new Testament (Rom. 12:13; 1 Pet. 4:9–11; 3 John 5). Church family ministry must not focus inwardly on the enrichment of the nuclear family, but instead needs to challenge Christians to expand the boundaries of the nuclear family, extending hospitality that enfolds others in expanded family systems.

Finally, Jesus' redefinition also provides a significant perspective for evangelism. In order to incorporate persons into the community of faith and help them grow spiritually, we have to deal with their relationship with and sustenance by families. The church has the task of developing family relationships—relationships beyond the bounds of kinship—which can germinate and grow Christians. God calls persons into a special relationship with God and others. Newbigin writes:

God is not solitary—but relationship between Father, Son and Spirit. Interpersonal relatedness belongs to the being of God. Therefore, there can be no salvation for persons except in relatedness. No one can be made whole except by being restored to the wholeness of that being-in-relatedness for which God made persons and the world and which is the image of that being-in-relatedness which is the being of God (Newbigin 1978, 76).

The role of the church, then, is not simply to nurture and support the families that already are members. The church must be about the task of nurturing and supporting new families and enabling all to be a part of a special family of God, including homeless mentally ill persons, teenage parents, children with special needs, the divorced father whose children live in another state.

The church is to provide a home for the homeless, love for the unloved, and grace for the disgraced . . . . The church is to be the seedbed for relationships in which we can parent and be parented, and in which we can give and receive brothering and sistering, regardless of biological kinship (Garland and Garland, n.d.).

Family services which serve as catalysts for the formation and development of ecological families thus stand on a firm biblical foundation. The definitive characteristics of the family can no longer be considered to be legal marriage and biological parenting; instead, they are summed up in *mutual commitment*. Neither can family ministry be touted as the centerpiece of the church's mission. As important as family ministry is, churches are not simply family service agencies. The church's mission includes also a prophetic role in larger social systems as well as attention to individuals, who have value and significance to God, and to the faith community beyond their role in a family system.

In its rightful place as one of several central functions of the church, family ministry needs to attend to the difficult task of bringing to fruition the ideals of a *family of faith*. The ecological family is a family born of mutual commitment to one another and to a common purpose: It is a "family of faith." The ecological family needs structures and supports that will enable it to develop and become functional and productive just as those exist to aid the nuclear family. The church, then, has the responsibility of providing this nurturing, sheltered environment for the formation and development of the ecological family. In doing so, the church goes a long way toward Jesus' ideal that all persons will have brothers, sisters, and parents in God's family.

References

Bailey, Kenneth E. 1980. *Through peasant eyes: More Lucan parables*. Grand Rapids: Eerdmans.

Bampfylde, G. 1969. Article John IX.28: A case for a different translation. *Novum Testamentum*, vol. 11:247-60.

Ellis, Ieuan. 1985. Jesus and the subversive family. *Scottish Journal of Theology* 38:173-88.

Garland, David E., and Diana S. R. Garland. n.d. The family: Biblical and theological perspectives. In *Theology as ministry, ministry as theology*, eds. Christian D. Kettler and Todd Speidell. Forthcoming.

Heller, Joseph. 1984. *God knows.* New York: Knopf.

Hengel, Martin. 1981. *The charismatic leader and his followers.* New York: Crossroad.

Leonard, Bill. 1988. The modern church and social action. *Review and Expositor* 85:243–53.

Mount, F. 1982. *The subversive family: An alternative history of love and marriage.* London: Jonathan Cape.

Newbigin, Lesslie. 1978. *The open secret.* Grand Rapids: Eerdmans.

Renan, Ernest. 1897. *The life of Christ.* London: n.p.

Tannehill, Robert C. 1975. *The sword of His mouth.* Philadelphia: Fortress.

3

Understanding How
Families Develop

Diana S. Richmond Garland

Individuals grow and change over time and so do the families to which they belong. The issues created by the development of individual members of a nuclear family are well known. For example, as teen-agers face the developmental tasks of establishing their own identity, taking responsibility for themselves, and launching their own careers and families, their parents must, in response, provide both a sense of security for them and space for their developing autonomy. At the same time, parents may be dealing with their own developmental issues, such as midlife career and marital changes and the inevitable processes of aging. In addition, their own aging parents may be increasingly frail and in need of care and assistance. The family itself grows and changes in response to these developmental tasks of its members, adapting and reacting to the complex interplay among the developmental issues of family members at different stages of the life cycle.

People adjust better to developmental changes when they know what to expect. And a church can minister more effectively to families if it understands the developmental crises and issues which families face. Yet if anything characterizes the current status of nonnuclear families, it is that there are no guideposts for family development. Developmental stages defined by the birth and growth of children do not readily provide direction for family ministry with therapeutic foster families, families who adopt a developmentally disabled adult as a special friend, or a close-knit community of widows.

Most models of family development describe the stages of family development by using as marker events both the ages and stages of children and changes in marital status. The stages of family development most common in family studies, then, are the following: unattached young adult, young married couple, the family with young children, the family with adolescents, the family launching young adults, the empty nest family, and the postretirement family. Family development occurs in the linear dimension of time, a result of three

35

and perhaps even four generations of kin growing up and growing old in interaction with one another.

Transition from one stage to another creates family stress and adds to any stress the family is already experiencing. Even stages marked by happy events, such as marriage, are stressful; the couple must form a new family unit that incorporates the partners' often-conflicting expectations. The birth of new members and the launching of adolescents have also been studied as stressful times for the family (Bradt 1989; Lewis, Owen and Cox 1988; McCullough and Rutenberg 1989). Families are more likely to have difficulties with developmental tasks when the stages of development are disrupted or occur at unusual times (McCubbin and Figley 1983). Pregnancy for an unmarried adolescent or for a woman approaching midlife often creates a significant crisis, for example. As a consequence, many family ministry programs have focused on providing education and crisis intervention designed to help families understand and cope more effectively with both normative and nonnormative family development tasks.

At first glance, stage models of nuclear family development appear to limit rather than expand our thinking about how we can nurture the development of ecological families. The names of the stages themselves assume marital and parenting roles, while our definition of ecological families includes but is not limited to families that are organized around marriage and parenting relationships. If we focus on how nuclear family life-cycle stages occur in response to the processes of (1) adding and losing members and (2) the interaction of developmental changes in individual members rather than on marital or parental roles, we can see that these processes take place in all family systems, not just nuclear families.

Carter and McGoldrick (1989) describe processes which have to occur at each stage of the family life cycle before the family can develop further. For example, a new marital couple must (1) form a marital system and (2) realign relationships with extended families and friends to include each other. These processes occur in all new families, not just new marriages. Ecological families also have to form a system since all families are social systems with accompanying rules, boundaries, and communication between members. They also have to realign relationships with other significant persons in the lives of each member. Roommates have to figure out, with little direction from societal norms, the extent to which they will be involved with one another's biological families. Should we go home with each other for Christmas or go separately to the homes of our respective parents?

Other stages of the nuclear family life cycle suggest similar developmental processes at work in the ecological family. In the families with young children stage, the processes described by Carter and McGoldrick (1989) include: (1) making space for child(ren); (2) joining in the childrearing, financial, and household tasks; and (3) realigning relationships with extended family to include parenting and grandparenting roles. In fact, these changes point to processes that occur anytime a member is added to an existing family—when a young couple and their children adopt a single older adult who lives nearby as a grandparent, when a foster child or young cousin moves into the family and takes on a siblinglike relationship with other children, when a tight-knit group of widows who are "closer to one another than we are to our own sisters" reaches out to a newly widowed woman and envelops her in their circle of support.

Family members have to make space for one another. They have to determine the extent to which they will become interdependent. Who has financial responsibility for a foster child or live-in cousin—for the daily costs of food, clothing, and school field trips? For an allowance? For college expenses? Does the adopted grandparent pay the young family for gas in exchange for transportation back and forth to the doctor or the grocery store? Or does the exchange remain implicit, with occasional loaves of homemade bread from the adopted grandparent's kitchen, a five-dollar bill slipped to a child "just because I want to," or child care so that the young couple can have dinner out together? The developmental processes at work in ecological families, then, parallel those in nuclear families.

The Family as a Group

Theories of group development provide a resource for thinking about ecological family development. The family is, by definition, a group, with the characteristic processes and dynamics that occur in groups (Spiegel 1971). A family differs in significant ways, however, from other kinds of groups, such as work groups, committees, and cliques. Structurally, it is often characterized by hierarchical rather than peer-power relationships: parents/adults usually hold more power than children. Unlike other groups, it has a longer history behind it and a longer future before it, a more extensive involvement of members with one another, and a structure which transcends the particular tasks it currently faces. Too often, however, family theorists have spent so much energy defining how family systems are unique that no attention has been given to some interesting parallels between group and family-development models.

Forsyth (1983) reviewed over 100 theories that seek to describe group dynamics and concluded that, for the most part, they take one of two basic approaches. *Recurring-phase models* suggest that certain issues (e.g., focus on the tasks of the group or focus on relationships between group members) dominate group interaction at different phases of the group's life, and that these issues recur off and on throughout the lifespan of the group. For example, families must develop and rework family rules and expectations over and over as the family changes over time.

The second group of developmental models are *sequential stages theories*. These models specify a typical order of stages in which groups develop over time. Interpersonal processes that build on one another define the specific group development stages. For example, a group first has to develop a group identity and cohesion—it must become a group. Conflict, the development of group structure, and working together on the group's identified tasks then follow in sequence (Hartford 1971; Tuckman 1965). These models of development differ, therefore, from the stage models of family development, because they define stages based on the developing relationships of the members with one another, not their individual ages and developmental stages.

At first glance, the stages of group development do not seem directly applicable to family relationships, but some interesting implications can be drawn from thinking about families as small groups. For example, group theorists locate a period of conflict immediately after the formation phase, a period which has parallels in family life. The phrase "the honeymoon is over" describes a frequently experienced period of conflict early in new marriages. This period of conflict is less well known but apparently just as real in other family relationships. For example, parents who adopt older children need to know that an early honeymoon phase of tranquility occurs only because the child does not yet feel attached. Once attachment begins, so does conflict, often with hostility and negativism that may shock the unprepared parent. The child tests the limits, preferring to be sent away now rather than risking further attachment and being sent away later (Hartman 1984). Such a phase of conflict may be common in other family types as well.

Group theorists do not argue that either stage or phase theories of group development ought to be dominant, but that a synthesis between them provides the strongest foundation for understanding and working with groups (Forsyth 1983). Similarly, the process model of family development presented in this chapter is not meant to replace, nor even to challenge the stage approaches to family life. Instead, it identifies the underlying processes at work in families of all types.

Relationship Issues in Family Development

Although many theorists have explored the processes of family relationships, few have tied these processes to the development of the family throughout the life cycle. Lyman Wynne (1984) has identified four relational processes that underly family development: attachment/caregiving, communicating, joint problem-solving, and mutuality. Kenneth Terkelson (1980) has posited that mutual need-attainment generates family development. And, as discussed in chapter 1, family members move from relationship contracts to deeper covenantal relationships.

Attachment/Caregiving, Communicating, Joint Problem-Solving, and Mutuality

Wynne's four processes that unfold in relational systems are: (1) attachment/ caregiving (complementary affectional bonding), (2) communicating (sharing foci of attention and exchanging meanings and messages), (3) joint problem-solving (sharing of tasks, interests, and activities), and (4) mutuality (renewing and deepening the relationship through the previous three processes as the family changes.

Each of these processes builds on and assumes those which precede it. Joint problem-solving, for example, must be preceded by attachment. A family will not stick it out through a difficult problem if they are not attached to one another. Evidence for this can be found in the higher divorce rates in the early years of marriage (Peck and Manocherian 1989) and the higher rates of adoption disruption in the first year after placement (Festinger 1986). Joint problem-solving must also be preceded by a communication system in which people understand one another. Many families embroiled in chronic conflict may not have developed effective communications that allow them to solve problems.

Wynne names each of these processes by its positive side, but he makes it clear that the negative side of the process is important for family development, too. The negative side of attachment/caregiving is separation, and Wynne suggests that "the intensity of attachment/caregiving is strengthened by appropriately timed separation, whereas excessively prolonged and poorly timed separation can lead to detachment/rejection" (Wynne 1984, 301). A healthy attachment of a child and the child's parents is strengthened by short separations, such as an occasional evening in which the child stays with a friend while parents have time alone. In contrast, when a child is separated from parents for long periods of time (in foster care, or while a parent serves in the military overseas), the family system may not be able to develop further because the process of attachment has been impaired. In the same way, occasional failures to communicate effectively or solve problems that confront the family may be seen as challenges to overcome. But if the family fails over and over in these relational processes, the relationships themselves may deteriorate.

Need-Meeting

Terkelson has also examined family development as the *consequence* of relational processes. He suggests that meeting one another's needs is the most important process that controls the development of the family. As family members meet one another's needs, from changing an infant's diaper to listening to an adult partner's woes or ironing a blouse for a hurried adolescent, families develop a sense of cohesion and create in family members a sense of "resource sufficiency" (Terkelson 1980, 31). Family members feel secure. Families that fail to meet one member's needs typically generate a sense of "resource scarcity" and family fragmentation.

Members' needs change over time. The infant son grows into a young child and no longer needs diapers changed; instead, he now needs a parent to take time to listen to his new reading skills. The adolescent girl as a young adult now needs support and encouragement in taking responsibility for her own finances. As new needs develop in family members, new responses are required from the family. These emerging needs lead to a period of instability in the family's structures, and then gradually to new structures.

Thus, new structures mark a new developmental phase. Physical need-meeting for the infant which occurred in bursts of frequent activity interspersed throughout the adult's other activities has given way to rituals of sitting on the couch for a half hour or more with a shared book. Care becomes less behavioral (dressing the infant) and more verbal ("Johnny, get dressed; breakfast is almost ready!"). Although these changes seem relatively small, they create a period of family instability. Children who are used to parents doing for them must learn to do for themselves, and parents must let them, with all the mismatches of clothing that this will mean. Gradually, the relationship between Johnny and his parents changes from an emphasis on physical caregiving to an emphasis on communicating. Wynne suggests that attachment/caregiving is succeeded by communication; Terkelson's emphasis on need-meeting and Wynne's relational processes are thus both illustrated in this example.

Commitment—From Contract to Covenant

Chapter 1 noted that interpersonal relationships often begin as implicit contracts. Each of the parties is in the relationship because it offers certain rewards (companionship, enjoyment, help with a difficult task). A contractual relationship is qualified and depends on evidence that others will fulfill their side of an exchange of benefits. If the relationship develops, however, the rewards, although still important, no longer are the foundation of the relationship. As people meet one another's needs, loyalty and commitment grow (Sakenfeld 1985). The relationship becomes more a covenant and less a contract. A covenant relationship continues unconditionally; it depends on a *leap of faith* in which members choose the relationship even when there is no evidence that the other will come through with what is hoped for (Kaplan, Schwartz, and Markus-Kaplan 1984).

Few relationships are purely contracts or covenants. Like the necessary negative counterparts of Wynne's processes, contracts are required by covenants, although the covenant itself is larger than any of the contracts that occur between covenant members. Contracts such as "if you'll do the cooking, I'll do the cleaning" ease family members through the maze of shared responsibilities. A breach in such a contract, however, does not signal the end of the family, as a breach in a business contract would signal the end of a business transaction. To be a family implies that there is commitment.

Like the processes of family development described by Wynne, a family's growth from a contractual to a covenantal relationship is nurtured as family members respond daily to one another's needs. Together, they provide an understructure for a model of ecological family development.

Ecological families dramatize the need for a process model of family development. Current family-development models that are based on marital and parenting relationships define development in terms of changes in roles and statuses. In families that are not nuclear in structure, however, family roles and statuses are rarely well recognized in our culture. We do not even have language to define these relationships, except to say what nuclear family relationships they resemble—foster parent, like-a-sister, stepmother, grandma, uncle. Yet these relationships sometimes differ significantly from their nuclear family counterparts in the roles and statuses they imply.

The Phases of Family Development

Ecological families move through phases of development which are described as relational processes that occur in all families, not as changes in specific roles and statuses.

Courtship

Family development begins with a phase of *courtship*. Whether intentionally or unintentionally, individuals go through a period of selecting other(s) with whom to form a family unit. In the case of the nuclear family in Western society, this is a time of dating and "going steady" or engagement that leads to marriage. But it may also be a time of considering adoption as a viable process for creating a family. Some adoptions begin before a relationship can develop between potential family members; an individual or couple may decide to adopt a yet-unborn infant or a child from an international adoption agency. Pregnancy may also be considered a courtship process; new parents are adjusting to the idea of adding a new family member.

Courtship may also be a time of selecting a specific other person as a family member, such as the decision to adopt a child with special needs, or to form a relationship with a mentally ill adult who is without family. Stepparents and stepchildren have to "court" one another; families do not instantly happen when remarriage occurs. Long-term friends may implicitly explore the options of committing themselves more fully to one another by sharing more of their resources and relating as a family unit to other friends and extended family instead of as individuals. In other words, persons may commit themselves to a new family member before they even know one another, or a preexisting relationship may evolve into a family courtship process.

Courtship is characterized primarily by a contractual relationship. Will this other person or these other persons meet my needs for being a family? Will adoption of this person bring me opportunities to love another that will fulfill my sense of purposefulness? These contracts are rarely openly spoken. Often, perhaps, they are not even allowed into conscious thought.

What is exchanged in these contracts may not be equivalent. Although each expects some return from the relationship, the expectation may be quite different for each. One may expect intimacy and companionship, the other security and protection. Sociologists have used exchange theory to describe the development of relationships, suggesting that persons choose to develop relationships because they expect to get better outcomes in exchange for what they themselves invest, or than what they perceive they could expect in competing relationships (Nye 1979; Sabatelli 1988; Thibaut and Kelley 1959). During the courtship process, then, the relationship is *conditional*, although none of the family members may be consciously aware of what those conditions are unless they are breached in some way.

Formation

The *formation* phase is entered with an increasing commitment and a decision, either implicitly or explicitly, to become a family. During the formation phase, the process of moving from a contract to a covenant relationship begins. The marital vows "for richer or for poorer, in sickness and in health, until death do us part," describe the covenantal ideal of family. As attachment and caregiving take center stage, family cohesion develops.

At some point, the commitment between persons becomes explicit. One friend says to the other, "We aren't just friends; you're like a sister to me." For some family relationships, this phase is marked by some formal recognition: wedding or adoption. In the case of the friendship that has become "sister-like," it may be a private recognition such as a special gift or an invitation to an extended family gathering. Or the recognition may come in an explicit agreement to share living quarters, resources, or responsibility with one another. This phase of moving from a primarily contractual to a primarily covenantal relationship occurs as the following developments take place:

1. *Persons feel intimate with one another.* This may or may not include verbal intimacy, but includes the intimacy one experiences with an infant because one is primarily responsible for the child's welfare. This is the intimacy that comes from sharing meals or other resources with one another, or with seeing one another's private selves not generally shared with others (as happens during sickness or personal crisis).

2. *Persons feel a sense of entitlement with one another.* They feel that they have a right to be in one another's lives and claim a relationship with one another. Persons in this stage feel freer than during courtship to offer advice or express opinions, even though doing so may cause disagreement. Stepparents and foster parents become entitled to the right to discipline, and stepchildren and foster children test the relationship until they feel secure that they will not be deserted, even when they show anger, change moods, or break family rules.

3. *People feel that they belong to one another and that their relationship with one another has permanence.* A breach of contract is far less likely to break the relationship in this phase of family development than in the courtship phase. People feel like family with one another; and just as biological ties are difficult to break, it is difficult to imagine dissolving the family commitment.

4. *People share tasks and commitments with one another.* They invest themselves in common ventures. If family members do not live in the same household, they nevertheless do not act like or treat one another like guests or hosts. They feel free to rummage in one another's kitchen cabinets and to expect sharing in kitchen clean-up. Sharp divisions between economic resources fade, sometimes to the point of sharing checking accounts or purchases (an automobile, furniture, canoe, or gas grill), or to a complete joining of financial resources for a common life.

The processes of attachment and caregiving undergird the phases of courtship and formation. Attachment is demonstrated when (1) family members experience a need to be with one another when experiencing distress, when (2) the presence of other family members brings a sense of comfort and diminished anxiety, and when (3) separation from the other and an inability to be reunited create anxiety (Weiss 1982; see also Bowlby 1975). Although these behaviors are most familiar in small children, adults too experience these expressions of attachment, although not in such overwhelming ways. Family members also demonstrate caregiving in a myriad of ways of meeting each others' needs, from filling the car with gas for the other to providing a listening ear or care during illness.

Partnership

If a family develops intimacy, entitlement, a sense of permanency through attachment of members to one another and caring for one another, and cohesion, it moves into the phase of *partnership*. Partnership is the working phase of family living. In this phase, families work through the shared life tasks and commitments that were undertaken in the formation phase, often before the meaning of those commitments was fully understood.

Families during the partnership phase often confront two major issues. First, the family's boundaries may be opening and closing as members are added and leave. Many families define their task as nurturing and parenting (biological parenting, adoptive parenting, foster parenting, or the informal parenting of children and adolescents in the extended family and friendship network). They may also nurture by maintaining open family boundaries, extending hospitality to others beyond their household. A family of unmarried adults (roommates, a religious order, grown unmarried siblings) may consider hospitality to others, either adults or children, as significant as parenting is to a married couple.

For many families, then, the partnership phase actually includes a period of recycling through the stages of courtship and formation as members are added and family relationships reshuffle to incorporate new members. In the television series, *The Golden Girls*, three unmarried retired women living together in a suburban home have created a family with one another. When Dorothy's aging mother needs a place to live, they incorporate her into their family unit, with necessary adjustments. It is obvious that Dorothy bears primary responsibility for "Ma," and that, in turn, this daughter is entitled to the nurture that children of all ages want from their parents. But the sharp divisions of responsibility and entitlement soften over time. The other two roommates also grow to treat her as Ma and to be treated as adult daughters.

In addition to the possibility of some recycling of earlier family phases, the partnership phase is also a time of settling down to being family together. Although the processes of communication have obviously been important throughout the family-formation process, communication becomes fundamental during the partnership phase. Communication means "to share meaning"; it is not only being good listeners and talkers, but achieving mutual understanding. Joint problem solving serves as the second major relational process of this phase. The feelings of being cared for and listened to without true understanding is not enough. Understanding is necessary if the family is to move forward.

James's first marriage was to Anne, who had two children, Bob, age 10, and Tom, age 9, from a previous marriage. Their biological father had deserted the family five years earlier, and they had not heard from him since. James loved the idea of being a father to two boys. He was careful to follow the suggestions of books on stepparenting he had read, suggesting that he hold off on discipline and other parentlike roles with his stepchildren while he developed a relationship with the boys and earned a right to be in their lives (the courtship and formation phases). During the year he was dating Anne seriously and in the first few months of marriage, he did everything he could to create a love for him in the hearts of Bob and Tom.

Anne agreed to continue as the primary rule-maker and disciplinarian with James's gradually increasing involvement. James spent lots of time with the boys, taking them on outings and watching ball games on television. He listened to them, and they warmed and opened up to him. He weathered their hostility and silence when they found themselves growing attached to him. He listened to their dreams about finally being able to do some things that they had never been able to do because of finances— go to Walt Disney World and buy backpacking equipment to trek through the mountains. And they in turn listened to James talk about his dream of moving out of the city onto a small farm. The conflict came six months after James and Anne were married, when James thought it was time to enact his dream. Buying the farm he had his eye on would mean that they would have to stay put to take care of the stock—there was no money or time to make trips away. The boys' dreams would have to be put on hold, at least for a little while. James believed that, in the end, his decision would be best for all of them and that he had earned the right to a fatherly authority in the decision process. Anne felt caught in the middle. The family was embroiled in conflict; everyone felt betrayed.

This family ran into difficulty with the communication processes of the partnership phase. Although they had felt understood, in fact, neither the boys nor James understood the intensity of the others' dreams for what being a family would mean. For the boys, camping in the woods with a dad carried much more meaning than simply the novel experience of camping. And for James, sharing the responsibility of a farm with growing sons was much more than an economic decision. Before they could confront and solve the problem, they needed to establish together a deeper understanding of the meaning of family to each.

A second issue during this phase of family development centers around the extent to which members' individual developmental phases and tasks parallel or conflict with one another. For example, the budding sexuality of a teenage girl raises her mother's anxiety level even as it parallels the sexual self-consciousness of the mother who is newly divorced after fifteen years of marriage.

Consolidation

The *consolidation* phase is characterized by processes of closure and the completion of life tasks and commitments that were central during the partnership phase. The major issues of this phase are the following:

- shrinking membership, whether this is voluntary (a roommate deciding to move out, adult children leaving the nuclear family) or involuntary (the death or incarceration of a member);
- changes in the family's environment (unemployment or retirement); and

- threats of loss or transformation of core family relationships (the terminal illness of a spouse or other primary life partner).

In contrast with the open boundaries of the partnership phase, which pushed the family toward a recycling of formation processes, this phase moves the family toward an end of the family in its current form.

Some family members may be leaving to start new family units of their own. Remaining family members feel like they are undergoing a "shake down"; although core family relationships may remain intact, they are altered by the changing family membership. When families define their primary task as the nurture of family members, the loss of the target of care involves change and often crisis in the family.

Other shared tasks such as retirement (from employment or volunteer work), unemployment, or career changes, may end during this phase as well. The family's boundaries and social networks change, then, not only because of changes within, but also because of changes without.

Lyman Wynne defines mutuality as a characteristic of relationships that survive differences between family members and, in fact, "thrive upon the recognition of such natural and inevitable divergence" (Wynne et al. 1958, 207). At times, mutuality is characterized by intimacy, but it may also include mutually comfortable distance between family members. Perhaps, in fact, the successful balancing of intimacy and autonomy create mutuality. The consolidation phase of family development emphasizes, as did the formation phase, a time of relationship definition and redefinition, resulting in the growth of mutuality.

Transformation

The next phase of family development is *transformation*. Core family relationships end and the remaining member(s) no longer constitute a family. The death of one of the members of a marital pair is the clearest example of this phase of family life. But the death of a lifelong roommate, the loss to a foster family when a foster child returns to the biological family, and the promotion of developmentally disabled adults from a group living arrangement into independent living are also examples of this phase. This is not the final phase of family development, however, but in fact the beginning of the next cycle. Usually core family relationships dissolve and family members are gradually absorbed into other intimate social networks and families (e.g., Goldberg et al. 1986). But these members of previous family systems are carriers of the family's values and norms into the new family they join, recreating in this family some of the patterns and lifeways of the past family system.

The phases are thus cyclical. Part of the process of transformation is courtship for a new or altered family system: A surviving spouse may assume a more central role in the family of an adult child. Or the surviving family member may develop or strengthen peer or neighborhood relationships that become the next "family."

Figure 3-1 summarizes the relationship between the relational processes and the phases of ecological family development.

Developmental Phases	Relational Processes
Courtship	contracting
Formation	attachment and belonging
	caregiving
	intimacy
	entitlement
	covenant development
	permanency
Partnership	defining common purposes/tasks
	communicating
	joint problem solving
Consolidation	mutuality
Transformation/Courtship II	redefining remaining relationships or absorption into other families in the social network
Forming II	
Partnership II etc.	

Phases of Ecological Family Development
Figure 3-1

Family Developmental Phases as a Focus for Family Ministry

Because families of all types go through these developmental phases, this model can serve as a theoretical framework for an ecologically based family ministry. This model is general enough to apply to many situations besides the nuclear family. For example, families may find support and new perspective on their own situations when they participate in family-life education programs with other families quite different from their own who are facing some of the same issues. The need to develop effective communication and joint problem-solving skills during the partnership phase belongs not just to married couples, but also to parents and their adolescents, roommates, and unmarried adults living with and caring for aging parents.

In the following pages, some suggestions for family ministry for each phase of family development are offered. Sheek (1985) suggested that the first step in promoting the well-being of families is "encouraging respect for and acceptance of all families through promoting the theological truth that there is no particular family structure, natural or chosen, that is more Christian than another" (119).

The suggestions in this section take family ministry the next step, from *respect* toward *action* that supports the development of ecological families. These suggestions are not designed to take the place of programs designed for particular family relationships at particular stages of the nuclear family life cycle (marriage-preparation programs, marriage enrichment, blended-family education programs, preparing-for-retirement seminars, etc.). Instead, the phases of ecological family development can provide an overarching framework that ensures the inclusion of *all* families in a community of faith. It also provides ways that families of different types can learn from one another and, in the process, develop more appreciation and support for one another.

Courtship

Family ministry has been little involved in the courtship process, because there appears to be little need to help nuclear families get started. There is evidence that persons are waiting longer to marry and that there is some decline in marriage rates, but these trends have not created much stir in the church. In fact, more effort has been expended in trying to head off courtships that are premature than in trying to help potential marital partners find and court one another.

Ecological families, however, are another matter; they often do not develop without nurture and support. In the public sector, family services have often focused on the courtship phase; programs designed to recruit and train adoptive and foster families for "special-needs" children and developmentally disabled or mentally ill adults help potential family members "court" one another. There are also some notable programs in churches designed for this phase of family development. The *One Church One Child* program recruits adoptive homes for black children through the black church and with the support of the church community as extended family for the child and adoptive family (Lakin and Hargett 1986). A community mental health center has collaborated with churches in a program designed to develop family-like friendships for the homeless mentally ill (Drouet 1989). Cross-generational programs, described in chapter 10, provide courtship opportunities for potential ecological family members. Family clusters around specific interests or ministries enable people to develop relationships with others who share common values; from these task-oriented relationships, the more extensive relationships of family may develop (Mpolo 1984; Otto 1979; Otto and Otto 1976; Sawin 1979a; Sawin 1979b). House churches and home-cell groups form seedbeds for ecological families to grow (Hadaway, Wright, and Dubose 1987). Concerned with the needs of persons to develop potential family relationships, family ministry aims to provide opportunities for people of a variety of ages, interests, and needs to mingle with one another and to interact in meaningful ways.

Such programs and services must begin and stand firmly throughout on a sound biblical and theological foundation in order to be accepted as an appropriate activity for the church community. A central image in the Bible describing our relationship with God is that of parent-child. Jesus stated that in order to be saved, we must be "born again"; this rebirth places us within the adopted family of faith with God as Father. This image points to the intentional creating of relationships—adoption—that provides that which is normally only available to us as biological children. It is ultimately appropriate, then, that the church actively seek to provide fertile ground for the development of *adoptive* family relationships in the community of faith (Garland and Garland n.d.).

One thorny theological issue that needs to be considered openly is that of special relationships within the larger community of faith. Few in a Protestant tradition have questioned whether nuclear-family relationships are appropriate in the faith community; but the process of courtship and formation of ecological-family relationships raises difficult issues. Our culture does not call these relationships *family*; they are called *inside groups* and *cliques*. How does preferring one another's company to the company of others fit with the Christian's call to love universally? Is it appropriate for Christians to choose a few "significant others" as special?

Jesus provides us with a number of examples that suggest that there is a distinction between love of family and the universal love of neighbor. John 11:5 records that "Jesus loved Martha and her sister and Lazarus." If Jesus loved all of his disciples, and, in fact, demonstrated love for all persons whom he encountered, why does the writer record that he loved these three? These were special persons in Jesus' life. He cried with Mary over her brother's death, experiencing her pain as his own. Evidently, these were like family to Jesus. We are also told that Jesus had a "beloved disciple." And finally, Jesus made special arrangements from the cross for his mother to care for and be cared for by this special disciple (John 19:25–27). They were to become family to one another. This was beyond the way the band of disciples cared for one another; *within* this community, Jesus designated a special family relationship.

The Christian community, then, is to nurture within itself the special relationships of family, whatever the biological or nonbiological foundation for those relationships. Jesus taught us to love our neighbors as ourselves, and he made it clear that we are to minister to the needs of all of God's children. That does not cancel our need for family, however. Neighborly love is universal, calling us beyond loyalties and special relationships. Family love is particular; it symbolizes our covenant with God. God singles out each of us, choosing us. Covenant love is not indiscriminate, including everything that is human in a social community; instead, covenant love "discriminates one from the other as particular and unique" (Anderson and Guernsey 1985, 39; see also Kierkegaard 1964, and Meilaender 1981).

Not only do these issues need to be sorted through by the leader of family ministry, but they also need to be a topic of discussion and study in the church community that seeks to nurture the growth of ecological families.

Formation

Nuclear families begin with one of the few major rituals of our society—the wedding. Weddings are followed by honeymoons, a time set aside in which the new family is expected to develop intimacy and establish their new life together. To a somewhat lesser extent, we also ritualize the advent of children with baby showers and birth announcements. The birth event is followed by a maternity leave, and paternity leave in some cases, that in some respects serves the same function as the honeymoon. We recognize that this early period of bonding lays the foundation for the family's continuing development.

No socially recognized rituals exist for the formation of nonnuclear families. Although some creative families invent their own means of celebrating and ritualizing their formation, the benefits of societal or community recognition are still not forthcoming. Churches can help families celebrate new family bonds and, in so doing, help families develop a sense of belonging to one another. A ceremony of adoption or joining gives family members a chance to *name* their relationship with one another and *claim* their identity as a family unit. They announce the rights, obligations, connections, and commitment which now and henceforth exist between them (Hartman 1984).

For example, a foster father and child may write together their pledges to one another, to be said in a small ceremony in the church sanctuary with close friends. The father says the words they have prepared together—"I will love you and support you from now on. I will not try to take the place of your biological father, but I will be your friend, and I will discipline and care for you the very best that I know how to help you grow into all that God has given you the gifts to become," and others in the family respond with their own pledges. As a consequence, the relationship takes on a deepened sense of attachment, entitlement, and permanency; they enter a covenant with one another. Not only have they defined their relationship for themselves, but they also have publicly explained and defended their family to others, another contribution to a growing sense of entitlement (Hallenbeck 1987).

In addition to ritualizing the formation process, ecological families can benefit from educational programs that help them understand the relational processes they are experiencing. Attachment, entitlement, permanency, and the relationship between contracts and covenants are all concepts that lend themselves to family life education (e.g., Garland and Hassler 1987; Garland and Chapman n.d.). Family members may need guidance in developing functional family roles; in deciding how much of their time, financial resources, and physical living space they will share and how much they will retain for privacy; and in negotiating relationships with one another's extended family.

Foster and adoptive families need to develop relationships with biological parents and siblings that work best for all involved. Ambiguous relationships create stress; a foster child may be confused and upset when the foster parent replaces clothes provided by a biological parent with new nicer things. The child may feel disloyal when wearing the new clothing on a visit with the biological parent, who is obviously upset by being replaced in the child's life. The foster parents and biological parents need help in bringing clarity to their roles and the boundaries between those roles.

Such discussions defining family relationships are not always comfortable. Adoptive parents may feel threatened and uncertain of how to respond to their children's need to discuss their biological background. Roommates may feel uncomfortable and embarrassed to speak explicitly about their need for privacy as well as their desire to share more fully in one another's lives. Family ministry services of the church can provide education concerning the importance of such communication and settings and experiences that encourage this kind of family talk.

Family ministry may also need to include crisis intervention as families flounder in the formation phase. A stepfather stormed out of the house and stayed gone several days when his adolescent stepson defied the house rules the stepfather had established and when the mother came to her son's defense. All blended families have to develop a sense of belonging and attachment—for both parents and children—and both generations often do so by testing the relationship with the other. The stepfather was testing his new parenting wings and his role in the family. The son was testing the limits of his entitlement to challenge the rules and still be accepted by the stepfather. And the mother felt caught in the transition from single parenting to blended-family parenting, with all its ambiguities. By identifying these developmental issues, the family can see their mutual share in working through the issues that face them rather than blaming their conflict on one another.

The Bible provides vivid images for the relational processes of this phase of family development. Jesus' words from the cross to his mother and his beloved disciple sound almost like a marriage ceremony: to his mother, he said "Woman, behold, your son!" and to the disciple "Behold, your mother!" Clearly this public pronouncement was a turning point, for "from that hour the disciple took her to his own home" (John 19:26–27). We would think that the disciples would have certainly looked out for Jesus' mother, but the actual speaking of the commitment made the difference. Family ties need to be spoken publicly. There is power in being named and recognized as family; it confirms loyalty and commitment.

Another biblical image is that of belonging. We want to belong to one another, to "abide" in one another, to be branches of the same vine, to belong to God (John 15:1–11), who knows and cares for us so much that God even knows how many hairs are growing on our heads. Families are to be examples, to the extent of human possibility, of this kind of belonging.

Belonging leads to entitlement. By belonging to God, our Heavenly Father, we are entitled to ask for what we need (John 15:7). What father, if asked by a hungry child for an egg, would hand the child a scorpion (Luke 11:11)? We can ask for what we need from God. We are witnesses in our families of God's love for each of us, as we ask for our needs from one another and bear responsibility for responding to those who ask from us.

Finally, our relationships are covenants in which we promise unconditional loyalty. In so doing, we bear witness to God's great covenant with us; neither life nor death nor things present or to come can separate us from God's love (Rom. 8:35–39).

These and the many other images of covenant making, belonging, and entitlement in the Bible show that forming functional family relationships is at the base a spiritual discipline for the Christian (Garland and Garland n.d.). The life of the Christian is to be a witness of God's love, the love of a Father. Those who are nearest and dearest—the family—provide the most rigorous training ground for Christian living.

Partnership

The partnership phase has received more attention from family ministry programs than other phases, with educational programs on communication, conflict management, values clarification, and family problem-solving. For the most part, these have been offered in marriage enrichment and parent education programs. Members of other kinds of family relationships face these same challenges and can benefit from educational programs and a self-help literature that recognize the relational processes of communication and problem solving in all kinds of families. Many family ministry programs for married couples or parents can be creatively adapted to include family relationships of all stripes.

All people who live together, whether roommates, spouses, parents/adults and children, or adults and older adults/parents, must come to terms with the daily tasks of living in one household. They must face anger and conflict that is generated when people share space and resources with one another, and must come to terms with differing values for guiding the family's life together. Family members who do not live in the same household have to negotiate similar issues, such as how much time and relationships with others should be shared, where is the boundary between concern for and intimacy with one another on the one side and intrusiveness on the other, and the extent to which finances and other resources are held in common or remain personal.

Consolidation

Families in the consolidation phase often have just experienced or are in the midst of a crisis, whether that crisis be death of a family member, divorce or separation, unemployment, retirement, or some other critical change. Crisis may not necessarily be experienced as a negative occurrence, as in the case of retirement or launching young adult members, but there is significant upheaval, nevertheless. Programs that provide information about survival strategies for families in crisis can be extremely helpful in normalizing what families are experiencing and in giving them coping strategies to fit their unique situations.

Educational programs on family crisis can be offered as part of an ongoing family ministry program. Much ministry with families in this phase, however, must be designed to fit the needs of particular family systems. The time around a funeral or memorial service, for instance, often is a time when friends tell stories about the loved one. Unfortunately, the family is often in too much turmoil at that point to take in all that they may hear. A family minister aware of the need for such a review of the family's life together may find a way to schedule a private family memorial service much later, at a time agreeable with the family, and encourage friends to write down the stories. The family can gather old family pictures and slides and prepare a scrapbook or find another way to review their life together during this memorial and, in the process, bring some closure to their relationship with the one who has died.

This kind of family ministry is even more significant in the lives of nonnuclear families, whose depth of grief may go largely unrecognized in a society that emphasizes the grief of spouses, parents, and children. The family members of a person dying with AIDS, for example, can benefit from rituals which recognize and affirm their grief, since this disease is met largely by denial and silence in our culture. Therapy with the family network can also be most useful.

In the best of all situations, all family relationships would end with this kind of review. Divorcing spouses might, in the presence of their children, overview their lives together and bring attention to the meaning they have shared that may have been forgotten in the heat of conflict that led to the divorce. The joy of birthing and raising children together, for example, could be reviewed. Following this review, then, parents can make their vows to one another and to their children to continue to do their very best to be good coparents, even though they have chosen no longer to be spouses. As a consequence of this explicit review of the past and plan for the future, parents and children are better equipped to enter the transformed family system that has been created by divorce and, perhaps, remarriage of one or both partners.

Transformation

Transformation brings the family back full circle to the courtship phase. The life situations are different, however. Now the aging roommate or spouse who has lost a lifelong partner is redefining relationships with close friends or grown children who are open to more closely knit bonds of relationship. The aging adult who has just moved into a retirement facility is developing peer relationships with others who live alone. The unmarried foster parent has watched the adolescent boy whom he has provided with a home return to his biological parents and, having dealt with the sense of loss and willing to risk attachment again, is considering adoption of a special needs child. Even though these families may in some respects seem different, the relationship issues they face are congruent with those in the courtship phase.

Summary

Imagine the map with which Lewis and Clark might have started their trek across the continent. No doubt, it hardly resembled what we now know of North America. Some basic landmarks might have been there, and some areas were probably fairly well defined. But some areas were markedly distorted, and other areas were simply blank spaces. One cannot criticize the map if no other exists, however, unless one is willing to explore and provide a better one. The explorers' map gives one a place to start and something to criticize and correct. It is a starting point.

No doubt, this model of ecological family development has about the same level of accuracy as Lewis and Clark's map at the beginning of their journey. There are some glaring blank spaces.

How can the development of families of all types and stripes be summarized in five phases, the last of which is actually the first played over again an octave higher?

How do these phases of family development interact with the individual developmental issues of children, adolescents, and adults in nonnuclear families?

The suggestions for family ministry emphasize educational programs that call for generalizing what we know about family-relational processes to all kinds of families. Little is mentioned, however, about how family ministry can advocate for families whose needs differ because they are at different places in their development, or who receive no recognition and support from other social systems because they are not nuclear families. Finally, and most critically, there is no longitudinal—or even cross-sectional—research that indicates that these are indeed the most basic phases of family development for the variety of family systems that we have called "ecological families."

But we must begin somewhere. This model is simply a rough map. Criticize it, test it, modify it, or replace it with something better. But by all means, let us design ministries with families that recognize the changing needs and challenges of living in all kind of families from their initiation to their transformation.

References

Anderson, Ray S., and Dennis B. Guernsey. 1985. *On being family: A social theology of the family*. Grand Rapids: Eerdmans.

Bowlby, J. 1975. Attachment theory, separation anxiety, and mourning. In *American handbook of psychiatry*. Vol. 6, ed. D. A. Hamburg and H. K. M. Brodie. New York: Basic Books.

Bradt, Jack O. 1989. Becoming parents: Families with young children. In *The changing family life cycle*. 2d ed., eds. Betty Carter and Monica McGoldrick, 237–54. Boston: Allyn and Bacon.

Carter, Betty, and Monica McGoldrick. 1989. Overview. The changing family life cycle: A framework for family therapy. In *The changing family life cycle*. 2d ed., eds. Betty Carter and Monica McGoldrick. Boston: Allyn and Bacon. 3–28.

Drouet, Claude. 1989. Family networks for the homeless. Manuscript. Louisville, Ky.: Jefferson Street Baptist Chapel.

Festinger, Trudy. 1986. *Necessary risk: A study of adoptions and disrupted adoptive placement*. Washington, D.C.: Child Welfare League of America.

Forsyth, Donelson R. 1983. *An introduction to group dynamics*. Monterey, Calif.: Brooks/Cole.

Garland, David E., and Diana S. R. Garland. n.d. The family: Biblical and theological issues. In *Theology as ministry, ministry as theology*, eds. C. D. Kettler and Todd Speidell. Colorado Springs: Helmers and Howard, forthcoming.

Garland, Diana S. R., and Kathryn Chapman. n.d. *Self-esteem: Parenting by grace*. Nashville: Baptist Sunday School Board, forthcoming.

Garland, Diana S. R., and Betty Hassler. 1987. *Covenant marriage*. Nashville: Baptist Sunday School Board.

Goldberg, Gertrude S. et al. 1986. Spouseless, childless elderly women and their social supports. *Social Work* 31: 104–21.

Hadaway, C. Kirk, Stuart A. Wright, and Francis M. DuBose. 1987. *Home cell groups and house churches*. Nashville: Broadman.

Hallenbeck, Carol. 1987. Magical mystical bonding. *OURS* (March/April): 25–26.

Hartford, Margaret E. 1971. *Groups in social work: Application of small group theory and research to social work practice*. New York: Columbia University Press.

Hartman, Ann. 1984. *Working with adoptive families beyond placement*. New York: Child Welfare League of America.

Kaplan, Kalman J., M. W. Schwartz, and Moriah Markus-Kaplan. 1984. *The family: Biblical and psychological foundations. Journal of Psychology and Judaism* 8: 2.

Kierkegaard, Søren. 1964. *Works of love*. Trans. by Howard and Edna Hong. New York: Torchbooks.

Lakin, D., and J. Hargett. 1986. The role of the black church in the adoption of black children with developmental disabilities. Paper presented to the NASW Clinical Social Work Conference, San Francisco, September 12, 1986.

Lewis, Jerry M., Margaret Tresch Owen, and Martha J. Cox. 1988. The transition to parenthood: III. Incorporation of the child into the family. *Family Process* 27: 411–21.

McCubbin, Hamilton I., and Charles R. Figley. 1983. *Stress and the family*. Vols. 1 and 2. New York: Brunner/Mazel.

McCullough, Paulina, and Sandra Rutenberg. 1989. Launching children and moving on. In *The changing family life cycle*. 2d ed., eds. Betty Carter and Monica McGoldrick, 285–309. Boston: Allyn and Bacon.

McGoldrick, Monica, and Betty Carter. 1989. Forming a remarried family. In *The changing family life cycle*. 2d ed., eds. Carter and McGoldrick, 265–94. Boston: Allyn and Bacon.

Meilaender, Gilbert. 1981. *Friendship: A study in theological ethics*. London: University of Notre Dame Press.

Mpolo, Masamba Ma. 1984. *Family profiles: Stories of families in transition*. Geneva: World Council of Churches.

Nye, F. I. 1979. Choice, exchange, and the family. In *Contemporary theories about the family*, Vol. 2, eds. W. R. Burr et al., 1–41. New York: Free Press.

Otto, H. A. 1979. Developing human family potential, In *Building family strengths: Blue-prints for action*, eds. N. Stinnett, B. Chesser, and J. DeFrain, 39–50. Lincoln: University of Nebraska Press.

Otto, H. A. and R. Otto. 1976. The more joy in your marriage program. In *Marriage and family enrichment: New perspectives and programs*, ed. H. A. Otto. Nashville: Abingdon.

Peck, Judith Stern, and Jennifer R. Manocherian. 1989. Divorce in the changing family life cycle. In *The changing family life cycle*, 2d ed., eds. Betty Carter and Monica McGoldrick, 335–69. Boston: Allyn and Bacon.

Sabatelli, Ronald M. 1988. Exploring relationship satisfaction: A social exchange perspective on the interdependence between theory, research, and practice. *Family Relations* 37: 217–22.

Sakenfeld, Katharine Doob. 1985. *Faithfulness in action: Loyalty in biblical perspective*. Philadelphia: Fortress Press.

Sawin, Margaret M. 1979a. The family cluster model of family enrichment. In *Building family strengths: Blue-prints for action*, eds. N. Stinnett, B. Chesser, and J. DeFrain. Lincoln: University of Nebraska Press.

———. 1979b. *Family enrichment with family clusters*. Valley Forge, Penn.: Judson Press.

Sheek, G. William. 1985. *The word on families*. Nashville: Abingdon.

Spiegel, J. 1971. *Transactions: The interplay between individual, family and society*. New York: Science House.

Terkelson, Kenneth G. 1980. Toward a theory of the family life cycle. In *The changing family life cycle*, eds. E. A. Carter and M. McGoldrick, 21–52. Boston: Allyn and Bacon.

Thibaut, J. W., and H. H. Kelley. 1959. *The social psychology of groups*. New York: Wiley.

Tuckman, Bruce W. 1965. Developmental sequence in small groups. *Psychological Bulletin* 63: 384–99.

Weiss, R. S. 1982. Attachment in adult life. In *The place of attachment in human behavior*, eds. C. M. Parkes and J. Stevenson-Hinde. New York: Basic Books.

Wynne, Lyman C. 1984. The epigenesis of relational systems: A model for understanding family development. *Family Process* 23: 297–318.

Wynne, L. C. et al. 1958. Pseudo-mutuality in the family relations of schizophrenics. *Psychiatry* 21: 205–20.

4

A Network Focus for Family Ministry

Diane L. Pancoast

Pleasant words are like a honeycomb, sweetness to the soul and health to the body.

Prov. 16:24

As illustrated by this proverb, the connection between positive social contacts and physical and emotional health has long been recognized. In our more scientific age, a growing body of research from physiology as well as sociology and psychology documents the wisdom of the biblical proverb. Supportive relationships and expressions of caring from significant members of our networks do indeed have health-maintaining and enhancing effects. Pilisuk and Parks (1986) have reviewed this research recently and conclude, "There is now a mass of evidence to indicate that such support may be one of the critical factors distinguishing those who remain healthy from those who fall ill" (29). However, their investigations also lead them to be apprehensive about the ability of people to find such support in the future:

. . . Though supportive, interpersonal relationships are important in health maintenance, the traditional sources for providing such support seem to be declining. . . . The very social currents of careerism, autonomy, mobility, privacy, and achievement that disrupt our traditional roots and ties also make difficult the continuity of new bonds (59).

Perhaps it is a perversity of human nature not to value something until we are in danger of losing it. Our forests, our seas, even the air we breathe have been

DIANE L. PANCOAST, M.S.W., Ph.D., is a consultant and trainer on informal social support systems. A former professor at the Portland State School of Social Work (Ore.), Dr. Pancoast has authored and coauthored books and articles on social support and natural helping networks.

taken for granted until they have become so threatened that there are serious questions about whether or not they can be preserved with any quality. We have recently come to recognize that a very complex system of interactions maintains our natural world. We have invented a science, ecology, to study these interactions so that we can better understand how to maintain them.

So, too, it seems that we have taken for granted the web of social relationships that sustains humans through thick and thin—our social ecology—until we are beginning to see that these relationships are diminishing in number and strength. We need a science of social ecology to describe these social relationships and understand their important functions. Until recently, the study of social relationships has not seemed to fit within the disciplines of either sociology or psychology. Nor does social psychology, which has begun to study the psychological elements of interpersonal relationships, encompass the social structures within which they are embedded or the cultural, historical, geographical, and physical conditions which affect them.

An earlier world of villages and extended families could take social relationships for granted. Kai Erikson (1976) has described one such community:

> The closeness of communal ties is experienced on Buffalo Creek as a part of the natural order of things, and residents can no more describe that presence than fish are aware of the water they swim in. It is just there, the envelope in which they live, and it is taken entirely for granted (187).

Relationships in such communities were unavoidable, sometimes oppressively so. Children grew up surrounded by people who knew them and their families. Crises and major life transitions were times for a gathering of ritualized and informal support. People who were not able to support themselves because of handicaps, illness, widowhood, or old age could generally count on the support of relatives or neighbors.

We know that this was not always a happy picture of villagers dancing around a Maypole. People frequently paid a high price for this form of social security: they had little privacy, they were expected to conform to narrow standards of behavior, and they often undertook the care of others out of a sense of duty. Certain people were heavily scapegoated in these societies, and others were cast out entirely, often to die.

With the disappearance of this world in industrialized nations, however, we can see that many basic human needs were met in ways that our modern substitutes—day care, schools, public assistance, hospitals, and nursing homes—cannot always fulfill. We could not return to this world even if we wanted to, but we can become more aware of its positive aspects and seek to recreate them in the modern context.

How can we create the basis for rich, sustaining social contacts? To borrow another analogy from ecology, we have learned that fish do not spawn in fast-running streams. They need water that is slowed and shaded by fallen trees and overhanging brush. Similarly, people are not able to form meaningful, coherent social worlds in large-scale, fast-paced, impersonal settings. They need what James Coleman (1987, 37) has called "institutional underbrush," the untidy but lively social environments created by groups and activities, neighborhoods, and casual encounters.

It is particularly difficult to insure the creation and maintenance of this institutional underbrush from the top down, by governmental planning. The task is even more complicated in a pluralistic society such as ours with competing value systems and a high regard for individual privacy and freedom of choice. The church seems to be one of the major institutions remaining that offers opportunities for rebuilding supportive social networks on a shared value base. It is also one of the few remaining institutions that welcomes people of all ages. This chapter will show how a network perspective can be used by church leaders to assess the supportive potential of their institutions.

A Network Perspective

We must examine our social environments and assess their potential to provide sustaining relationships. We are like fishermen who must periodically spread out their nets to look for holes, loose knots, and fraying lines. We can no longer take for granted a social world which will provide us with the social contacts we need to build an adequate social support system. Findings from research on social-network analysis, as well as the experience of intervention efforts to strengthen networks, can suggest ways in which we can improve social networks.

In the past fifteen or twenty years sociologists, anthropologists, and psychologists have developed social-network analysis as a way of describing the social world of individuals, communities, and corporations when the more general sociological categories (e.g., social class, groups, roles) fail to correspond closely enough to the reality of experience in our rapidly changing, mobile society. As an example, the discussion of families in chapters 1 and 2 shows that our operational definition of a family is not as precise as we may think and that a shared understanding of what constitutes a family cannot be taken for granted.

When we take a closer look at the families we see around us, we realize that there is really quite a lot of variation in them, even if we focus on those who are living together in one household. Some include grandparents or grandchildren on a part-time or full-time basis, some are blended families from previous marriages, and some include foster children or other people unrelated by blood. Even though all of these people may be living under the same roof, they may not have equally strong ties to one another. In fact, some of them (a teen-ager home for the summer from college, or a young boy who is a member of a street gang, for example) may have stronger ties to people outside the household than within it. If we describe this collectivity as a specific network of persons linked by a mutually understood tie, an ecological family, we have a more precise picture than if we use the designation of "family" and assume we all know what is meant by it.

J. A. Barnes defined the essential characteristics of a network twenty-five years ago. "[A social network is] . . . a set of points which are joined by lines: the points of the image are people or sometimes groups and the lines indicate which people interact with each other" (Barnes 1954, 43). A network can be diagramed and while each network forms its own pattern, certain common characteristics can be described and compared.

Personal Networks and General Networks

Networks described from the perspective of an individual are called *personal* networks. Networks can also be described within a particular social setting such as a neighborhood, a school, or a church congregation, again according to a common criterion such as knowing one another. These are called *general* networks. Either way, network analysis focuses on the pattern of relationships and the implications of this pattern for the behavior of the individual members.

Several methodologies have been developed for mapping personal networks and helping individuals or families assess their networks (Attneave 1976; Maguire 1983; Hartman 1979; Rueveni et al. 1984). In this chapter, we will discuss general networks since they provide a useful approach for a church setting. However, church leaders might very well find it useful to map the personal networks of members of their congregations or to conduct workshops to enable others to map their own networks. Church-based social workers and other helping professionals in the church will certainly want to take personal networks into account when working with individuals and families.

Boundary Setting

One usually starts to map a general network by deciding on a boundary. It is common to study general networks within a group or organization. In this case, membership defines the boundary of the network. For our purposes, a church congregation plus the direct links of its members form the network of interest. Of course, denominations differ in how they draw their boundaries. Some have a parish concept; others use baptism, confirmation, or some other form of declared membership. Most would consider their doors open to all. Churches typically have a core group, however, who are regular participants in the life of the church and might be considered the nucleus of a general church network. Figure 4–1 shows a highly simplified example of such a network based on hypothetical friendship links among the members of a congregation.

Within a congregation we find individuals with many ties to other members as well as some comparatively isolated individuals. Some persons who have few ties within the congregation have many ties outside of it while others would have very few connections to nonchurch members. Studies of personal networks have shown that the size of individual networks varies considerably, particularly in the area of less intimate ties (Fischer 1982). Most people seem to have between six and ten persons in their intimate circle, that is persons whom they see very often, care about very much, and with whom they

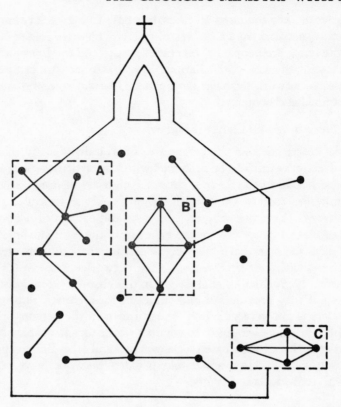

Friendship Networks in a Church Setting
Figure 4-1

exchange goods, services and emotional support (Hammer, Makiesky-Barrow and Gutwirth 1978).

The part of the network that involves less intimate ties varies more in size. This probably reflects individual variation in opportunity and enthusiasm. Looking at each point in our diagram as the base of a personal network, it can be seen that these individuals vary considerably in the size of their church-based networks. Of course, individuals have other potential members in their personal networks: family, workmates, neighbors, old friends, etc. A person with few relationships within the church might therefore have an extensive network outside of it. Another person, perhaps the center of the star in box A, might derive a large number of his significant relationships from within the church.

These overlapping personal networks in a church congregation form an overall, general network pattern. Tight cliques (boxes B and C) can be seen as well as individuals who form bridges between various parts of the congregation's network. Some people appear to be hubs of a great deal of network activity while others are more on the periphery. Some people may have a few key ties within the congregation and many others outside of it, serving as links between the church community and the larger environment.

The potentially rich web of association in a church congregation or other social setting offers an individual many opportunities to form new relationships and to strengthen the interconnections in his or her network. Here is institutional underbrush graphically displayed! We need to know how to maximize the potential of such settings in our increasingly impersonal world. Obviously, not all ties offer social support, actual or potential. But social support must be offered through interpersonal relationships. Network analysis offers us a set of tools to measure and monitor the social support potential of a particular setting, in this case, a church.

Network Analysis

We can illustrate some of the usefulness of this approach by referring to our diagram. The center of the star in box A, sometimes called a network *nexus*, is essential to the existence of the star. The nexus might be a person who has a strong link to a powerful outside person, and the other members of the network rely on the nexus for access to this outside person. Perhaps the nexus is very needy and dependent and keeps the network focused on him or her by discouraging contact among the other members. Whatever the dynamics and personalities involved, a star is inherently unstable over the long run for most of its members, since it ceases to exist without the nexus person. The network might be strengthened by creating ties among the members independent of the nexus and building another link to the outside person. However, network analysis would also alert us to the profound changes this would make in the social world of the nexus person. These effects would need to be dealt with as well.

Box B illustrates a clique within the congregation. It is a strong one since all four of the members are connected to each other. It is not exclusive, however, because two of the clique members have ties to others in the congregation. An example of this pattern might be a church board or planning committee which can draw cohesiveness and support from its interconnections while it maintains linkages to other segments of the church membership.

The one person in the clique diagrammed in box C who is a church member appears to have most of his or her significant relationships with persons who are not part of the congregation. This might be a teenager, who comes to church only because of family pressure, or a person who participates in church programs but receives social support elsewhere. In the first case, a goal might be to link the teenager to other congregation members to strengthen the commitment to church membership, or the teenager might be encouraged to involve more of his peer group in church activities. In the second case, one might simply want to recognize and respect the wishes of this person to keep various aspects of his or her life separate. It would be worth exploring, however, whether this person would like to expand and deepen her relationships with church members. These examples are speculative, and one should not assume that interventions are always necessary or even possible. They illustrate, however, the sort of information that a network analysis can provide.

So far, we have only looked at structural elements of the network, the patterns formed by the ties. The content of these relationships will also influence how the network functions. Among the most useful aspects to consider are the strength of the tie, the number of different types of content (called multiplexity in network terminology), and the frequency of interaction.

Strong and Weak Ties

Strong ties are based on a deeply felt commitment or a sense of intimacy and trust. It is possible to feel strong ties based on a common heritage or residence in a particular community, but most strong ties are based on kinship or strong personal attraction. Weak ties may be based on casual acquaintance, membership in the same organization, or having a friend in common. Weak ties can develop into strong ones. In our own lives, this may be how we found a spouse or made new friends after a move or a divorce. To help someone rebuild an intimate sector of his or her network or help an isolated person create one, it may be most productive to look for weak ties to build on rather than starting from scratch by introducing a total stranger. Church activities can be planned to allow participants to maximize opportunities for low-key interaction that will help them decide whether or not they would like to deepen the relationships.

Weak ties are also important because they offer us access to information and influence, opportunities to experience different values and lifestyles, and pathways out into the wider social world. The number and type of weak ties we have are related to race and social class; the families we are born into, the schools we attend, the neighborhoods we live in, and the work we do all affect the opportunities we have to develop weak ties. Healthy and effective networks, whether an individual's or a congregation's, have both strong and weak ties. It is especially important for church leaders to cultivate weak ties continuously in order to keep the church responsive to its environment and to reach out to new people and ideas which can contribute to the continual renewal of the congregation.

Multiplexity

Ties become stronger when they carry more than one type of content. If Johnny's Sunday School teacher also lives down the street and is the mother of his best friend, she is likely to be a much more significant person in his life than a teacher who is only seen on Sunday morning. In multiplex relationships, there is more pressure to resolve conflict in one aspect in order to preserve another. Thus, Johnny's Sunday School teacher might be more likely to deal with his disruptive behavior in class by trying to work out the problems instead of expelling him because she might know that he is having a rough time at home or because she wants to preserve the friendship between him and her own child or between herself and Johnny's mother. Naturally this is a two-sided coin since she is also more likely to know when he is playing hooky and be sure that his parents hear about it! The point is not that multiplex relationships are better or worse than single-stranded ones, only that they operate differently.

Interaction

It is a mistake to assume that frequency of interaction and intimacy are strongly and positively correlated. We can have very strong ties with family members and old friends that we seldom see. On the other hand, we may be thrown together daily with persons with whom we maintain a distanced relationship. There needs to be some sort of interaction, however, to maintain a tie. It is important to realize that for some isolated members of the congregation, even fairly limited associations in the church context may provide some of their only opportunities for social interaction. In the past few decades, many churches have responded to the decrease in the opportunities for spontaneous social interaction available to people in their everyday lives by increasing those opportunities in the church setting. From brief interactions during the worship services to more extensive "family-fests" and other gatherings, churches are providing social contexts which will facilitate informal interactions on which more lasting ties can be built.

Problem-Anchored Helping Networks

Donald Warren (1981) developed one very useful application of network concepts, problem-anchored helping networks (PAHNs). Instead of focusing on the ongoing relationships in a network, as we have been doing, he highlights the process of mobilization to respond to a particular problem. The salient linkage in a PAHN is that which ties together those people who offer assistance, whether it be to an individual or in helping to resolve a community or organizational problem. On our diagram we could highlight those pathways in the congregation's network that were activated in order to solve a particular problem.

We could imagine a situation in which a member of the congregation had a critically ill family member. The assistance this person would be able to receive from the congregation would depend on his or her location in the network as much as on personal help-seeking style and norms within the group. If the distressed individual contacts church members who are connected to others in the congregation, his or her problem-solving efforts can draw on these indirect ties as well. Those contacted can "spread the word" about the crisis and organize help so that efforts are combined more smoothly to bring in meals, care for children, or visit the hospital. When the crisis subsides, there is likely to be a lower level of interaction again in most of these connections.

In his research, Warren found that it was not an absence of problems that was associated with individual or community well-being but the ability to cope successfully with the problems that came along by mobilizing an effective helping network. In surveys of the PAHNs of individuals, Warren found that the most effective ones used three or four different helpers who were able to provide a variety of types of help (i.e., active social support as well as listening and offering advice). Ineffective problem-solving networks had too few links, or the helpers offered too limited a range of support, or, at the opposite extreme, were too large or complex to offer coherent support. An entire congregation of several hundred members would not serve very effectively as a PAHN. In the effective networks, direct linkages, besides being helpful in themselves, were pathways into the larger network. In ineffective PAHNs, linkages were dead ends, blocking access to others.

Building on Warren's research, a church wanting to provide a social environment which facilitated the problem solving of its members would have the following characteristics:

- A general climate which encouraged people to draw upon each other for help and which legitimated many different ways of helping
- A variety of helpers with a variety of helping styles
- Members who were willing and able to serve as effective links to outside resources such as professional services

In Warren's research, communities as well as individuals were found to have different modal patterns. In some communities, different sources of help were not connected to each other, so that turning to one source blocked access to others. In others, each potential source was a gateway to others as well as a source of direct help.

The scope of Warren's work did not include a thorough investigation of what caused the variations in community patterns but many of the findings are suggestive and have implications for a church setting. Social class and occupational status played a part, since the more affluent communities tended to have more effective networks. Also not surprising was the association between economic and residential stability and effective networks.

However, other important factors were not as obvious. Population density was a significant factor. Moderate density seemed to be optimal, providing "enough behavior settings and chance contacts to stimulate helping exchanges, but not such a high density as to reduce privacy options that are conducive to keeping one's helping confined to known intimates and primary group members" (Warren 110–11). More effective communities also showed more integration into the larger society, as evidenced by more voter participation and more interest in national problems. Their PAHNs included professionals and formal service agencies, but these contacts were combined with informal ones and generally mediated through informal network members. Effective communities had ethnic associations and many strong churches. Warren notes that the presence of many flourishing churches was especially important in distinguishing healthy black communities from those in which problems were not effectively solved.

These findings, too, have implications for strengthening a church as a social environment which facilitates problem solving. Churches should seek to strengthen the following characteristics in their congregations:

1. Economic and occupational diversity.
2. Stability: rapid turnover in membership makes it difficult to form relationships.

3. Moderate density: the congregation should be sufficiently large to allow for a variety of relationships among the members. The church should provide a number of behavior settings in which relationships can be formed.
4. Integration into the larger society.
5. Ties to professional sources of help through members of the congregation.

Beyond the resolution of the problem at hand, Warren identified three ways in which Problem-Anchored Helping Networks strengthen the larger community. First, the mobilizing of a PAHN offers a reason to keep alive a weak tie with someone who was formerly closer. Secondly, the PAHNs serve as spawning grounds for the creation of new, close-knit ties, forged in the process of responding to a crisis. Finally, they strengthen ties by creating a base of reciprocity, so that future efforts to help resolve a problem are ways of paying back help received in the past. In these ways, resolving problems through networks becomes a way of building community and thus benefits the whole network as well as the individual. Similarly, churches which develop their problem solving capacities can expect to reap benefits as organizations as well as contribute to the welfare of their members.

Warren raises two interesting cautions, however, to a general enthusiasm for encouraging the use of a congregation for building PAHNs. On the personal level he feels that it is possible to distinguish helping from social intimacy. In fact, they may often be antagonistic to each other. Asking for help, especially if it is done repeatedly, may undermine close relationships. Additionally, if the close friend fails to meet the request for help, the whole relationship is jeopardized. Many people prefer not to risk being disappointed, relying on weaker ties for explicit help. Therefore, an effective PAHN should include both the sort of strong relationships that can provide more generalized social support that one hopes to get without having to ask for it, and looser, weaker ties which can provide specific help and information. It is not a good idea to encourage someone with a problem to rely on his intimates for all types of help, and people in a congregation should not be made to feel any pressure to offer more extensive help in personal networks than is normative for those networks. While it is good to foster a general climate of helping and caring, for example, it is better to let specific offers of help occur spontaneously rather than making formal requests of individuals. Likewise, potential helpers should not feel pressured into drawing upon their connections to outside resources. They will be best able to judge whether or not such a request would be appropriate and what effect it might have on future interactions. On the other hand, a person in need of help may be reluctant to presume upon a weak tie by directly asking for assistance. In this case a "matchmaker" in the church network may be in the best position to judge whether or not this request would be well-received and to make the connection.

On the general network level, churches, like neighborhoods and other social contexts, vary in the richness of the resources their networks have to offer. If people are encouraged to look within their churches to find help in solving problems but the church has only a few members who are able or willing to extend themselves to others, these scarce resources will be exploited and the few helpers will soon feel burned out. If a church has only one member with medical expertise, for example, he or she may feel that Sunday mornings are the busiest day of clinical practice and start to avoid attending church. If the church lacks ties to other resources in the community or encourages isolation for ideological reasons, members who are urged to keep their problems in the church family may be badly served and fail to get the expertise of alternative options that they need.

In order to function effectively as a supportive social environment, a church needs to cultivate a variety of helping options, allow a great deal of latitude for the expression of varying levels of concern, and maintain open boundaries and good connections to other parts of the community that can also offer assistance in PAHNs—community groups, professional services, ethnic and cultural groups, kinship systems, and the workplace. A church can provide a rich culture for the growth of PAHNs, but it must be aware of the pitfalls and limitations and be appropriately cautious in attempting to alter or influence the problem-solving efforts of members of the congregation.

Much can be done, however. Warren's survey of over 2500 randomly chosen residents of metropolitan Detroit found that 14 percent of them did not turn to anyone for help, and 24 percent turned to only one person, typically the person's spouse. Fischer (1982) found similar results for a large sample of Californians. If we can assume that the old adage "two heads are better than one" still holds, there should be plenty of room for expanding the problem-solving resources of many people without overtaxing church members or other potential members of PAHNs.

A Role Perspective: Key Helping Figures

A third way of assessing helping activities is to see the offer of help as the performance of behavior associated with a certain role. Although our society is not particularly clear in its rules about what forms of assistance may be expected from different roles, there are, nonetheless, certain generally held assumptions within a particular community or subculture. One way a program which tries to enhance informal helping activities can get into trouble is to violate these assumptions.

Helper Types

In a national study of informal helping activities conducted several years ago, we identified six types of informal helpers (Froland et al. 1983). Although each type of helping has certain unique characteristics, it is probably more useful to think of them as roles rather than separate categories, since a particular individual may have different helping roles in different parts of his or her network, either simultaneously or at different times. Informal helping is, and should be, fluid, flexible, and defined by the participants.

Social Intimates: Family and Friends. Christians are told to love one another, but these feelings are not held with equal intensity toward all members of the network. Even within the circle of his disciples, Jesus had those whom he especially loved and confided in (John 13:23). It is the close circle of intimates from which one would expect to draw the generalized social support described by Donald Warren. Intimates can be expected to rally around when we have a crisis. These relationships, in their ideal form, are the prototypes for all helping relationships. When we want to describe an intimate helping encounter we often compare it to familial relationships: "like a brother," "motherly advice," "play sister." Helping among intimates is generally based on commitment and concern rather than on special skills or knowledge. The circle need not be large, as long as it contains at least one person who can be a confidant.

Neighbors. Generally, people think of their neighbors as those who live quite close to them, although sometimes the definition is broadened, especially if there is a strong sense of community, to include residents of a wider area. There are certain expectations of general neighborliness, but they may be violated in practice. These might include help in an emergency, watching for criminal activity, and, perhaps, the loan of tools or small acts of assistance. Most people can also name several neighbors with whom they have more extensive helping relationships that include taking in the mail or watering plants, sharing rides to events or to shop, and exchanging local gossip. In general, however, while the level of knowledge about many aspects of one another's lives may be fairly high, the level of involvement is low.

Natural Helpers. While we are all involved in giving and receiving help from time to time, there are some people for whom helping is a more central activity than it is for most of us. These people are sometimes called *natural helpers* (Collins and Pancoast 1976; Patterson 1977). They are willing to make themselves available to people in need in their families, neighborhoods, workplaces, or the organizations to which they belong. They have the sort of personal skills, similar to those of helping professionals, which make them particularly effective problem solvers. Some natural helpers hold positions of leadership, but many prefer to work behind the scenes. Their importance can only be detected through the sort of network analysis we have discussed previously, when they stand out as nexus people on a network map, or by observation over a long period of time.

Natural helpers exhibit what we have called "freedom from drain." Although they share many of the life circumstances of those they help and do not hesitate to get heavily involved in helping if it becomes necessary, their own life circumstances and their helping activities do not drain them of the ability to function or to be enthusiastic about helping someone else. Natural helpers have usually developed a good sense of the limits of their abilities and capacity to be helpful.

Although natural helpers know a great deal about the lives of those they help, they respect confidences. If they did not, word would quickly get out in the community and people would stop turning to them for help. Chapter 13 will focus specifically on natural helpers as a resource.

Role-Related Helpers. While these people may also have the interpersonal skills that are typical of the natural helper, they are more likely to fill an influential role in the community and be turned to for help primarily because of that role. Some fill roles, such as a pastor or a public health nurse, that are considered to include helping as part of the role definition. Others have positions that locate them at crossroads where they are likely to be turned to for help because of their visibility: storekeepers, postmasters, teachers, bartenders, and beauticians.

Not all people who have jobs that bring them into contact with the public are willing or able to provide help, of course, but some see this as an important and satisfying part of their daily routine. A man who runs a neighborhood shoe-repair shop fills it with folding chairs to encourage passersby to come in and sit for awhile. "A lot of people don't like people to come in and just sit, but I don't mind. I love people, I just love people," he says.

People with Similar Problems. To deal with the specialized problems of modern life, people are increasingly motivated to look for help from someone who has shared the same problem. This person is not likely to be found among the limited number of relationships in a personal network. A PAHN can provide linkage to someone else who has recently lost a husband, been divorced, or undergone a cancer operation. This shared experience is the primary basis of the relationship and interactions are usually directly focused on the particular problem. Interactions are more likely to be structured with specific appointments or meetings, in the case of support groups. There is no initial expectation that the relationship will become multiplex or that the individuals will become ongoing members of each other's networks, although more generalized friendships frequently do form from such contacts.

Volunteers. Volunteers are probably the helper type that comes most readily to mind when thinking of types of informal helping. This form of help is usually stranger-to-stranger and is channeled through a formal organization. Of all the forms of helping we have discussed, it is the most likely to involve inequality of status between the helper and the recipient—both in terms of socioeconomic status and of general coping ability. There is also an unequal exchange, with the volunteer clearly defined as the helper. Relationships are usually structured and time limited; they frequently involve the provision of some form of instrumental assistance. All of these role characteristics imply that volunteering, unlike any of the other helping roles, requires a formal structure and some outside initiative to develop and sustain helping relationships.

Keeping the Roles Straight

Each helping type has something unique to offer in an overall plan for informal helping in a church context but will not be effective if the characteristics of the role are not respected. A neighbor may be very willing to keep an eye on an elderly neighbor but not willing to become a confidant. A natural helper will freely offer help when he or she perceives a need but may not accept an assignment to offer assistance to a stranger. A support group is likely to be more useful to its members when it consists of people who do not associate otherwise and when instrumental assistance is not expected. It can then provide a new sector in its members' networks, and the common problems they face will not become a burden.

This is not to say that a relationship begun on one basis may not evolve into another type, only that the expectations should be consistent and mutually determined. Any enhancement program initiated by a congregation should be clear about the expectations for participation.

The Church as a Support Base for Key Helping Figures

In surveys, informal helpers frequently cite religion as a motivator (Patterson 1984; Kelley and Kelley 1985). People expect to find aid, comfort, and encouragement in a church setting. The Good Samaritan is cited in the Bible because he was willing to help a stranger, perhaps even an enemy, the ultimate act of charity. The Bible also leaves no doubt as to the proper Christian response to the universal question, "Am I my brother's keeper?" The church is in an excellent position, then, to offer validation and support to the types of informal helping we have been discussing.

It was mentioned earlier that the church is one of the few inclusive milieux left in modern society. Ideally, it meets Robert Frost's definition of home as the place where, "'when you have to go there, they have to take you in.'" The door of the church is always open. The rituals of the church provide, among other things, an opportunity for people of all ages and backgrounds to join together in a collective activity. Out of this association, friendships can be formed, PAHNs mobilized, volunteers recruited, needs expressed, common problems identified, and natural helpers made aware of opportunities to offer help.

A religious setting provides a common ground for people to come together to explore their mutual needs: to help as well as be helped, to care for as well as be taken care of. Ecological family relationships can be fostered in a church setting to build stronger, more flexible families that can meet the challenges of today's society.

References

Attneave, C. L. 1976. Social networks as the unit of intervention. In *Family therapy: Theory and practice*, ed. P. Guerin. New York: Gardner Press.

Barnes, J. A. 1954. Class and committees in a Norwegian island parish. *Human Relations* 7 (1):39-58.

Coleman, J. S. 1987. Families and schools. *Educational Researcher* 16 (6): 32-38.

Collins, A. H. and D. L. Pancoast. 1976. *Natural helping networks*. Washington, D.C.: National Association of Social Workers.

Erikson, K. T. 1976. *Everything in its path: Destruction of community in the Buffalo Creek flood*. New York: Simon and Schuster.

Fischer, C. S. 1982. *To dwell among friends: Personal networks in town and city*. Chicago: University of Chicago Press.

Froland, C. and et al. 1981. *Helping networks and human services*. Beverly Hills: Sage.

Hammer, M., S. Makiesky-Barrow, and L. Gutwirth. 1978. Social networks and schizophrenia. *Schizophrenia Bulletin* 4:522-45.

Hartman, A. 1979. *Finding families: An ecological approach to family assessment in adoption.* Beverly Hills: Sage.

Kelley, P. and V. R. Kelley. 1985. Supporting natural helpers: A cross-cultural study. *Social Casework* (June):358–66.

Maguire, L. 1983. *Understanding social networks.* Beverly Hills: Sage.

Patterson, S. L. 1977. Toward a conceptualization of natural helping. *Arete* 4 (3):161–73.

———— 1984. The characteristics and helping patterns of older rural natural helpers in the Midwest and in New England. *Dissertation Abstracts International* 8428892.

Pilisuk, M. and S. H. Parks. 1986. *The healing web: Social networks and human survival.* Hanover, N.H.: University of New England Press.

Rueveni, U., ed. 1984. Applications of networking in family and community. *Family Therapy* 6:2.

Warren, D. I. 1981. *Helping networks: How people cope with problems in the urban community.* Notre Dame: University of Notre Dame Press.

5

The Church as a Context for Professional Practice

Diana S. Richmond Garland and
Sister Ann Patrick Conrad

Professionals who work with families in church settings need to consider the role and function of the local church as well as understand the congregation's perception of itself as a service provider. This chapter will address key issues in professional practice in church settings. Examples from various Christian denominations will be used to illustrate central concepts and principles.

Church settings can be considered either primary or secondary settings. In *primary settings*, providing a supportive context for professional practice is a primary organizational or agency function. For example, family specialists usually practice in family and children's service agencies; mental health specialists practice in community mental health centers and other appropriate settings. Many church agencies can be considered primary settings.

By contrast, *secondary settings* host the family professional's practice but do not identify primarily with the professional's goals. In secondary contexts, the professional provides services that enable the organization to achieve its primary goals more effectively. In hospitals, family professionals help families of patients provide adequate care upon release from the hospital so that recovery or rehabilitation can occur. In schools, the professional helps families and teachers deal with the needs of children so that the children can learn more effectively.

Family services are only one of several major goals of churches and their agencies, not the core of the church's justification for existence. Family ministry

DIANA S. RICHMOND GARLAND, M.S.S.W., Ph.D., is associate professor of social work in the Carver School of Church Social Work at The Southern Baptist Theological Seminary. An author of books and articles on family issues, Dr. Garland has served as a social worker and director in a community mental health center. ANN P. CONRAD, M.S.W., D.S.W., is assistant professor at the National Catholic School of Social Service, The Catholic University of America, Washington, D.C. She has conducted national research and published articles on parish social ministry, social justice, and professional ethics.

may be a major focus of a church, but rarely is it *the* major focus. In order to be effective in leading the church's family ministry, then, the professional must be knowledgeable about the church and its levels and variations of organizational structures and purposes. This chapter attempts to give the family professional some skills for assessing a particular church organization and making an appropriate place in that organization for family ministry.

What Is the Church?

Daniel Moberg, in *The Church as a Social Institution*, provides a useful foundation for assessing church organizations as contexts for family ministry. Moberg defines the church as "organized religion," which includes all organizations which seek to develop, renew, and guide people's religious lives (Moberg 1984, 1). The church is by definition a social organization with a structure based on (1) a division of responsibility and privilege between persons, (2) tasks to be performed, and (3) defined processes, rules, and norms for performing them. It embraces a body of beliefs that is codified in creeds and doctrines. Members identify with one another and with the organization. Despite variations in structures, churches are groups of people acting together on behalf of religious interests. Before further discussing the nature and role of family ministries, we will define concepts which we consider central to understanding the church as a context for practice.

First, *the church*, as used here, refers to the universal church—all followers of the gospel tradition in the past, present, and future. The church provides a value system that, at least to some extent, motivates and guides the self-critique and continuous modifications and development of church organizations. Acts 2 describes the embodiment of this ideal in the early church:

> And all who believed were together and had all things in common; and they sold their possessions and goods and distributed them to all, as any had need. And day by day, attending the temple together and breaking bread in their homes, they partook of food with glad and generous hearts, praising God and having favor with all the people. . . . Now the company of those who believed were of one heart and soul, and no one said that any of the things which he possessed was his own, but they had everything in common (Acts 2:44–47, 4:32).

The fellowship of the church is based on Jesus' promise to be with his followers whenever and wherever they congregate: "where two or three are gathered in my name, there am I in the midst of them" (Matt. 18:20).

Paul instructed Christians to consider themselves part of one body, the body of Christ, each with an indispensable function (Rom. 12:3–9; 1 Cor. 12). In another image, Christians together are members of the "household of God" who with Christ as the cornerstone, grow into a holy temple, a dwelling place for God in the Spirit (Eph. 2:19–22).

Although actual groups of Christians may vary dramatically in the emphasis they place on different aspects of these ideals, the scriptural descriptions of the church provide a common ideal and identity for churches across denominations, varying theologies, and organizational structures.

Second, a *congregation* or *local church* refers to a group of persons banded together for religious purposes who have a shared group identity. They often have a central meeting place such as a church building and may be referred to as the group which meets in that location. A local church may also be identified as a *parish*, which usually refers to a geographic community within which the members reside.

Third, a *denomination* refers to an organization of many congregations who share certain beliefs and practices and choose to cooperate together. Examples include the Methodist denomination or the Baptist denomination. Denominations frequently sponsor various social service and social-action agencies and projects, publication houses, colleges and seminaries, and national and international mission projects. Denominations are organized into overlapping levels, such as local, state, and national bodies.

Fourth, *ecumenical organizations* are organizations of local churches, denominations, or both which choose to cooperate in activities and goals through which they transcend theological, ecclesiastical, and historical differences. Ecumenical activities also occur at several levels, from community ministries composed of churches of various denominations that are located in the same neighborhood or community to the World Council of Churches, the World Evangelical Fellowship, and other international organizations.

Family ministry perspectives and programs have significant roles to play in congregations, denominational agencies and structures, and ecumenical organizations. Denominational and ecumenical organizations depend upon and are composed of congregations, requiring that even the family professional employed by these church organizations understand the nature and structure of the local church in order to develop effective family ministries.

The Local Church Congregation

The local church can be viewed as a "mediating structure" which, like the family, stands between individuals' private lives and large social institutions (Himes 1985). It serves as a buffer that protects individuals from having to deal with these large social institutions alone. For example, individuals in a neighborhood who are opposed to the use of alcohol may use a local church as their advocate when a local government considers changing zoning ordinances so that neighborhood restaurants can serve alcohol. In the sanctuary movement, some local churches have become advocates with national government for voiceless political refugees (Bau 1985).

The mediation role of the church can operate in the opposite direction as well; the local church might provide a means for large social institutions to reach individuals. Community mental health and other social service agencies often need a pastor's endorsement to gain access to individuals within a local congregation. Churches that sponsor preventive and educational programs such as parent training, help for adult children of frail, elderly parents, or divorce adjustment provide access for social services to families who might never consider seeking such help from an agency.

Not only do churches provide an avenue for professional services. They frequently enhance the effectiveness of those services. When professionals offer family services through a local church, they have access not only to particular target families but also to an actual or potential social network for those families. For example, a parenting course in a church often includes participants who are potential or actual friends who can continue to support and encourage one another in any new parenting skills they learn long after the course has ended.

Although many families who may need services cannot be reached through local churches, the numbers of those people who do participate in local congregations indicate that the church continues to be a significant mediating structure in our society. In a national study, seven out of ten adults indicated that they were members of a church or synagogue, and many others stated that they regularly attended (Moberg 1984, 32). Churches, through the outreach of their members, have contact with and access to many more persons in their community beyond those who hold formal church membership.

Churches also serve as mediating structures because, despite the exception of large mega-churches, most churches are relatively small, allowing for frequent and personal interaction among the members. In 1982, the average American congregation had 456 members. This number varied considerably by denomination, with Roman Catholic parishes averaging over 2,000 persons per parish and Protestant denominations ranging from a low of 98 persons (Church of God) to 464 persons (Lutheran) per congregation (Jacquet 1982). Some churches deliberately have restricted congregational size, beginning a new congregation when a critical number is reached. Many large churches are moving toward the use of cell groups which provide face-to-face relationships between members.

Wach (1951) described three major forms of Christian religious communities which still have relevance in today's church. *Ecclesiastical* bodies (Lutheran, Calvinists, and Anglicans) claim exclusiveness (at least they did so initially) as the one true church and have authoritatively defined doctrines and structures. *Independent* bodies (Baptists, Quakers, etc.) emphasize congregational church polity and are less institutional; they stress a more spiritual notion of Christian fellowship and oppose the identification of the church with any human institution. *Sectarian* bodies (Holiness and Pentecostal groups) oppose the religious practices of other church organizations, insisting on their own exclusive role in the kingdom of God. Their fellowship is based on sharing norms of faith and ritual, and upon disciplined individual conduct.

In the United States, these three forms of church organizations tend to blend, with a church beginning as a sect and evolving into a denomination (group of independent bodies) or, less often, an ecclesiastical body. Perhaps *cults* should also be considered in any typology of church organizations. Cults tend to be small, exclusive groups, often built around a charismatic leader, and short-lived. They usually concern themselves mainly with the problems and spiritual experiences of the individual, not with families or other levels of the social order (Yinger 1957).

Organizational Structures

Denominations vary dramatically in the nature of their formal structures. Congregational structures often reflect the organizational structures of the denomination to which they belong, but considerable variation occurs even within denominations. These variations do not simply grow out of organizational development processes; they also reflect a church's or denomination's theology and belief about the nature of the church.

A church's governance can be described using one of three basic types: episcopal, presbyterian, and congregational. These correspond roughly to political monarchies, aristocracies, and democracies, respectively (Moberg 1984, 94).

In *episcopal* polity (Roman Catholic, Episcopal, Lutheran), authority is vested in an ecclesiastical hierarchy which has control of the clergy. Authority flows from central church government down, so that clergy can operate independently of local congregations. The congregation may protest the actions of the church leader but cannot initiate action against that leader without the involvement of higher authority.

In *presbyterian* polity (Presbyterian, Methodist), local congregations theoretically have the authority, but, in fact, the clergy who control the middle levels of church organization along with the elders in local congregations tend to operate as an aristocracy. Clergy are subject to control by both the congregation, operating through its elders, and the middle levels of church organization, the presbytery.

In *congregational* polity (Baptists), churches loosely organize themselves using a democratic form of government. Local churches retain their autonomy and right to choose and control clergy. The congregation itself operates as a democracy.

Even the denominations named often mix these types of government. Episcopal and Presbyterian churches show increasingly democratic tendencies. From the other direction, congregational churches increasingly vest power in their centralized governments (Moberg, 1984, 95). Nevertheless, the key characteristics remain salient.

A church's polity directly affects the choices the effective professional makes in seeking to influence decisions made and programs implemented. For example, episcopal polity allows the church leader to use the power of a secure office to take a stand on social issues and to develop programs that might not receive the required majority vote in a locally autonomous congregational church. In addition, denominational levels of church government develop policy statements, provide materials, and develop programs that have a significant impact on the family ministry of many local congregations. In 1988, for example, the National Conference of Catholic Bishops published *A Family Perspective in Church and Society: A Manual for All Pastoral Leaders*. This document urged all Catholic parishes throughout the United States to consider the family as a system, to be sensitive to the changing needs of families today, and to incorporate a family perspective in all the Church's policies, programs, ministries, and services.

On the other hand, local autonomous congregational churches may develop creative services to meet particular local needs or may create innovative family ministry programs that can serve as models for other churches because they are not required to follow the direction of any central denominational government. They may also involve themselves in activities that would not be endorsed or supported by a central denominational government.

Of course, within these formal structures, churches vary in the actual informal structures through which they operate. A congregational church with a highly charismatic leader may in fact operate on an authoritarian decision making model: the church leader dictates the primary policy and practice of the congregation. Similarly, episcopal structures may in fact be quite democratic with major decisions made by general consensus. The general typology of church organizations presented here can be used, however, to formulate hypotheses from which the professional can then develop a more refined assessment of the particular formal and informal decision making and organizational processes within a particular congregation.

Assessing the Individual Congregation

Historical Identity

Each congregation has its own historical identity. It may have begun as a small rural congregation that became a rapidly growing suburban church. A church may itself have moved, sometimes more than once. Or, it may have identified itself with a particular population group and then relocated to the suburbs along with its membership. Thus, the Broadway Baptist Church may be located miles from its initial location on Broadway.

A church's identity also includes its historical role in a community. It may have been the first church of its denomination in a community, and therefore has served as the mother church for other congregations as well as being the major denominational representative in the community. A church may have been formed from a splinter group that developed in another church's divisive conflict. Or a church may have begun because of a particular vision of its founders, with a particular emphasis and concern that gives direction to its life.

Finally, a church's identity also includes its current vision of itself. It may see itself as a mainline church which attempts to meet the needs of a diverse group of members. Or, it may see itself as a denominational or community gadfly, committed to trying new forms of worship, beginning programs and ministries, and taking stands on controversial denominational or community issues.

Stage of the Life Cycle

According to Moberg (1984), churches have life cycles just as families do. As a church develops, it creates or takes on formal structures; if it is a member of a denomination, it usually mirrors the structures of the governing body. It also develops its own informal structures, traditions, mission statement and goals, rules and norms, division of labor between clergy and members, dreams and visions, cohesiveness, and identity. Increasingly, it imposes formal rules upon members, producing conformity. Efficiency becomes a major value. Because the church is a voluntary organization, however, this increasing formalization may begin to impair the effectiveness of the organization in maintaining the involvement of its members. Renewal comes through relaxation of formal rules or greater emphasis on informal processes and social interaction and support among members.

Moberg has identified five stages in a church's life cycle; a sixth stage has been added by the authors as follows:

1. *Incipient organization.* Unrest and dissatisfaction with existing churches grow until leadership arises for beginning a new congregation, sect, or cult. There is often a high degree of collective excitement.

2. *Formal organization.* Followers commit themselves by becoming members of the new church which now separates itself from any parent church. The church formalizes and publicizes its goals to attract additional members. It develops a creed and behavioral norms. The congregation emphasizes ways it is different from nonmembers.

3. *Maximum efficiency.* Leadership becomes less charismatic and emotional and more rational and bureaucratic. Rapid growth requires new committees, boards, and executives. Leaders are committed and efficient, and the processes of decision making and the rituals that symbolize the beliefs of the congregation serve as means to shared goals.

4. *Institutionalization.* Formalism takes over. The leadership becomes more concerned with perpetuating its own interests than maintaining the distinctiveness that brought the group into existence in the first place. Worship becomes formal. Conflict and consciousness of distinctiveness with the outside world is replaced with toleration. Sermons become topical lectures rather than the fervent discourses of the church's youth.

5. *Disintegration.* The institution becomes unresponsive to the personal and social needs of its members. Symptoms of disintegration include formalism, indifference, patronage, and corruption. The church becomes inactive and financial support dwindles (Moberg 1984, 118–22).

6. *Organizational renewal.* From the dying ashes, a new group may begin the life cycle again. In this stage new leadership emerges, with an interest in reevaluating the church's mission in the light of current trends in theology, mission, and the needs of society and the congregation.

Just as a family professional would not intervene in a family system without first assessing and understanding the issues that the family is dealing with in the family life cycle, so the professional concerned with leading the church in family ministry needs to assess the church's life cycle issues. For example, intervention in a congregation in the institutional phase may need to address the needs of families and also the congregation as a whole for renewal and revitalization. Renewal can be encouraged through family ministry programs such as family clusters or programs that develop and nurture social support networks.

Size, Staff, and Decision Making

Churches come in all sizes, from house churches with less than twenty members with no paid staff to memberships numbering in the thousands with a substantial group of paid full-time and part-time professional and clerical staff. The staffing arrangements will, to a certain extent, influence the nature and extent of activities that can be carried out. Churches also have vastly differing roles for paid staff and nonpaid members. In some, a board of nonpaid members —deacons or elders—may control the decisions and activities of the church community. Others, who may have the same formal structures, may informally leave control of the church to the paid staff which merely reports its decisions to the church boards and committees for approval. Finally, in some, the entire church membership makes decisions together in a democratically run business meeting. A family ministry perspective is needed wherever decisions about the life of the congregation are being made since these decisions may have an impact on the family life of the members.

Stability

Professional intervention needs to be carried out with sensitivity to the relative stability or flux in which a church finds itself. Is the congregation in a period of rapid growth or decline? Is the membership relatively stable, with many lifetime members, or does the membership experience relatively rapid turnover? Does the church carry a heavy debt because of a building program, or is it relatively debt-free and able to commit itself to the projects and programs it chooses? How stable is the leadership of the church? Has the pastor been in the church thirty years or three months?

Ties to Denominations and Ecumenical Groups

Churches with the same denominational affiliation may vary dramatically in the degree to which they identify with their denomination. In some denominations the congregation decides the degree to which it will support the denomination financially and programatically. Denominational issues may be central or peripheral concerns for a congregation. Churches may even choose to affiliate with two or more denominations, or to withdraw from its denomination. A congregation may also choose to involve itself in or eschew ecumenical efforts in its community or at national and international levels. In contrast, within the Catholic tradition, parishes have well-defined ties to diocesan and archdiocesan structures, and there is a clear mandate to collaborate in ecumenical efforts.

The Nature of the Church

A Voluntary Organization

Members choose or choose not to participate in a church congregation. If they do not like the direction, the decisions, or the processes of a church, they may choose to disaffiliate themselves. In some denominations, if local churches are not in agreement with the directions of their denomination, they may choose to withdraw support. Conflict can be particularly problematic in local congregations since members have the often-used option of simply withdrawing.

The voluntary nature of the church requires a distinctive response on the part of the professional. This is true even of the professional employed by a denominationally sponsored child welfare organization, such as Lutheran Social Services, that may appear to be more similar to than different from state sponsored child welfare programs. Professionals must relate not only to the organization which employs them but to other levels of church organization, including local congregations. Significant amounts of time need to be spent consulting, speaking, and developing resources in local churches; hence, skills in encouraging participation, collaboration, and enabling are essential.

Mission and Goals

Providing family services is vital to a church only as these services are demonstrably integral to the overall purposes of the church. The mission of the church is to proclaim the Good News and to serve as a living witness to the love of God as shown in the life, death, and resurrection of Jesus Christ. Effective family professionals articulate the relationship between family ministry and this overarching mission of the church community (Garland 1988). The mission of the church is expressed in worship and evangelism, fellowship, and service (Conrad 1980). Family ministry perspectives and programs can be incorporated into all aspects of the church's mission, although they do not dominate any one.

Evangelism and Worship. A primary purpose of a congregation is to worship God and to proclaim the kingdom of God to others. The incarnation of Jesus into a human family highlights the dignity and worth of the family. Evangelism is "being, doing, and telling the gospel of the kingdom of God, in order that by the power of the Holy Spirit persons and structures may be converted to the Lordship of Jesus Christ" (Miles 1988, 275). Entire family structures can be evangelized (Acts 16:33). In chapter 2 we saw that the very form of the family has become a target of change in contemporary society.

Fellowship. Importantly, churches provide a sense of support and fellowship among the members. Fellowship of church members, the "communion of saints," is modeled on family relationships, symbolized by the use of family names in referring to one another—sister, brother, mother, father, children of God.

Service. Service to one another, usually referred to as social ministry, has traditionally been an indispensable function of the church (Conrad 1980). Social ministry refers to ministries of care and service to those both inside and outside the church family. Social ministry, which requires a diversity of approaches and pluralistic forms of service, includes both direct social services as well as social action in the cause of justice. Social services are defined as communal provisions to promote individual and group well-being and to aid those in difficulty. They include those helping and developmental services offered to individuals, groups, and families. Christians are called to serve, whether or not the service leads to conversion of those served. Social action includes such social-organizational activities as community organization and class advocacy, which are directed to systems change. Social service ministries often lead to social action in an attempt to change the noxious environmental forces that created the service needs in the first place. For example, instead of helping poor families pay exhorbitant utility bills, a church becomes involved in lobbying for legislation that will limit utility bills to a fixed percentage of income, or for legislation requiring landlords to weatherize low-income rental properties.

Delos Miles says that the story of the Samaritan illustrates the difference between social service and social action. What the Samaritan did was social service. If he had sought to change the conditions which led to robbing and mugging on the Jericho road, that would have been social action (Miles 1988). Rahner (1978) referred to these forms of ministry as newly developing models of the spiritual and corporal works of mercy. Clearly, family ministry needs to include both social service and social action.

The Role of Members

Unlike social service agencies, the nonpaid members, not professional staff, provide the heart of Christian social services. Ideally, professionals act primarily as facilitators (Joseph and Conrad 1988), usually involving recruiting, training, and supervising church members in their ministries to one another and to others outside the church fellowship. Professionals do not become paid substitutes for friends and social support. The body of Christ is composed of *all* believers, each having an indispensable role in ministry that goes far beyond paying the salaries of a professional staff. Church members share actively in ministry.

Church members need family professionals to empower them with knowledge about the intrapersonal, interpersonal, cultural, and social dimensions of the issues they address in their ministry. They need the support of continuing training and consultation in their work. Finally, they need encouragement and recognition for their ministry (1 Thess. 5:11–13).

Culture

Professional practice with families in a local church or church agency in many respects resembles practice with an ethnic group. Churches have their own language, nonverbal symbols, codes, norms, and patterns of relationships—their own culture. If professionals have not been a part of this cultural context, they will find themselves, for all practical purposes, in a cross-cultural practice setting.

The professional needs to be able to operate within and use the language and cultural patterns of the church community; the Bible, theology, and Christian values and lifestyle become resources for practice (Whipple 1987). For example, biblical concepts of forgiveness, confession, and repentance can provide a foundation for helping Christians work through family conflict. The concepts of the family of God and Christian hospitality provide justification for social action on behalf of homeless and isolated persons as well as for social-ministry programs that strive to include them in the life of the community.

Shared Lifespace of Professionals, Members, and Clients

The professional working in a church often shares the same social networks, community, and social lifespace of church members and even of clients. Professionals often are expected to be members of the denominations and congregations they serve. Professional relationships with clients may originate in shared church functions—church committees, groups, or educational and other social ministry programs led by the professional (Taggart 1962).

Boundaries of client/professional relationships and between professional and private life therefore are much less well-defined than in other contexts of professional practice. At times, they may be virtually absent (Garland 1988). These permeable boundaries allow clients and church members greater access, both formally and informally, to family professionals than in other social-service settings. The family professional also has greater potential knowledge of the social networks of clients and members as well as other resources and barriers for intervention. It must be recognized, however, that the professional may then have to cope with overlapping personal and organizational roles (Joseph 1988); church professionals must guard against burnout from being almost constantly "on duty."

The Church as a Natural Support System

Pattison (1977) suggests that effective natural systems are characterized by: (1) *Multiple interactions*—Persons stay in touch with one another; interaction with one another is a significant part of members' social exchange system. (2) *Multiple spheres of activity*—Natural systems are not centered in a single task, or if they begin around a single task, other tasks evolve as the support system develops. For example, people are colleagues at work, play on a softball team together, and worship together in the same church family. (3) *Varied times and places*—Relationships last over time and are not just reserved for a single place—the church building or the office. (4) *Both affective and instrumental dimensions*—Emotion is felt for one another which is normally positive unless persons are forced to remain in contact, such as in some extended-kin systems. Not only do members like one another, but they need one another in a variety of ways. Goods and services are mutually exchanged. (5) *Multiple connections*—Group members are not all connected through a single person but are connected by a web of relationships (Pattison 1977).

Churches differ significantly in the degree to which these characteristics of natural support systems describe them. The small rural community church most likely exemplifies churches that approximate natural support systems. By contrast, the large urban church, which attracts persons from all over a city because of a dynamic preacher or special programs, is least likely to be characterized as a natural support system. In such churches, people may have few or no connections with one another other than attendance at worship services; they do not work together, go to the same schools, or live in the same neighborhood. Interactions tend to be limited to one sphere of life, at a prescribed time and place, with little affective and instrumental exchange, perhaps held together by a single person—a charismatic speaker.

Denominational and Ecumenical Organizations

The local church congregation is frequently the touchstone for denominational and ecumenical organizations, although in some instances the local diocese or a national church body may be the sponsoring group. These organizations may either closely or remotely resemble the local church in the dimensions described previously, but they must always be able to understand and communicate effectively on these dimensions with their supporting churches. Accordingly, some organizations are closely tied to their supporting church congregations; professional staff are active members and may have professional roles in both local churches and denominational and ecumenical organizations. At the other extreme, some denominational and ecumenical organizations may be so in name only, perhaps receiving only partial or nominal support from local churches. They may be receiving government funding of various kinds or be supported in large part by client fees. Many church programs and agencies receive over half of their funds from grants and other nonchurch funds (Netting 1986). Staff may or may not be Christian and may not have any relationship with the churches who support them.

The denominational and ecumenical agencies and organizations with which this book is concerned are those that clearly identify their mission and goals with those of the church, and with the denominations and local congregations that support them. They do not simply view churches as resources to be maintained but see their role as being a support to and an enactment of the shared ministry of their constituent churches.

Denominational Agencies and Boards

Many denominations support social-service programs and social-action committees or agencies that serve families. These agencies and boards are considered ministries beyond the communities of the local churches which support them or as responses to those needs that require professional competence beyond the resources and capabilities of congregations. Examples of these social ministries include residential child care; shelters for the homeless, pregnant teen-agers, and abused families; family counseling agencies; facilities for persons with AIDS; professional lobbying and government legislation watch committees; and community development services.

Ecumenical Agencies and Organizations

Ecumenical agencies and organizations resemble denominational agencies and organizations, in that they represent the cooperation and coordination of various local congregations for the purpose of providing ministry beyond what any one local congregation could do alone. Their goal, however, is to bridge differences that may otherwise be divisive in order to achieve the ultimate vision of the church.

Ecumenical activities occur at every level, from the local community ministry in which the churches of various denominations within a community join together in cooperative ministry, to international organizations. Family ministry as both perspective and program can occur at all levels in an ecumenical context.

In a local community, a cluster of churches may join together to assess community needs and provide services that may include emergency assistance, nutrition programs, senior-adult programs, child-care centers and after-school clubs, single-parent groups, self-help groups, counseling, and advocacy efforts. Some churches choose not to join such ecumenical endeavors.

Presently, Louisville, Kentucky—a community with which the writers are familiar—has seven of these cluster ministries, involving twenty to twenty-five churches each. Six to ten staff members are employed by each cluster ministry, as well as an army of volunteers. Cross-Lines Cooperative Council in Kansas City involves forty denominations and six hundred cooperating churches and, in addition to the services offered by most cluster ministries, teaches job skills and develops businesses staffed by former welfare recipients and retired volunteers (Bakeley 1986). In the Catholic tradition, parishes in the United States are engaging in collaborative social ministries within an ecumenical perspective (Peeler 1985).

Professionals in ecumenical organizations have the complex task of understanding and articulating for their constituents the common ground which unites churches in ministry. They need to know the particular cultural and theological milieu of member churches so that the family ministry of the organization is congruent with the expectations of church congregations, and the unique emphases and resources of members can be used and nurtured in the ministry.

Summary: Principles for Family Ministry

In summary, these characteristics point to a number of principles for working with families in a church context.

- The organizational structure and form suggest important points of entry for family ministry. Democratically controlled congregations require the professional to present family-ministry perspectives and programs to a congregation in ways that are congruent with the church's mission, goals, and culture. Episcopalian and presbyterian church polities require the professional to develop and nurture contact with those in positions of authority who can authorize programs and whose decisions can affect families.
- Every church is unique in its historical and developmental identity and community context; family ministry programs and perspectives need to be developed in response to this uniqueness.
- The voluntary nature of the church requires sensitive presentation of family ministry programs and perspectives to the churches, a presentation which can engender enthusiasm and commitment on the part of church members.
- The goals and process of family ministry need to be congruent with the church's mission and goals of worship and fellowship, evangelism, and social ministry. They need also to be culturally relevant to the church community.

- The empowerment and enabling of church members as ministers needs to be a primary focus of family ministry (Edge 1983).
- The professional on the church staff needs to define with the congregation the role expectations, responsibilities, and limitations of both professionals and church members.
- The professional working with a church in an advisory or consultative role needs to learn the language and culture of the church community similar to preparing for a cross-cultural practice setting.

A Model for Family Ministry

Ideally, the church can be considered a social support network, an ecological family, or perhaps a family of families. As such, an ecological perspective seems most appropriate for family ministry. An ecological practice model assesses and intervenes in the networks of interpersonal relationships. The primary form of intervention is the development and sustainment of these networks, focusing on ministry to one another rather than replacing the functions of the network with professional services.

For example, in a church setting the professional would choose to help friends and family understand a child's emotional turmoil over the death of a parent and provide the needed listening, loving, and support. Providing the child with intensive professional counseling would be a back-up plan in case of special need, not the initial intervention plan (Garland 1988).

When family needs are shared by two or more family units, the professional may provide intervention by offering educational groups designed to enhance the resources of social networks. Examples are parent training, educational groups for adult children of aging parents, or educational programs for helping church members respond to friends in crisis.

When natural support networks cannot meet the needs of their individual members, they can be supported by self-help and professional groups designed to deal with specific problems, such as Alcoholics Anonymous and Al-Anon for family members. From a family ministry perspective, these supplement, not re-place the resources of the natural support network.

Finally, the family professional may become directly involved with members of a social network who have needs beyond those which the network or self-help groups can address. A married couple may need help in resolving conflict. A young man with schizophrenia may need to learn social skills which enable him to participate in and not drain a natural network. Even in these situations, the goal is to provide needed services so that the client system can be sustained by a mutually beneficial support network. The couple in marital conflict, after work-ing through the immediate conflict, may benefit from a marriage enrichment group (educational group) or married couples support group (self-help group). The young adult with schizophrenia needs to develop friendships and family relationships in which he can contribute as well as receive instrumental and

Level of Intervention	Form of Service
Primary Intervention	Social support networks Consultation with networks Educational services
Secondary Intervention	Self-help and issue-centered groups Creation of support networks
Tertiary Intervention	Client-professional contract for counseling or other clinical services

Levels of Intervention for Family Ministry
Figure 5-1

affective support. Figure 5-1 illustrates these levels of intervention for family ministry, highlighting the role of church members in ministry to one another and suggesting that ministry can be carried out in five basic roles.

1. *Members of natural support networks.* The first level of ministry is with people who are already in or accessible to the minister's (church member's) network—neighbors, work colleagues, and family members. The professional may serve as a consultant in strengthening existing relationships, renewing relationships, and providing needed intervention through these personal channels.

2. *Members of created networks.* When networks have some deficit, the minister (church member) may seek to create a supplemental relationship. For example, a father may become concerned that one of his son's friends, who lives with his mother and three sisters, has no adult male family member to provide a male role model. He consequently seeks to develop a friendship with the child. Or, when the professional becomes aware of such a need he or she may seek a minister (church member) to meet the need, providing consultation and support when appropriate. When such relationships become mutually rewarding, the created network may be absorbed into an ongoing natural support system. The goal of the professional is to make a successful match between need and minister and then provide supportive services so that what begins as ministry can become a mutually rewarding support system.

3. *Members of self-help networks.* Church members not only benefit from but also contribute to the artificial networks in which they participate. For example, widows or widowers who have benefited from the outreach services of a group for widows often stay in the group after they have worked through their own grief and have reorganized their lives. They stay to minister to others in the ways that they found helpful.

4. *Central figures.* Central figures are the key people in a social network to whom the network turns for advice and resources (Froland, et al. 1981). In churches, they are often key leaders in the church community, serving on a number of committees and boards, teaching religious education, or serving as deacons, trustees, or elders. These ministry roles are most visible and consequently most

recognized in many congregations. These people often serve as community gate-keepers, the first to know about illness, tragedy, and crisis in the church family. Chapters 13 and 14 describe work with central figures in greater depth.

5. *Volunteers.* Finally, church members minister as volunteers in the church's organizations. They may serve as leaders of children's socialization groups, leaders of worship services in nursing or retirement facilities, and a myriad of other roles in which they develop helping relationships with others in need. From an ecological perspective on family ministry, the goal of volunteering is to create social networks or to include persons in existing networks, and in so doing, to strengthen ecological families.

The role of the professional is to identify and fill gaps in care that cannot be met by existing social support networks and ecological families. Professional intervention is interwoven with any existing network and family relationships so as to use and strengthen these networks (Froland 1980). The network of family and friends who provide emotional support and respite care to parents with a developmentally disabled child may need the professional to: (1) augment the network with someone who would like to offer respite care while parents have needed opportunities for rest and relaxation; (2) refer parents to a support group of parents with developmentally disabled children; (3) provide an informal training session for friends and extended family who help with the child's care so that they will know how they can encourage physical and emotional development; (4) offer informal or formal counsel to parents as they adjust to the demands of their situation and balance the needs of their special child with the needs of siblings; and (5) generate church support in advocacy efforts with local government for developing adequate preschool education for developmentally disabled children.

In summary, an ecological perspective for practice responds to the unique organizational structure, historical context, goals and mission, culture, and ecology of the church. It requires competent professional assessment and creative intervention. Effective family ministry maintains a focus on the needs of individuals and families, moving outward from this center to identify and support ecological families and social support networks, to the social and cultural context in which families and networks live, interact, and worship.

References

Bakeley, D. 1986. Cross-lines. A presentation at building family strengths: Ninth national symposium. University of Nebraska, Lincoln, Nebraska.

Bau, Ignatius. 1985. *This ground is holy: Church sanctuary and Central American refugees.* New York: Paulist Press.

Conrad, A. P. 1980. Social ministry in the early church: An integral component of Christian community. *Social Thought* 2:41–51.

Edge, Findley B. 1983. Faith and mission: God's call to the laity. *Faith and Mission* 1:23.

Froland, C. 1980. Formal and informal care: Discontinuities in a continuum. *Social Service Review* 54, 572–87.

Froland, C. et al. 1981. *Helping networks and human services.* Beverly Hills: Sage.

Garland, Diana S. R. 1988. The church as a context for social work practice. *Review and Expositor* 85:255-65.

Himes, Kenneth R. 1985. The local church as a mediating structure. *Social Thought* Winter: 22-30.

Jaquet, Constant H., ed. 1982. *Yearbook of American and Canadian churches 1982.* Nashville: Abingdon Press.

Joseph, M. V. 1988. Religion and social work practice: An exploratory study. *Social Casework* 69:443-52.

Joseph, M. V., and A. P. Conrad. 1977. *National trends in parish social ministry.* Washington, D.C.: National Conference of Catholic Charities.

————. 1988. *The parish as a ministering community: Social ministries in the local church community.* Hyattsville, Md.: Pen Press.

Miles, Delos. 1988. Church social work and evangelism: Partners in ministry. *Review and Expositor* 85:273-83.

Moberg, Daniel O. 1984. *The church as a social institution.* Grand Rapids: Baker Book House.

Netting, F. Ellen. 1986. The religiously affiliated agency: Implications for social work administration. *Social Work and Christianity* 13:50-63.

Pattison, E. Mansell, 1977. *Pastor and parish—A systems approach.* Philadelphia: Fortress.

Peeler, A. 1985. *Parish social ministry: A vision and resource.* Washington, D.C.: National Conference of Catholic Charities.

Rahner, K. 1978. Practical theology and social work in the church. In *Theological investigations,* Vol. 10. Trans. D. Bourke, 349-70. London: Dartman and Todd, Ltd.

Taggart, Alice D. 1962. The caseworker as parish assistant. *Social Casework* 43:75-79.

Wach, Joachim. 1951. *Types of religious experience: Christian and non-Christian.* Chicago: University of Chicago Press.

Whipple, Vicky. 1987. Counseling battered women from fundamentalist churches. *Journal of Marital and Family Therapy* 13:251-58.

Yinger, J. Milton. 1957. *Religion, society and the individual.* New York: Macmillan.

PART TWO
Application in Churches and Agencies

In some respects, to say that this part offers applications of the theoretical, methodological, and biblical content of Part One of this book stretches reality. Most of the programs and research about which these authors have written were taking place prior to our articulation of the content of Part One. Some of the authors were operating out of similar conceptual frameworks as they developed their work; others were not. Nevertheless, these authors offer creative programs and perspectives on family services that are congruent with an ecological definition of the family.

The chapters in this part are not comprehensive of all the dimensions of family ministry and the reader will readily think of many other examples we have not included. For example, we have not addressed family ministry in the arenas of special-needs adoptions and of homelessness, both of which cry out for the involvement of the church's family ministry. Many churches and church agencies are already engaged in such ministries, such as a church in Louisville, Kentucky, that has been working closely with a community mental health center to provide emergency shelter for the homeless mentally ill. This church also has a befriending program designed to include these people in their faith community, providing friendship, support, and help in the tasks of living (Drouet 1989).

The World Council of Churches has been developing family clusters designed to support individuals and families in countries around the world, with varied outcomes: influence on governmental family policies, the development of food co-ops and cooperative credit unions, and obtaining clean water supplies (Mpolo 1984). A number of congregations and agencies have been involved in providing tangible and social support for teen-age parents, in developing adoptive and foster homes, and in advocating for families with developmentally disabled members.

Part Two does describe innovative ways of thinking about and shaping family ministry, even though they may not represent the whole spectrum of family ministry. They each help define family ministry from an ecological perspective and call forth creativity from readers in their own particular ministry contexts. The first three chapters address directly the needs of existing families, particularly those within the congregation. The next four chapters address the ways in which the church can create and nurture social support networks and ecological families which address the needs not only of people within the church community but also those on the fringes or outside of functional support systems and/or the church. Chapters 13 and 14 are concerned with the role of natural helpers in family ministry.

As you read these widely diverse examples of family ministry as defined by an ecological perspective, we challenge you to think about how this perspective suggests applications in your own ministry with families.

References

Drouet, Claude. 1989. Family networks for the homeless. Manuscript. Louisville, Ky.: Jefferson Street Baptist Chapel.

Mpolo, Masamba Ma. 1984. *Family profiles: Stories of families in transition.* Geneva: World Council of Churches.

6

Developing and Empowering Parent Networks

Diana S. Richmond Garland

Like other parents in churches of their denomination all across the country, a group of parents in Nashville, Tennessee, has just completed a parenting course consisting of thirteen weekly sessions, offered during the regular Sunday evening programing of their congregation. They have studied Scripture passages which define the ways Christians are to relate to others, including their children. They have learned ways parents can nurture their children's self-esteem as they talk with, listen to, and discipline their children.

In this course, parents have broadened their views of family life to include the contribution other significant adults and peers make to healthy self-esteem in their children. They have discussed ways they can shape relationships with these significant others in behalf of their children. As a result, parents in the group have:

- agreed to continue calling and talking to one another about their parenting concerns.
- begun to call the parents of their children's friends, whether they are acquaintances are not, to get answers to questions such as: What activities are being planned at a party? Will the chaperones allow alcohol or drugs? Are other parents really letting their children attend that concert in a distant city and how do they feel about it?
- found ways to communicate appreciation for special persons in their children's lives, such as special relatives or adult friends. They have included them in family celebrations and children have made them homemade gifts. The message has been, "you are part of our family."
- started a child-care co-op with other parents, so that parents can develop closer relationships with one another's children and give one another some respite from the demands of child care without incurring babysitting expenses.

- developed a relationship with a single mother of a developmentally disabled child, who is relatively isolated, to provide friendship to the mother and child and to share in her responsibilities for child care.

Parent education has been extremely popular in churches. For example, in two years' time, an estimated eight thousand churches and fifty thousand parents (Hauk 1987) participated in a parenting program prepared by the Sunday School Board of the Southern Baptist Convention (Crase et al. 1986). Many parent-education programs used in churches focus on teaching parents knowledge, attitudes, and skills deemed functional for child rearing. Parents learn how to listen to children, how to talk to children so they will be heard, how to shape children's behavior and discipline them effectively, how to teach values to children, how to deal with sibling rivalry, how to instill courage and responsibility in children, and how to nurture children's spiritual growth (Crase et al. 1986; Gordon 1975; Popkin 1983). If popularity is any indication of the usefulness of these programs, they are meeting a real need.

Most parent education has focused on the parent-child relationship and sibling relationships; relationships with others outside the nuclear family have received little or no attention in most programs. An ecological perspective suggests, however, that in addition to knowledge of child development and skills for instilling valued characteristics in their children, parents need skills in dealing with other significant relationships in their children's environment and in developing relationships which support their parenting. The parenting program described at the beginning of this chapter is based on this ecological perspective.

Why Include Parent Network Development in Parent Education?

Changes in our culture have led to the need for parents to be intentional about developing and nurturing a supportive network of relationships for their children and for themselves as parents.

Cultural Changes in Parent Support

In decades past, neighborhoods were often composed of social networks. Most women worked in the home and their friendships thus were neighborhood-centered. Children walked to the nearest school; their families lived near one another in the same neighborhood. Churches were also neighborhood- or parish-based. As a consequence, mothers, who were the primary parents, usually knew the parents of their children's friends, and those parents usually lived in the same neighborhood.

Today, with the majority of women working, adult friendships are more likely to be based in work settings than in neighborhoods. Many children find themselves transported to a distant school, either for desegregation purposes or because of the increased specialization of schools (e.g., centers for certain ages, interests, or abilities). Schools are larger and more impersonal, with few links to other social relations in a child's life and with little community life within, as children are segregated in classes that change their composition yearly. The school has become "one of the most potent breeding grounds of alienation in American society" (Bronfenbrenner 1979, 848). Churches also have become specialized; members often drive across town to reach the congregation that best suits their interests and needs (Schaller 1986). Mega-churches provide a context in which persons may stay strangers and spectators.

As a result of these changes, socialization links are often individual to individual instead of family to family. Our friends are more likely to be the people with whom we work or go to school, not those who live in the same neighborhood. Consequently, parents often do not know the parents of their children's friends. Because friendships are not neighborhood-based, they are less likely to have the informal quality of visiting across the back fence or of borrowing a cup of sugar. Instead, socialization is planned, often as generational groups instead of as families. Birthday parties for children often include only other children; parents go out with other adults and leave their children at home with a baby sitter.

Parents therefore face the task of childrearing with much less involvement from neighbors and other adults than they did thirty years ago. If Mrs. Jones who lives down the street sees Burt Smith picking on little Susie Collins, she is far less likely to call Burt's parents or intervene than she would have in 1950.

The Importance of Networks for Parents and Children

So much attention has been given to the stresses of single parenting that most parent educators have not addressed the more subtle limitations of the nuclear family for socializing children. Children and adolescents need relationships with other adults in addition to their parents. Two parents are not enough. Observations from anthropology and sociology indicate that families in differing cultures often include more persons than the nuclear family. Mudd and Taubin (1982) found that healthy families have a talent for friendship and relate regularly with a group of about twenty persons in addition to their families. We live in constructed psychosocial families composed of "fictive kin" which provide us a network that resembles the kin networks of other societies (Pattison 1984).

Research also supports a significant correlation between a strong network and healthy, effective parenting. In an early study, Young (1964) found that 95 percent of severely abusive families had no continuing relationships with others outside the family. Young reported also that 85 percent of the abusive parents in the study did not belong to or participate in any organized groups. Vogel and Bell (1960) discovered that families with emotionally disturbed children often have relationships with neighbors which are either minimal or hostile. Colletta and Gregg (1981) found that an active support system is positively related to a mother's mental health and negatively related to the frequency of restrictive, demanding, and rejecting interactions with children. Those with high levels of support were more affectionate, closer, and more positive with their children, while those with low levels of support were more hostile, indifferent, and rejecting (see also Hetherington, Cox, and Cox 1976; Reis, Barbara-Stein, and Bennett 1986; and Turner and Avison 1985).

Gray et al. (1979) identified parents considered high risk for abuse at the time of their child's delivery.

From these, a group was randomly chosen to receive support services (weekly home visits by a nurse and friendly visits designed to offer emotional support). These parents fared far better in measures of child abuse than other high risk parents who did not receive such services. Garbarino and Sherman (1980) found that mothers considered low risks for child maltreatment are willing to exchange child supervision with other mother. Mothers who are high risks for child maltreatment, on the other hand, are less likely to engage in these neighborhood exchanges. Finally, Dunst, Trivette, and Deal (1988) report research demonstrating the significant relationship between informal social support and "good" parenting of children who are retarded, handicapped, and developmentally at risk (see also Beavers et al. 1986; Kazak 1986; Trute and Hauch 1988).

The influences of a network extend beyond the support of positive parenting behavior in the adult, however, and affect children directly. Children need a network of adults with whom to relate: parents of peers, single persons, married persons without children, older adults, and both kin and nonkin. Such a network provides a child with security, respite from parents, additional life models, and a source of developing identity.

Security. An informal network of adult friends and extended family gives a child a sense of security, rootedness, and belonging; it takes some of the power out of a child's fears of being solely dependent on the heartbeat or good will of a parent. Children need a neighbor to turn to if they come home from school to an unexpectedly empty house. They need persons in their neighborhoods who know them and their families and who can exercise gentle and unobtrusive surveillance as children wait for a school bus, walk home from school or the grocery store, or play with friends up and down their street.

Many times, of course, adult-child relationships may develop out of role-related contacts such as teachers and children's activity leaders. As lovers of children, many a teacher, coach, and social worker has provided the special attention so desperately needed by a child that goes far beyond the expectations of their role in the child's life. Although professional and volunteer children's workers are critical in the lives of children, they usually do not form life-long intimate relationships with most of the children with whom they work.

Respite from Parents. Network members can offer respite for both children and parents. Network members can provide family-like child care based on a loving relationship with the child, not simply on a baby-sitting arrangement. Also, staying with a trusted adult friend or family member for a few days—or longer—may provide an acceptable alternative to running away or even emergency shelter for a child when parents are incapacitated or unable to cope with the intensity of family relationships (York, York, and Wachtel 1984).

Additional Life Models. Adult network members can offer balance and alternatives to parents' values, views, and blind spots. Children can survive and even thrive in difficult home situations if they have adult allies elsewhere.

Thus the child from an abusive or neglecting home may be able to overcome the damage that that mistreatment inflicts if he has enduring relationships with helpful adults outside the home, relationships that can help compensate for the developmental damage inflicted by the abuse and neglect. (Garbarino 1979, 131–32)

Zelkowitz (1987) found that children of mothers living in poverty who are either depressed or likely to become depressed because of stressful life circumstances behave in less aggressive and more socially acceptable ways when they receive nurturance from other significant adults in their lives.

Children in loving, nurturing homes also can benefit from enduring ties to adults that provide different perspectives and values. A family friend who is skilled with crafts or who is an art lover may see and encourage a child's creativity that would go unnoticed by parents concerned with other issues.

Identity. Finally, networks help children develop an identity rooted in mutuality and significance in the lives of others. A child not only is offered role models, caregiving, and security from an informal network; he or she can also be encouraged to give in return. Other adults may delight in receiving a child's lovingly made gifts (e.g., art projects) and services (e.g., a teenager who uses a new driver's license to run an errand for an aging neighbor). As children learn to share with others beyond their own family units in meaningful ways, they develop an identity as a functional member of the social network.

Networks can also be sources of difficulty as well as solutions to problems. Clearly, not all network relationships are supportive or helpful; social networks are not equivalent to social support (Gottlieb 1981; Wellman 1981). Children may be used and abused instead of nurtured. The models offered by other adults may not be those we would wish children to have. Recognizing that some network members, like some parents, can be threats to a child's development rather than resources does not detract, however, from the needs children have for a network of relationships with loving, supportive adults.

Yet most children do not benefit from such relationships. In a study of the social maps of children approaching adolescence, Garbarino and others (1978) found that children hardly have any adults in their networks. Urban children named an average of 2.3 adults among the 10 people they know best and see at least once a month. Rural children named 1.5 adults, and suburban children, 1.0. In fact, 60 percent of the suburban children reported no such relationship with an adult. The number of adults in a child's life also decreases with the age of the child. The researchers concluded that "the results reinforce the widely held concern over age segregation in American life as a developmental and historical trend" (Garbarino et al. 1978, 426). We might hypothesize that those children who are most troubled by family concerns, peer pressures, and emotional issues are least likely to have supportive adults in their lives. A research study with sixteen-year-old boys in Norway supports this hypothesis; Cochran and Hogskolesenteret (1987) found that larger numbers of nonkin adults in a boy's social network were related to better school performance, less absenteeism, and more positively evaluated social behavior.

Why Are Churches and Agencies Appropriate Contexts?

Creating parent networks can be a major goal of family ministry. Parent-education programs focusing on child development and parenting skills, especially if offered within an ongoing network of relationships like a congregation, can encourage the development of supportive adult relationships for children and parenting networks for adults. For many children and adolescents, the church's programs for children and youth are a significant context for peer relationships. Unlike in the peer groups in a public school, their parents are at least potentially acquainted with one another and are sometimes even close friends. Parents may consult with children's activity leaders and discuss and plan activity programs for their children as a group. Such meetings can easily include agenda relevant to the development of parent support. Churches may also sponsor groups such as Parents Anonymous, Toughlove, and Stepparents, Inc., which are support and self-help groups for parents sharing common issues and problems.

Parent networks do not have to be organized from scratch. They may work better if they develop out of another program such as those mentioned above—parent education programs, parents' councils and committees, and self-help groups for parents. Sunday School classes and other programs in the church which have a different focus than parent support provide a conducive environment for relationships to develop between parents and with other adults who are involved in or concerned about their children.

The biblical and theological foundations described in chapters 2 and 3 provide the rationale for expending church resources in developing parent networks. Specific biblical examples can also be used to illustrate to a congregation the importance of other adults in the lives of children. The following examples have been used as one piece of the biblical foundation for a parenting program (Garland, Chapman, and Pounds n.d.).

Timothy learned to be faithful from the example of his grandmother. She evidently played a key role in his becoming a missionary (2 Tim. 1:5; 3:15).

The prophet Samuel visited Jesse, seeking the next king of Israel among his sons. Jesse assembled his boys for Samuel's inspection but did not even think to include David, his youngest son. It took the special vision of someone outside the family, Samuel—and then only by special revelation from God—to recognize qualities in the young David which his father and brothers had missed. Samuel called for David and named him the new king (1 Sam. 16:1–13).

As a young child and growing adolescent, Jesus experienced the recognition of his special gifts by other significant adults besides his parents. The teachers in the temple in Jerusalem were "amazed at his understanding" and talked and shared with him (Luke 2:46–47). His understanding of himself and his gifts and calling must have grown as these others blessed him and encouraged him. He found favor in their eyes (Luke 2:52), even when his own parents did not understand.

Jesus' parents were no doubt influenced and supported in their parenting by other adults. Jesus' cousin Elizabeth pronounced a blessing on Jesus before he was even born (Luke 1:41–44), a blessing which must have had special significance to the young girl Mary. While Jesus was yet an infant, two people clearly recognized how special Jesus was and shared their vision with Joseph and Mary. When they took the infant Jesus to the temple, righteous Simeon took Jesus in his arms and spoke of his expectations of who Jesus would be and what he would do (Luke 2:25–33). The prophetess Anna also gave thanks to God for Jesus and blessed him (Luke 2:36–38). These encounters must have impressed Mary and Joseph and been a source of support to them in the difficult days ahead of them as a young family (Luke 2:33, 51).

As an adult, Jesus stretched the circle of the family. His last act confirmed his care for his mother and his intention to expand family relationships beyond biological bounds (John 19:26–27). Jesus had an even broader view of the possibilities of family-like relationships. As Christians, our families are no longer limited to kinfolk; we are to be a family of faith, to care for one another as parent and child (Matt. 12:48–50).

Expanding Parenting beyond the Nuclear Family

Parent networks begin by linking parents with one another so that they can begin to share common questions, concerns, and experiences. In addition, networks can link parents with others who can be their partners in nurturing children, such as teachers, church children's group leaders, and caring relatives and neighbors.

Extended family members also provide key support to parents. A major effort needs to be made to counteract the popular assumption in our society that a healthy family is a nuclear family which is independent of the extended family. Some families in our culture feel a certain embarrassment to admit that they spend Sunday afternoon with the in-laws, or that they make frequent trips "back home." Older adults express concern that they not "interfere" in the lives of their adult children. As important as independence and noninterference may be, families need to hear also that it is healthy to need one another.

Many nuclear families do not have extended family to provide a network of support. Geographic mobility has placed hundreds of miles between many parents and their nearest kin, and as wonderful as the telephone may be for keeping in touch, it cannot provide an evening's child care nor easily be a channel for other reciprocated services. With the dropping birth rate, many extended families may be limited to two sets of grandparents and one aunt or uncle. More and more couples are having only one child. When two *only* children marry, the roles of aunt, uncle, and cousin are nonexistent for their child(ren). A death or two in an extended family may shrink the extended family below an adequate number even to call it a network.

Programs for empowering parents by involving significant others in child rearing therefore need to include both (1) educating those potentially significant others—kin and friends—of the need, and (2) providing them with resources that will develop and/or strengthen their relationships with parents and their children. Perhaps no institution is as suited to developing such programs as the church, where people of all ages congregate and can form webs of relationships.

How to Develop Parent Networks

In the Local Congregation

Sermons and Educational Materials. Church members need to hear that we are called to share the responsibilities of nurturing and guiding the children of the faith family. Parents need to hear that they should not expect themselves to be all things to their children. Other adults need to hear and acknowledge the gift they can offer to children. "We must be a people who stand ready to receive and care for any child, not just as if it were one of ours, but because in fact each *is* one of ours" (Westerhoff 1983, 127).

Being a special person in the life of a child is just as important a ministry as any other. It is a living witness to the love and Good News of Jesus Christ just as much as talking about one's faith with an adult. This content can be shared with a congregation in a special sermon or series of sermons during the special family-emphasis times of a church's life or in a series of adult Sunday School lessons.

Cross-Generational Programs. Many church programs are segregated by age, so that the only ones with whom children have contact at church are their teachers and leaders, who may be relating to a dozen or more children at the same time. This makes it more difficult to show individual love and concern for a single child. Churches who want to nurture family networks need to provide for individual relationships across generations. Peace and justice groups, for example, frequently become strong networks of cross-generational support in addition to their involvement in social action (McGinnis and McGinnis 1981).

Many churches have experimented with family clusters, which are support groups composed of various nuclear-family units and single persons who meet together periodically for contracted periods of time and from which enduring networks of support can grow (Newcomer 1972; Sawin 1979). Special caution needs to be taken that a cluster program structures children in interaction with adults, so they are not merely appendages of adult relationships. Games and discussions can pair each adult with a child as partners in the activity. Every child in the church can be *adopted* for a year by a member adult who acts as a special friend (Johns 1988). Chapter 10 provides other suggestions for developing cross-generational programs.

Dedication of Families. Children born into the families of the church are often baptized, dedicated, or otherwise presented to the church family in a worship service. These occasions can be used to dedicate and recognize the significance not only of the child and parents, but also of the church family in this child's life. Church families can commit themselves to love and guide and share the responsibility for this new person in their fellowship. People who pledge special support to a child and parents (godparents), whether they are kin or not, can be recognized and dedicated as the church's representatives in the child's life. Westerhoff graphically describes the use of the ritual of infant baptism to symbolize the church as a family:

> By baptism we are made Christians. However, we often miss the radical nature of this symbolic action. In the case of children, godparents, who represent the "faith family" and act as sponsors for the child, bring the child before the community so that the child might be drowned (killed) and reborn and thereby begin life afresh, outside the bounds of biological kinship. The child is given up by its parents for adoption into a new family and acquires both a personal baptismal name and a new faith–family surname— Christian (Westerhoff 1985, 11).

In Crescent Hill Baptist Church in Louisville, Kentucky, as in many other churches, the pastor symbolically communicates this new family relationship. He takes a child who is being dedicated into his arms and walks through the midst of the congregation, talking with the child (and to the congregation) about this new family of faith and the congregation's promise to nurture and love and stand with the child throughout life. The congregation together then speaks its covenant to be faithful family for this new member.

Blessing of Family Bonds. Children often make gifts in their church classes for parents on Mothers' and Father's Day. They can be helped to identify the special adults in their lives to honor similarly on a Church Family Day. They can make gifts or cards, or can prepare coupon books that the special adult can redeem for services from the child such as washing the car, weeding a flower bed, running an errand, or playing a game of checkers. When these activities are done together, the relationship is further strengthened.

In Parenting Programs

A church's parenting programs should stress the significance of support networks for parents and children and include skills for developing and nurturing these networks. The Sunday School Board of the Southern Baptist Convention developed the program described earlier in this chapter, *Parenting by Grace: Self-Esteem* (Garland, Chapman, and Pounds n.d.). Professional staff train laypeople in churches to lead this thirteen-session program for parents. A notebook for leaders offers guidance in conducting the program; parents also receive a handbook containing the content of the program and learning activities which they complete as preparation for each program session. Parents adopt goals, such as the following, for participation in this program:

- State ways other adults are important to my children.
- Name the important adults in my children's lives.
- Identify ways I and my children contribute to these important persons' lives.
- Plan a way I and/or my children can strengthen one of these relationships.
- Explain the importance of a network of parents and other significant adults for good parenting.

- Decide how our group will continue to support and care for one another after the course has ended.
- Identify children besides my own who need my love and support.
- Plan and carry out a ministry activity in which I share in the parenting of at least one other child.

As an introductory activity in this program, parents identify the myriad of influences in their children's lives. A large weekly calendar on which parents can write their children's normal activities can be helpful in this task. They include not only activities away from home such as school, clubs and sports, but also time spent with peers in the neighborhood, watching television, talking to peers on the telephone, and so on. For many parents, such an activity is shocking; the time they can circle on such a calendar during which they are the primary influence in their child's daily activities is often relatively little. From the age of six on, the majority of children's waking hours are spent in institutions and with adults and peers apart from parents. The majority of preschool children have parents who are both working, so that the children spend up to ten hours each working day with people other than the family.

In a second assessment activity, parents ask their children to name their best friends (other than parents and siblings). Separately, parents list their own best friends. A number can be given ("name your five best friends") or the number can simply be left open-ended. Parents then take their children's lists of friends and figure a *parent network score*. If children have listed adults among their best friends, parents receive a +2 if they know the person very well, a +1 if they are well-acquainted with the person, and a 0 if they do not consider themselves to have a relationship with the other. Similarly, for children listed as their child's best friends, parents received a +2 if they know the child's parents very well, a +1 if they are well acquainted, and a 0 if they do not consider themselves to have a relationship with the parents, even if they know the child. The total score is then divided by the number of friends listed.

Parents' lists of friends can be scored in a similar way, based on the degree to which their children consider their parents' friends their own friends and acquaintances. This activity supports several avenues for discussion. Parents can think about the relative numbers of adults children consider best friends and whether or not children have adults other than their parents to whom they feel close. Parents can also look at the degree of overlap between a parent's network of support and a child's network.

The following activities for parents can be presented in parent programs as ways of developing more supportive parent networks:

- Contact and become acquainted with the parents of their children's friends.
- Talk with other parents about concerns (What helped when your children had chicken pox? What do you think of the T-ball program? Are you letting your children see that movie?).
- Swap child care and other services, such as transporting children and chaperoning activities.

- Share resources such as portable beds, humidifiers, and outgrown scout uniforms.
- Meet together to talk over shared concerns (drugs in the school, the need for a community sports program).
- Include other adults involved with children in such a meeting when it would be helpful to the children and/or the adults (church children's workers, school teachers, grandparents).
- Work together to offer alternative activities to those in which parents do not want their children involved (a party instead of going to a rock concert in a city three hours away).
- Use their combined strength to advocate for the needs of children, both their own and the children of others (for resources, see The Children's Defense Fund 1982).
- Offer one another help in a crisis—a meal, child care, calls on an elderly parent.
- Tell "significant others" how important they are to parent and child and include them in family celebrations.
- Celebrate important family relationships with special days and gifts.
- Provide support and nurture to the children of others.

In Professional Relationships with Parents in Churches and Church Agencies

Parent networks are not only a significant focus for educational and prevention programs in family ministry. They also deserve attention by family professionals working with families in crisis or with problems. Professional help is more effective if it is sensitive to and promotes the family's use of informal support networks (Dunst, Trivette, and Deal 1988).

Teaching Network Skills to Parents at Risk. Many of the families who receive services from church-related child welfare agencies, counseling centers, and church-related medical facilities may benefit from involvement in parent networks. Examples include abusive or neglectful families that are isolated or overwhelmed with the demands of parenting, parents of children with special needs, parents who themselves have special needs, and foster and adoptive families. Many of the principles and strategies used in a parent-education group can be used or adapted to fit the unique context of a particular family. The professional helps parents to develop the social skills needed to learn and maintain a social support network.

Linking Parents at Risk with Networks. Second, the professional may develop links between families at risk and social networks. One program, for example, links pregnant and teen parenting teenagers with "stable, achieving women who themselves had children as teens" (Silvern 1984, 3). In this program and similar programs both with teen parents and with abusive or potentially abusive parents, volunteers serve as positive role models, advocates, parental figures, friends, and helpers (Duncan et al. n.d.; Height 1985; Nickel and Delany 1985; Johns 1988;

Program aids pregnant teens 1986). "In one case, a team member 'drank more coffee than I ever imagined I could consume' while regularly taking an isolated and psychologically trapped young mother out to chat in a nearby restaurant" (Johns 1988, 12). In a family with a paraplegic father, the father was helped to go to ball games with his two sons and to record his comments about being a paraplegic for other paraplegics. The children were taken on outings by their special friends, who were willing to spend hours playing games with them and simply being available, caring adults.

In another program, friends, relatives, and volunteers were involved in providing a variety of support services for handicapped children and their families. These extended family members (which included volunteers recruited for the program) were trained to care for the children so that they could provide respite child care, help parents with transportation, and offer additional help with the tasks of caring for the children's special needs. The program was particularly successful in helping socially isolated families develop support systems that enabled them to continue care in their homes instead of placing their children in foster or institutional care (Moore et al. 1982).

Other programs, such as the Pilot Parent Program and the Visiting Parent Program (Poyadue 1988) provide supportive experienced parents who have been trained to pilot new parents through the initial difficulties of accepting a child's handicap or illness, learning about it, and finding needed services for the child. Recognizing the isolation and despair that often comes with learning that one's child has a major handicap, these parents can become lasting friends in their shared experience (Porter undated). Finally, parents in Ohio formed the Family Consortium Program, which develops and manages homes in which adults with developmentally disabling conditions reside. Parents administer the home, supervise employees, manage the funds, relate to one another, and handle the inevitable crises (Grosh 1988).

Providing Consultation to Central Figures. The professional may also provide consultation to a natural helper or central figure in a church community who has contact with the family. A child's Sunday School teacher may be concerned about the needs of a family and consult with the church staff. If appropriate, the teacher's role with the family may be strengthened and encouraged by giving him advice in how best to help child and family rather than the professional "taking over" the problem by becoming directly involved. Church members—Sunday School teachers, deacons, and friendly visitors, for example—who have potential relationships with families who may be isolated or in crisis can be trained and encouraged to provide informal helping and social support. Their involvement with families may be sufficient intervention in itself, or it may be an essential component of a larger intervention plan for a family in crisis. These central figures in the church may become aware of and be able to alert professionals to developing family crises such as child abuse, neglect, or mental illness (Johns 1988).

Developing Self-Help and Support Groups. Finally, the professional may link parents with other parents dealing with similar issues in a self-help or parent-support group. Parents Anonymous is such a group. It provides self-help groups led by a volunteer professional for parents who have abused or neglected their children or are afraid that they might do so. Members exchange phone numbers and are encouraged to support one another between meetings (Lieber 1983).

In Toughlove groups, parents frequently accompany one another to court appearances or to social services when they are dealing with their children in trouble. They help one another develop action plans for dealing with their children who are acting out, and they emotionally and even physically back one another when confronting their children's unacceptable behavior. They may stand in for one another, taking one another's children into their homes until the children agree to return home under agreed-upon conditions of drug treatment, school attendance, or other expectations parents have for changed behavior (York, York, and Wachtel 1984).

Getting parents who most need such services to participate may prove difficult. These parents often are by definition isolated and not skilled at social interaction, so that voluntarily presenting themselves for services is not likely to happen. Mediating people such as a neighbor, a child's school teacher, a social worker involved with the family, or a community pastor may be able to encourage participation. Free child care, transportation or money for public transportation to meetings, snacks, and recognition awards serve as incentives for initial attendance and continuing involvement in a parents' group (Garbarino, Schellenbach, Sebes, and associates 1986).

Drop-in centers for parents and children can provide respite care for children, a professional or knowledgeable volunteer available to talk over a parents' concerns, parent education programs, and the opportunity to socialize with other parents. A teen mother's program found, for example, that the support young mothers gave to one another as they sat and talked and rocked their babies was a source of "encouragement and respect that only they could give to one another" (Nickel and Delany 1985, 31).

For those concerned about preventing some of the common problems parents of children and adolescents experience in our culture, Deerfield Citizens for Drug Awareness offers a prevention program entitled *The Parent Peer Group Solution* (Houghton and Grant 1982; see also McDonald 1989). The program addresses the need for parents to help their adolescents deal with drugs, but it could be adapted to address any number of parental concerns.

The parent peer group begins with a professional working with one parent to make a list of her child's friends (approximately fifteen) and inviting those friends' parents to a meeting in which common concerns are discussed (Houghton 1986). Together, parents are encouraged to agree on a few overall guidelines that they will share in governing their children, such as tolerating no alcohol or drug use by minors in their homes, calling to confirm the presence of an adult before their children can attend parties in the homes of others, and setting common curfews.

The Deerfield group provides detailed guidelines for conducting such a program and a written pledge to be signed by participating parents to strengthen their agreement (Houghton 1986; Houghton and Grant 1982). The guidelines parents want to develop together may cover a whole range of issues and depend to some extent on the ages of children. In addition to drugs and alcohol, parents of teenagers may also want to address driving privileges. Parents of younger children can discuss permitted toys, television shows, and acceptable discipline for visiting children, although the focus is more likely to be sharing common concerns and learning from one another than it is developing a set of guidelines.

Such a programing model has a number of advantages. First, it has potential for preventing problems such as drug use and unsupervised parties. Second, it enables families to meet their own needs rather than relying on professional intervention. Third, it is simple to implement. Fourth, it addresses children's issues within the context of the family rather than as isolated individuals. Fifth, it is inexpensive, requiring little professional time other than getting the network started. Finally, and perhaps most importantly, parents feel supported in the struggle to set appropriate guidelines for their children and their children know clearly what is expected of them. The professional empowers parents to face issues that concern them by joining forces with others who share their concerns.

Houghton and Grant (1982) add some cautions in conducting such a program. The focus needs to be broader than simply setting limits on children's behavior. Parents and children need to think together of acceptable and satisfying alternatives to the behaviors being limited and plan activities that meet the guidelines. Second, a parent network may become an overpowering adult peer group, with parents feeling powerless in decisions or fearing disagreement with other parents. The voluntary nature of parental agreements needs to be highlighted, and the emphasis more on sharing educational resources and experiences with one another and supporting one another than developing legalistic rules.

Finally, networks are based on personal relationships, not organizations, and are best kept small enough that each member can contact all the other members easily either directly or through a linkage with a mutual acquaintance or friend. It is also helpful to include children in the network so they can discuss their concerns and have a voice in decisions that will affect them.

Parent networks can provide a means for parents to work together in advocacy efforts in behalf of themselves and their children. Together, parents can accomplish more than an isolated parent knocking on the doors of unresponsive school, health, and social-service systems.

Many of these programs were not developed in a church context. Even so, they suggest exciting directions for family ministry that are particularly relevant to the definition and goals of family ministry. In implementing replications of these programs in a congregational or church-agency setting, it is important to articulate the biblical and theological bases for offering family services. A church community needs to recognize that such parenting programs are appropriate expressions of their mission. Educating a congregation not only about the need for a particular program but also about the appropriateness of their taking the responsibility for it may take considerable more time and energy on the part of the professional than would be the case with a public agency. The program will also take on the character and culture of the supporting church, so that it may not end up being what the professional had originally envisioned. The result, however, may be a more creative program that responds to the culture and value systems of the community, with broad based support in the community.

Evaluation

Parents Anonymous is reported to be the most effective intervention for families troubled with child abuse, when compared to individual therapy and group therapy. "Someone who stays in P.A. for a year or more will probably not go back to abusing his or her children," says L. L. Lieber. "If a parent stays in the program for three years or longer, he or she actually ends up becoming a better parent than the norm in a community" (Lieber 1983, 289). Beyond this isolated study, there is an amazing lack of evaluation of network and self-help approaches to parent services, except for the personal testimonies of parents and professionals who have been involved in these programs.

Developing and intervening in informal social-support systems often involves professionals in less direct roles, and often with lessened control over the processes of intervention. Evaluation is thus more difficult and the need for evaluation may seem less compelling to the professional, at least when compared to professional services such as family counseling, in which the means for accomplishing objectives are spelled out by client and professional for their work together.

Even so, a critical assessment of the results of intentional efforts to develop and influence parent networks is needed. Simple self-report and retrospective evaluation instruments completed by parents participating in such programs would be a place to begin. Comparisons between retrospective baselines of children's behavior prior to and after the parents' involvement in parent networks, and between children whose parents are included in such programs and those whose parents are not, would also offer indications about the effects of these programs.

Not all the programs described in this chapter have been positively received by professionals. Toughlove, for example, has been criticized for its assumption that all children of participating parents have perceived themselves as valued and respected by their parents. Toughlove does not address the needs of children who may have been emotionally neglected or even abused. Toughlove groups urge parents to coerce children into living by parental rules and give little attention to other parenting attitudes and skills (Garbarino et al. 1986). Since no evaluation of program outcomes has been conducted, professionals will want to exercise some caution in recommending participation in Toughlove, as with any other program which has not been evaluated.

Even with the lack of evaluative data, other cautions can be intuited about the limitations of parent networks, based on the experience of professionals who have been involved with these programs and on what we know about social networks.

The Limitations of Parent Networks

1. Those who need network support are the least likely to benefit if these are the only services offered. Isolated parents by definition do not readily involve themselves in parent-education programs or in receiving services from helping professionals unless some crisis or problem develops that brings them to the attention of others. Professional services with isolated parents and children need, therefore, to look at the development of such a network as a significant goal of service that may require active involvement from the professional (Hartman and Laird 1983). Saying, "you need to develop some friendships" is not enough. Part of the helping professional's work with the parent may be teaching social skills which the parent can use to develop friendships and participate in church programs.

2. Some parents who have significant problems and are most in need of social support may have *burned out* their support network. Networks need to be characterized by mutuality and reciprocity, at least in the long run, in order to function effectively. This reciprocity may be even more important for emotional support than for instrumental support (Wellman 1981), yet it is more subtle and difficult to learn to give emotional support when one does not have effective relational skills. Kin, friends, and central figures who serve as a network of support need to have their own needs met by the network as well as serve as resource people to parents and children. Professionals can develop and support motivations and rewards for social-network members other than direct reciprocity from the overburdened parents. Network members may feel supported by (1) recognition from the church community that informal helping is a significant form of ministry; (2) opportunity to share in a supportive group with other central figures and network members who are serving others in similar ways; and (3) informal consultation as a member of the ministry of the team with the professional church leader.

3. Programs which encourage the development of networks of support need to be indirect. One cannot directly assign persons to be networks for one another; one can only provide a climate in which relationships can develop and then support them as they grow. Opportunities can be presented, such as pairing senior citizens with teen-agers for a recreational event, but these need to be considered blind dates, not weddings. There needs to be a period of courtship, of waiting for mutuality and affection to develop; this requires time and opportunities for sharing meaningful activities.

4. Natural support systems can only absorb a limited number of families in crisis or with chronic problems. Ecological families are not treatment groups; if they are to remain natural support systems, there must be a variety of resources and mutual support available within the system. On the other hand, churches usually contain many strong families and a variety of natural support systems, so that the larger faith community can minister with many more families in crisis than one natural support system could absorb.

5. Working with parent networks makes client confidentiality virtually impossible. The expectations and limitations of confidentiality need to be carefully and

clearly articulated with professional, client, ecological family or network members, and social-service agencies and other professionals involved. In the church, the recognition that "we are all sinners" and "we all struggle with problems" provides a foundation for dealing with information about one another gently and confidentially.

6. Finally, not all networks are nurturing. The stereotype that in-laws are interfering and adult children need their independence has endured because in some families, it is true. Networks can both support and divide a family against itself (Bott 1971). Networks can be stifling of creative life changes, narrow and crippling in their value systems, and can scapegoat members. Professionals may have to help clients alter the nature of network relationships or diminish the strength of such relationships in their lives, not strengthen them. Often, however, an effective intervention to accomplish this is the gradual growth of a new or altered network which is more supportive and nurturing.

Parents who perceive themselves as helpless and powerless to influence their children's lives in the face of peer-group pressures, school systems with which they are unfamiliar, and cultural influences they cannot control cannot empower their children. Empowered parents take an active role in shaping the environment not only at home but in all the other arenas that affect their children. In so doing, they model empowerment for their children.

References

Beavers, Jeanett et al. 1986. Coping with families with a retarded child. *Family Process* 25:365–78.

Bott, E. 1971. *Family and social network.* London: Tavistock Publications.

Boukydis, C. F. Z., ed. 1986. *Support for parents and infants.* New York: Routledge and Kegan Paul.

Bronfenbrenner, U. 1979. *Contexts of child rearing: Problems and prospects.* American Psychologist 34:844–50.

The Children's Defense Fund. 1982. *It's time to stand up for your children: A parent's guide to child advocacy.* Children's Defense Fund, 122 C Street, N.W., Washington, D.C. 20001.

Cochran, M. M., and Inge Bo Hogskolesenteret. 1987. Connections between the social networks, family involvement, and behavior of adolescent males in Norway. Paper presented at the 1987 Meeting of the Society for Research in Child Development, Baltimore, Md., April 20–24.

Colletta, N. D., and C. H. Gregg. 1981. Adolescent mothers' vulnerability to stress. *Journal of Nervous and Mental Disease* 169:50–54.

Crase, D. R. et al. 1986. *Parenting by grace: Discipline and spiritual growth.* Nashville: The Sunday School Board of the Southern Baptist Convention.

Duncan, D. et al. n.d. *Adopting child protection workers: A new response by the religious community to the crisis of child abuse and neglect.* Texas Department of Human Services, 701 West 51st Street, Austin, TX 78769.

Dunst, Carl, Carol Trivette, and Angela Deal. 1988. *Enabling and empowering families.* Cambridge: Brookline.

Froland, C. et al. 1981. *Helping networks and human services.* Beverly Hills: Sage.

Garbarino, J. 1979. Using natural-helping networks to meet the problem of child maltreatment. In *Schools and the problem of child abuse,* eds. R. Volpe, M. Breton, and J. Mitton, 129–36. Toronto: University of Toronto.

Garbarino, J. et al. 1978. The social maps of children approaching adolescence: Studying the ecology of youth development. *Journal of Youth and Adolescence* 7:417–28.

Garbarino, J., C. J. Schellenbach, J. Sebes, and associates. 1986. *Troubled youth, troubled families.* New York: Aldine.

Garbarino, J., and D. Sherman. 1980. High-risk neighborhoods and high-risk families: The human ecology of child maltreatment. *Child Development* 51:188–98.

Garland, D. S. R., K. C. Chapman, and J. Pounds. n.d. *Parenting by grace: Self-esteem.* Nashville: The Sunday School Board of the Southern Baptist Convention.

Gordon, T. 1975. *P.E.T.: Parent effectiveness training.* New York: Wyden.

Gottlieb, B. H. 1981. Social networks and social support in community mental health. In *Social networks and social support,* ed. B. H. Gottlieb. Beverly Hills: Sage.

Gray, J. et al. 1979. Prediction and prevention of child abuse and neglect. *Journal of Social Issues* 35: 127–38.

Grosh, V. 1988. The Family Consortium Program. *Family Resource Coalition Report,* 7:20.

Hartman, A., and J. Laird. 1983. *Family-centered social work practice.* New York: Free Press.

Hauk, G. 1987. Personal communication.

Height, D. I. 1985. What must be done about children having children? *Ebony,* March, 78–84.

Hetherington, E. M., M. Cox, and R. Cox. 1976. Divorced fathers. *Family Coordinator* 25:417–28.

Houghton, E. W. 1986. *Organizing parents into an effective prevention network.* Informed Networks Inc., 200 Ramsey Rd., Deerfield, IL 60015.

Houghton, E. W., and N. J. Grant. 1982. *The parent peer group solution.* Deerfield Citizens for Drug Awareness, 2440 Forest Glen, Deerfield, IL 60015.

Johns, M. L. 1988. *Developing church programs to prevent child abuse.* Austin: Texas Conference of Churches.

Kazak, Anne E. 1986. Families with physically handicapped children: Social ecology and family systems. *Family Process* 25:265–81.

Lieber, L. L. 1983. The self-help approach: Parents Anonymous. *Journal of Clinical Child Psychology* 12:288–91.

McDonald, M. M. 1989. Involving the community in prevention efforts. *Prevention Forum* 9 (3):1–4.

McGinnis, K., and J. McGinnis. 1981. *Parenting for peace and justice.* Maryknoll, N.Y.: Orbis.

Moore, J. A. et al. 1982. *Extending family resources.* Children's Clinic and Preschool Spastic Aid Council, Inc., 1850 Boyer Ave. East, Seattle, WA 98112.

Mudd, E. H., and S. Taubin. 1982. Success in family living—Does it last? A twenty-year follow-up. *American Journal of Family Therapy* 10:59–67.

Newcomer, D. M. 1972. The family of the future? A nonkinship model. *Social Action* 39:24–30.

Nickel, P. S., and H. Delany. 1985. *Working with teen parents: A survey of promising approaches*. Chicago: Family Resource Coalition Report.

Pattison, E. M. 1984. The church and the healing of families. Paper presented at conference, A Consultation on a Theology of the Family, Fuller Theological Seminary, Pasadena, Calif.

Popkin, M. H. 1983. *Active parenting*. Atlanta: Active Parenting, Inc.

Porter, F. Undated. *A design for developing a program for parents of handicapped children*. Omaha: Greater Omaha Association for Retarded Citizens, 3610 Dodge Street, Omaha, Nebraska 68131.

Poyadue, F. M. 1988. Parents helping parents. *Family Resource Coalition Report*, 7, 18.

Program aids pregnant teens. 1988, April 3. *Chicago Tribune*.

Reis, Janet, Linda Barbara-Stein, and Susan Bennett. 1986. Ecological determinants of parenting. *Family Relations* 35:547-54.

Sawin, M. M. 1979. *Family enrichment with family clusters*. Valley Forge, Penn.: Judson.

Schaller, L. E. 1986. From the neighborhood to the workplace. *Search* (Fall): 13-18.

Silvern, J. 1984. Building community alliances. *Family Resource Coalition Report* 3(2):3.

Trute, Barry, and Christopher Hauch. 1988. Building on family strength: A study of families with positive adjustment to the birth of a developmentally disabled child. *Journal of Marital and Family Therapy* 14:185-93.

Turner, R. Jay, and William R. Avison. 1985. Assessing risk factors for problem parenting: The significance of social support. *Journal of Marriage and the Family* 47:881-92.

Vogel, E. E., and N. W. Bell. 1960. The emotionally disturbed child as the family scapegoat. In *A modern introduction to the family*, eds. N. W. Bell and E. F. Vogel. New York: Free Press.

Wellman, B. 1981. Applying network analysis to the study of support. In *Social networks and social support*, ed. B. H. Gottlieb. Beverly Hills: Sage.

Westerhoff, J. H. 1983. *Building God's people in a materialistic society*. New York: Seabury Press.

Westerhoff, J. H. 1985. *Living the faith community*. Minneapolis: Winston Press.

York, P., D. York, and T. Wachtel. 1984. *Toughlove solutions*. Garden City, N.Y.: Doubleday and Co.

Young, L. 1964. *Wednesday's children*. New York: McGraw-Hill.

Zelkowitz, Phyllis. 1987. Social support and aggressive behavior in young children. *Family Relations* 36:129-34.

7

Using Church and Family Ritual

Joan Laird

The church has always understood the beauty and power of ritual in reflecting, expressing, recreating, and perpetuating shared meanings. Furthermore, for most families, the church has been one of the most central locations for family ritual, a place where families can mark and celebrate their most important events, sharing not only their weekly worship and spiritual meanings but their social and family-life transitions in community with others. Both church and family define and renew themselves in the process.

While this marriage between religion and ritual remains intact for many families, some observers (Kimball 1960) suggest that rituals that formerly involved town, village, and church now tend to take place in more private and isolated settings, inside the family and even inside the therapist's office. For example, the family's Fourth of July picnic in the back yard has taken the place of the town's community celebration. Although many weddings still take place in churches, the church often simply provides a traditional, convenient place for the bride and groom to assemble their guests; it is usually not the church community's celebration.

Clergy today often are asked to marry and bury people they have never seen before. As a result, such rituals, besides lacking meaning, can be occasions for awkward participation by clergy. I recall attending one funeral service for an elderly friend some years ago. The minister remarked on her long and faithful wifely devotion to husband and children. But she had divorced her husband sixty years earlier after discovering he was having an affair with another woman; her "long and faithful" devotion was to her two children and to her lifelong career.

JOAN LAIRD, M.S.W., is associate professor at Smith College School of Social Work, Northampton, Mass. She taught twelve years at Eastern Michigan University and founded the Ann Arbor Center for the Family. An author and experienced therapist in family-centered practice, Professor Laird is pursuing a joint doctorate in social work and anthropology at the University of Michigan.

In many cases, families have lost the richness and importance of shared ritual life not only because of the disillusionment, cynicism, and "me-centeredness" so prevalent in contemporary society, but because of particular losses. Perhaps migration has cut off the family from all that is familiar, as in the case of the black middle-class family in a white community or the Jewish or Cambodian immigrant family whose holocaust losses have been so unspeakable they cannot be told. Other families, through poverty and despair, cannot mobilize themselves to seek order and definition through family ritual. Traditionally, the family dinner has been a time of day when the family could remember that it was a family, as members connected with each other, symbolically redefining the family's sense of itself. Today family members are often together yet strangely apart and unconnected. Many of us are simply too busy; ordering pizza, reading the newspaper, and watching television has become the family routine, a daily ritualized pattern that in some families has taken the place of the family dinner.

Members of the church community, professional and volunteer alike, are in unique positions to help families shape their ritual lives, enriching both the connections with the church and the family's own systems of meanings and beliefs, and sometimes helping the family heal old rifts and wounds. In the discussion which follows, *ritual* is defined and its many functions reviewed. The various events in individual and family lives that can be mastered with the help of ritual are described, illustrated with case examples, and the steps and necessary ingredients in designing effective rituals are proposed.

Ritual Defined

Ritual encompasses an extremely broad category of human action. While politicians, anthropologists, and the clergy have been our ritual experts, all of us know something about it and engage in multiple rituals everyday, although we may not realize that is what we are doing. In an urban ritual game, children don't step on the cracks in sidewalks; the senior skit is performed every year in a college; and the alcoholic wanders purposefully to the same bar six nights a week or, better yet, in recovery, to the local AA meeting. These are ritual actions in the same way as are the crowning of a queen or the ordination of a cardinal.

A cluster of characteristics unites these widely differing events (Moore and Myerhoff 1977). Rituals are *performances*. They involve action and spoken words. They are *repetitious*. Some are performed only occasionally, while others are highly repetitious, such as the way members of a family enter or leave the home, greet each other, perform the chores, or put the children to bed. Some are common to many societies or widespread in our own, while others are quite unique to individuals or families, such as the annual opening of the summer cottage in *On Golden Pond* or the extended extramarital affair in *Same Time, Next Year*. Most rituals are *stylized* or contain some degree of *drama*, as in the taking of communion, placing the hand over the heart in the pledge of allegiance, or the father of the family raising the knife to slice the first piece of the Thanksgiving turkey.

While rituals contain *order*, there is also room for *spontaneity*. The football game or rock concert provide dramatic examples of the shifts between elaborate rules for behavior and times for planned chaos. Rituals often involve role reversals; for example, in the family, once a year children may dress in their parents' clothes, performing a grown-up skit for the family; or every Sunday a husband may serve his wife breakfast in bed.

Rituals usually occur at *specified times and places*, such as the annual Oscar awards; they make *extensive use of symbols* which provoke an emotional charge: the Christian cross, the American flag, the family heirloom, the candles lit on Sabbath.

Furthermore, rituals *communicate* a family's most profound and mundane "truths." They speak on many levels at once, often metaphorically or analogically, transmitting powerful messages that may be heard and experienced both consciously as well as out of our awareness. At Easter Sunday dinner, for example, the family may be aware of the religious significance of their celebration but unaware of the many levels on which specific family traditions and gender-role balances are being expressed and reinforced.

Finally, of particular relevance to the ecological perspective in this volume, the ritual has or should have a *collective dimension*. It contains a social message; it joins and connects people or inducts a person into a community of peers and thus is a very powerful force in developing and maintaining the continuity of the group. The sharing of family rituals in a faith community, for example, strengthens the social network and creates a system that is not unlike a large extended family.

Rituals vary a great deal in terms of the degree to which they are widely practiced or are relatively unique or idiosyncratic. This means that they also vary in terms of how much cultural material is available for their shaping (Wolin and Bennett 1984). Our society, through its religious and other institutions, provides a repertoire of available symbols for various holidays, religious celebrations, and rites of passage. The Christmas gift, the Halloween pumpkin, the bread and wine of Communion, the wedding dress and garter are all familiar symbols which are widely recognized and easily incorporated. Other rituals, such as the family vacation or the birthday, adopt more idiosyncratic symbols and particular kinds of food, dress, and actions, even though these rituals may be widely practiced. These often mix cultural symbols and symbols which are unique to a particular family. For example, our society provides some rather universal birthday symbols, such as greeting cards and candles, but families also tend to celebrate birthdays in their own unique ways. Families have opportunity for diversity and creativity in the rituals and ritual symbols of everyday life, in patterned family interactions such as the goodbye kiss, the walking of the dog, and the way that day and night are separated inside the family.

Still other situations often faced by ecological families call for ritual, for which very little cultural symbolic material is available (Laird 1984). Many transitions occur, in our urbanized world, in isolation from community, extended family, and other potential networks of human relationship and support. I will return to these issues. For now, however, mention might be made of divorce, a phenomenon now at least half as common as marriage; the joining of individuals in committed relationships; the entering and leaving of hospitals, prisons, or other institutions; the placement of children in adoptive or other homes (Imber-Black 1988a); the onset of menstruation, or the birth of a child (Laird 1988). Many other similar transitions might be mentioned, but the point is that in some of these instances little help is available from the wider community in incorporating new statuses and roles. Because of social disapproval or stigma, the transition can be accompanied with secrecy and shame.

The Functions of Ritual

We cannot live without ritual, because *ritual orders our lives*. It is the way we organize ourselves and our interactions with others in time and space, the way we mark the seasons, the weeks, the days. It enforces our rules for living, proclaiming when and how we eat, what we can talk about to whom, when and how we shall celebrate our travels through life. It is often through ritual that we define and express the nature and quality of family relationships and, indeed, define the very boundaries of families. Rituals of greeting and farewell order comings and goings, and rituals of entering and leaving draw boundaries, defining who is inside and who is outside. Various family and community rites of passage, such as baptisms, graduations, weddings, anniversaries, and funerals celebrate new statuses and redefine family relationships and commitments. Since ritual, as it occurs in the ordinary life space of ecological families, has enormous power to mark and facilitate change, so too can it serve as a very powerful helping tool.

Rituals *express, reflect, create, and recreate*. They reveal and express our deeply shared meanings, serving as windows into an individual's or family's identity. For the family minister, asking a family about its rituals or having the privilege to share in the enactment of one provides rapid and vivid access to family beliefs and organization. Rituals convey to the individuals or families involved a sense of themselves and of their own coherence. As enactments or performances, rituals create; no matter how unchanging some may seem, each ritual enactment occurs in a new context and some sort of changes are made. Thus they not only recreate, in the sense of providing continuity, but they create anew; they are adaptive as well as transformative.

Ritual, and this is most important for the social worker, the pastoral counselor, the teacher, and others who are in a position to help families, is *one of the most powerful socialization mechanisms* available. As we participate in the rituals of our society, our churches, or our families, we are socialized; we learn who we are and how we are to be. Such rituals communicate and sanctify particular values and norms, such as how to be a woman or a man, how to lead a worthy life, how to be a parent. Family recreational rituals provide one example. One family may communicate the importance of role sharing and a close connection

with nature through its frequent picnics, camping trips, and wilderness adven-
tures. Another may express the importance of culture with special outings to
concerts and museums. As family members participate in such rituals, they learn
whether cooperation or competition is valued, the appropriate behaviors for each
sex, and family rules for togetherness.

Rituals also help individuals and families *master separation and incorporate
change* in their lives. Life-cycle ceremonies, or family rites of passage, perhaps offer
the best examples of this function of ritual. Life-cycle rituals such as weddings or
funerals help families cope with old and new losses, to consider how they will hold
on and let go, as family boundaries are expanded and contracted and family rules
and relationships are renegotiated and redefined. As Friedman (1985) points out,
life-cycle ceremonies are also unique opportunities for healing and for the enhancement of holiness, for the strengthening of the church-family ecology.

> No other aspect of our duties so unifies our major responsibilities. . . . At no other
> time can we so effectively fulfill the pastoral part of our ministry without having to adopt
> modes and metaphors from outside our calling. And, at no other time are the two major
> dimensions of our healing potential so apparent: the uniqueness of our entree into family
> life, and the power inherent in our community position. But more than healing is in-
> volved. A family approach to life-cycle events also embraces the holiness inherent in the
> tradition, because religious values are far more likely to be heard when family process is
> working toward the success of the passage, rather than against it. (p. 163)

Church process, too, must work toward the success of the life-cycle passages,
helping families express their particular meanings as they blend with and differ
from the larger ecological family. So-called nontraditional or "alternate lifestyle"
families need particular help and encouragement in determining how they will
express their own "familiness" and their connectedness to the larger church
community through the life-cycle ritual, a point to be expanded upon later.

Not all functions of ritual are positive or desirable, however. Rituals are
"conserving" forces and thus are sometimes used in rigid, self-protective, and
self-maintaining ways that can close family members off from each other and
from the community, preventing necessary healing opportunities and warding off
new information. Churches and families, for example, have often excluded
women from playing certain central roles in their most important rituals, and in
some cases women and children are demeaned. Such rituals tend to *maintain
vested interests and particular balances of authority and power.* The Inquisition,
the infamous witch trials, the inhuman uses of political rituals in Nazi Germany
and in Cambodia, and family rituals of violence are extreme examples of situations in which the power of ritual is misused to maintain some in positions of
power and others in positions of subordination and dependence.

Rituals can *ward off change and gloss over contradictions.* Immersed in our
experiences of participating in ritual, we can fail to notice the anomalies and
paradoxes inherent in some of our relationships or roles. Thus the family secret or
a particular set of family rules and relationships can be protected from comment

or change. Or a congregation's uncharitable or discriminating practices can be glossed over and dismissed from awareness, the power of the ritual promoting a false sense of togetherness. A father and son may only come together through sports rituals, a pseudo-close togetherness in which both fail to acknowledge that there are many painful subjects that cannot be discussed. Tithing rituals or the Sunday collection in church may foster the illusion that wealthy congregants have adequately helped their fellow human beings, supporting denial of homelessness and other forms of suffering in the community.

Finally, while ritual can be used to sanctify or consecrate, it also can be used to *degrade*. Some families, for example, use repetitive rituals of humiliation to maintain a rigid homeostasis or a particular set of rules for communication and interaction in which one or more family members may be scapegoated (Reiss 1981). Such rituals may be maintained unintentionally, covering over losses, uncertainties or fears. Bermann (1973) illuminates the patterns in a family that scapegoats a particular child with demeaning communication rituals while avoiding the father's imminent death. In one family I worked with, the father's ritualistic and authoritarian humiliation of one son and his fostering of his wife's drug dependency masked his own unresolved losses and fears. Family ministers who understand the form and power of ritual can help families create new, more growth-enhancing rituals for family life.

The Use of Ritual in Work with Families

How can the power of ritual be more effectively harnessed in family ministry? In the next section, a number of opportunities for using ritual will be described and illustrated. While the emphasis will be on work with individual families, on a more general level the church and the ministry need to begin with a reexamination of their own ritual practices, asking:

- What is it we hope to accomplish through our church rituals? Is it being accomplished?
- Are our ritual practices relevant to the contemporary spiritual and social needs of the congregation?
- Can older interpretations of ritual be rethought and reclaimed so that they can enrich the present with new meaning and connect with the special needs of the congregation?
- Are our existing ritual practices patriarchal, at times excluding women and insensitive to their particular experiences? Are they ethnocentric, failing to appreciate the potential cultural contributions of particular groups?
- Are there ways our congregants can participate more fully, more meaningfully, enhancing their connections with and support from the church community?
- Has the ministry creatively reached out to know and understand the individual stories of its people and its families, helping them to express particular meanings as they participate in widely practiced rites?

Each family needs to shed outworn and meaningless rites, renew, reclaim, and preserve those that hold promise for contemporary experience, and create new traditions relevant to the demands of today's world. In the same way, the church has renewed and must continue to renew its ritual practices.

The Family Ministry and Ritual

Family ministry, through its counseling, education, and prevention programs, may discover many ways to tap into the power of ritual in helping families and strengthening the relationship between church and community. In terms of counseling, there are many parallels between the roles of the modern day minister and the contemporary counselor or therapist, as well as between these helpers and the shaman or healer in more traditional societies. For example, many clergy today are schooled not only in the rituals integral to their theology but in psychology and in pastoral counseling. In the latter role, clergy and other professional helpers provide contexts in which the power of ritual is joined with knowledge of individual and family dynamics. A family minister may work with a family to help a young person learn to leave home in a more healthy and planned way. He or she may help a family plan a rite of passage that will mark and celebrate the transition, linking family and church community. A pastor may help a young husband gain healing from the impact of a divorce through counseling and through sponsoring self-help or ministry-led groups for community members who experience such transitions. Special efforts should be made to connect the newly isolated family member with social and other events.

Losses are most profoundly felt at times of central family ritual, particularly throughout the first year after a divorce, death, a child's leaving home, or placement of an elderly family member in a nursing home. These are times when families may be encouraged to join with other families to participate in church-sponsored events and rituals in which the lost persons or relationships are remembered and perhaps mourned again through commemoration or sharing of experiences and stories.

The power of rituals may be harnessed by the professional helper in several ways. In fact, the counseling or therapeutic relationship itself, like a tribal healing ceremony, has many powerful ritual aspects and sometimes an elaborately prescribed form. Rules for greeting, for beginning and ending, and for communication among the participants may be quite ritualized. The power of the ritual form may be consciously used in giving the family homework assignments, thus increasing the possibility of the family's enacting the change. Therapeutic prescriptions hold much more potential for change if they are presented in repetitive, ritualized ways, ways that contain drama and demand attention. For example, a family may be instructed to hold a family meeting once a week, in which complaints are heard and differences renegotiated. Several professionals in the family-therapy field have taken leadership in the use of ritualized prescription or assignment (Selvini-Palazzoli et al. 1977, 1978; Byng-Hall 1973).

Carefully constructed and elaborated rituals, rich with symbolic words and actions, rituals that are often intended to be performed only once, can be designed to be enacted in the counseling session itself, in the home, or in some other context relevant to the problem or need. Such rituals may be designed to undo a limiting or destructive family myth, help a family bridge a transition, or move a family toward a more complete resolution of a loss (Imber-Black, Roberts, and Whiting 1988; Laird 1984; van der Hart 1983). Examples of such rituals will be presented in some detail in the pages to follow.

Family-Life Transitions—Normative

Normative family-life transitions present the most obvious and frequent opportunity for strengthening the role of family ministry in the area of family ritual. Birth, death, and marriage usually imply tremendous change for families. Family conflict and tension can escalate during times of transition, as old, unresolved pain may be reexperienced and unresolved conflicts renewed. At such times, as van Gennep (1909/1960) outlined, the family must experience a separation, a letting go, a liminal time betwixt and between the old way of being and the new, and the reincorporation into society in changed form. In the case of marriage, for example, the partners must relinquish the freedoms associated with singlehood and their closest attachments to family and to same-sex peers (the separation), experience a liminal time in which they are "engaged"—neither single nor married but in preparation for a new phase—and be wed (the reincorporation), from which they emerge into society in a new status, with new expectations for commitment and role performance. While the wedding itself—the formal life-cycle ceremony, with its elaborate symbolization—provides the bridge over which the couple crosses, the actual transition may take many months and sometimes years to accomplish. If it is short-circuited, or its symbols meaningless or contradictory, or if it occurs without the sanction and support of family and/or community, its functions and thus its success are likely to be impaired.

Family ministry has a special role to play on these occasions. Many families may ignore the importance of ritual in accomplishing their major life transitions. They may do this to avoid painful feelings caused by the loss of significant family members (e.g., the death of a parent whose absence will be felt), or to sidestep family tension or conflict. For example, perhaps a family member has said he does not want any fuss over his death, no service or other special observance. This same family may experience the next cycle of family rituals as painful and lonely affairs. Or perhaps parents are adamantly opposed to a daughter's marriage and will not accept her choice or his family. Perhaps a woman is pregnant out of wedlock and marries hastily and secretively, without sanction or celebration and cutting herself off from both extended family and community. Perhaps a Hispanic or Vietnamese family has recently moved to the church neighborhood and has no one with whom to share their wedding anniversary. Perhaps too many Christmas holidays have been spoiled by a husband's drinking binges. Perhaps the onset of a young girl's menstruation is accompanied in the family by secrecy, shame, and a confused sense of meaning rather than new definitions and celebration of womanhood and of life. In all of these and many more which might be mentioned family ministry can play a significant role, identifying families who need connection with others and helping them figure out how to share their important transitions in community with others. The church can offer a safe environment for resolving conflict and mediating difference, providing a sense of what Turner (1969) has termed *communitas* or a sense of community. It also can encourage the formation of natural helping networks.

Families may pay too high a price when, for whatever reason—intended or unintended—they avoid attending to their rites of passage. The resulting incompleteness of the passage and the lack of connectedness of the family to a wider community can exact severe costs which span generations, as in the following example:

Myrna, a forty-six-year-old woman in counseling, would still cry every time she remembered her grandmother, who lived with her parents and with whom Myrna shared her room. When Myrna was eight years old, her grandmother became ill and Myrna was sent to visit an aunt. When she returned home, her grandmother was not there, but no one would tell Myrna where she was. Finally, Myrna overheard her father on the telephone telling someone that the grandmother had died. There was no sitting shiva in this Jewish family and Myrna was not allowed to attend the funeral. Almost forty years later she still shed tears of rage and loss.

The counselor suggested, at one point, that Myrna, who was also quite cut off from the remaining members of her small family of origin—her sister, an aunt, and two cousins—might consider holding a memorial service for her grandmother. She became very excited over the idea and with the counselor's help and a blending of ideas, planned such a ceremony. The work included educating the rabbi she chose (he initially was quite disconcerted about the idea of a service memorializing someone who had died almost forty years earlier) concerning the purpose of the service, telling him the meanings Myrna wished to have expressed, and planning how to invite and include others who had meaning in her life and in the life of her original family.

The replacement of the lost ritual, a very moving experience for all concerned, achieved the primary goal of helping Myrna complete a long-delayed mourning process. But it triggered other changes as well, some anticipated and some unanticipated. Through the careful planning of the rite, Myrna became reconnected with members of her extended family from whom she had been alienated; old wounds connected with old feuds began to be healed. Further, she had long felt "stuck" and unable to deal actively with her anger at her husband who had had a continuous series of extramarital affairs for many years. Her inability to confront her husband mirrored her childhood sense of paralysis in relation to her anger at her own parents and her fears of further separation and loss. Myrna also felt paralyzed in her relationship with her daughter, whom she saw as "fragile," like her own mother who had been mentally ill. In the months following the memorial service, Myrna made clear her expectations for her marriage. A separation was initiated in which she and her husband would take stock of their lives and the future of the marriage. Also, her husband entered a church-connected rehabilitation program for men with sexual addictions. Furthermore, Myrna began to work on renegotiating the relationship with her daughter—a relationship in which her daughter was valued for her competence rather than her dependence. The daughter, interestingly, became very involved with a fundamentalist church, symbolic of her own efforts to be "born again."

In the above example, the original ritual is lost or missed. As in crisis therapy, because of the heightened emotional energy present during family transitions, an anticipated rite of passage can be used not only to help incorporate new or anticipated changes, but to rework insufficiently resolved transitions from the past. The counselor can help the family (1) consider the meanings of the anticipated changes in their lives, (2) plan a rite of passage which enables the members to let go of and to grieve whatever must be left behind, (3) plan for the future, and (4) celebrate the new, incorporating where possible the words and symbols that will best express their meanings and will connect them to the wider family, church, and community.

Other normative family transitions may be underritualized for other reasons. For example, the significant events in a married woman's life in general are contingent upon the movement through the family-life cycle of others—her parents, her husband, and her children. It is usually she who does the preparatory work for the major family holidays, for the church supper, and other events while her own transitions can be amorphous and poorly marked. Family migrations and moves, for example, are often dictated by the husband's career. "The trailing spouse," the woman partner who follows her husband's work, often experiences multiple losses of affiliation and status, without the accompanying rewards of the clearly marked new status, prestige, and built-in social world that welcomes the husband. Even in childbirth, one of the most significant events in a woman's life, it is the infant who is celebrated and welcomed—through gifts, through the baptism or the *bris* (the Jewish rite of naming and circumcision), through ceremonies that give the child the name of the father and attach it to a male lineage. Few rites in American society prepare the woman for motherhood, recognize the enormous implications of her change in status, or welcome her into a new community of women. While some men and women find help in birth education or other parenting programs, the church too can take leadership in providing contexts in which families can prepare for important family transitions.

Life transitions can be poorly marked for the unmarried person and particularly for the unmarried woman. Although families have begun to prepare both their sons and daughters for multiple life roles, in many families the son has been and continues to be clearly prepared for public life, the daughter for marriage and mothering. Many rituals connect males, single or married, with the public world —the rituals of politics, the corporation, the military, sports, the local bar, and the church. The unmarried woman, on the other hand—since women's rituals are so domestically centered—can be in some ways forever viewed as an incomplete adult or even a child. Her life may not be defined as separate or special, and her personal relationships and choices are often subordinated to family demands.

Pat, thirty-eight years old and the second youngest in a family of six children, remained in the same town as her long-divorced mother and three siblings, two married sisters and a bachelor brother. Pat was frequently "on call" to help her mother prepare for family events, to transport her to and from the airport, to pay her mother's bills and water her plants while she was away, and to be available for breakfast, lunch, or dinner when her mother wanted company and had no other plans. As is common in such situations, Pat's resentment and occasional complaining were labeled as disloyalty or lack of caring. It was frequently pointed out that her sisters had many responsibilities and her brother's job was very demanding. Interestingly, her own career goals languished, she was underemployed in relation to her talents, and afraid to take risks. She had never invited her mother or any of her siblings to dinner, always going to the homes of the "real adults" for family occasions.

In this situation, Pat was helped to redefine her relationship to her family and to their ritual lives. She "resigned" maturely and affectionately from some of her family responsibilities, which forced the redistribution of some of the family tasks. This realignment, which implied some risks and some losses for Pat because of the ways in which the caretaker child's role is often maintained through the threat of loss of affection or approval, nevertheless freed her to examine her own priorities and to reach out for healthier connections to potential friends and eventually a partner. She marked the completion of this phase of her treatment with the preparation of a family dinner at her apartment, which she privately labeled her "independence" party.

The church can provide a context for "singles" with varying kinds of social and emotional needs and can help families consider how they may more fairly distribute the work of family caretaking that working women continue to shoulder.

Men tend to struggle with a somewhat different set of issues. Because of the very powerful social forces that define home and family as woman's world, women often lack the language or the skill to navigate well in the public world. Similarly, men often lack the words or comfortable skills for full participation in family life. Many men exhibit discomfort and a sense of isolation, sometimes expressed as boredom, in family gatherings. A wife may discount her husband's ability to parent or to have a significant role in the care of an infant. Men may feel excluded from the often warm, busy networks of women and female children who take major responsibility for family culture, events, and stories. While men sit at the head of the table, and have many other prerogatives in family life that symbolize their greater status, and perhaps must be deferred to in a variety of ways, they are often labeled the outsiders in family life, their domestic roles peripheral to the family's most central events. Men often pay a price for patriarchal family divisions of role, possessing a more limited range of expressive tools for sharing loss, for experiencing intimacy and connectedness through family transition. Again, family ministry can help families reclaim and revitalize their family rituals in ways that better express the needs of modern men and women rather than encouraging families to preserve the outdated gender-role divisions implicit in many traditional family rituals. Premarital and marital self-help groups sponsored through the church, as well as marriage-enrichment programs, can play an important role in helping couples share ideas about the effects on their families of changing social constructions of gender and consider more flexible, egalitarian, and growth-enhancing relationships.

Family-Life Transitions—Idiosyncratic

In our rapidly changing society with newly emerging family forms, the culture has yet to devise accepted and available rituals. Yet, as Imber-Black (1988a) points out, the same complex reworkings of relationship that are required in any transition need to occur in these.

For example, as a society we lack meaningful rituals that might help the traditional wife and mother face the "empty nest" syndrome, or assist a husband and wife to comfortably adjust to the husband's retirement. For other families, contextual support may be lacking or the family may be stigmatized, promoting isolation and secrecy from extended family and community. For example, the church community may shun the lesbian family, rather than reach out to them. With unmarried persons adopting children or, through modern technology, giving birth to and raising their own, it is not hard to visualize the obstacles such children will face in a school system, for instance. Other families may be shunned because a sense of shame or fear is attached to their transitions. For example, clergy and church members may avoid the family in their congregation whose daughter has AIDS, or they may fail to help the family whose son will be leaving for prison or a drug treatment center. These families, too, are facing losses and need help in mastering the transition. Family ministry can play an important role in helping to educate the community and in reaching out to particular families. The fact that these and other unusual transitions are ritualized at all and are well mastered must be credited to the extraordinary, spontaneous creativity of individuals, families, and some institutions.

The Alternate Rituals Project of the United Methodist Church (1976), for example, has had a two-fold mission:

1) To suggest ways in which those who shape and use traditional worship forms can be increasingly sensitive to the realities of a changed and changing society and 2) to suggest new rituals and acts of worship which may now be appropriate for optional or trial use within the church. (6)

In their work, they have explored five rituals in contemporary contexts, (1) footwashing, (2) naming, (3) rituals with the dying, (4) rituals with the divorced, and (5) rituals for endings and beginnings.

Footwashing. Footwashing, as a ritual for special liturgical occasions, is a very old practice in the Christian church and one that apparently is reemerging. Referred to in John 13:1–17, footwashing is said to symbolize and disclose Christ's messiahship, to mark the participants as people who are obedient to God, to define a relationship of closeness and mutual service among church community members, and to convey a sense of humility. Footwashing "serves to enable all who are at worship more fully to experience, express, and symbolize the depth meaning of their faith" (Alternate Rituals Project 1976, 27).

Naming. Naming, in Genesis, is to call into being. There is great power in naming and similarly, the potential for great power in a name. Naming not only points to but helps to define who one is, linking person with family and with the larger community. Many societies have naming ceremonies which recognize and admit newborns into the community. In the Jewish ritual of *bris*, the male child is circumcized and named. In certain of the churches, baptism has served as both an admitting and naming ritual, although some argue (Alternate Rituals Project 1976) that the two functions are different and that the naming purpose is indistinct and should perhaps be separated from ceremonies of baptism.

Some churches are making naming or renaming a much more clearly defined part of the wedding ritual or are helping families devise naming ceremonies in special services after the birth or adoption of a child, the incorporation of stepchildren in a remarriage ceremony, or in bestowing a Western name to serve as an additional name for a child adopted from another culture. In recent times, some women clearly have understood the meaning and power in a name and have created ceremonies in which they take new names which liberate them from assignments to male lineages through birth or marriage. Some churches have begun to attend to the renaming ritual, providing contexts in which the newly named or renamed person is joined to a larger community.

Rituals with the Dying. The construction of rituals with the dying is a delicate and complex task, especially in a society such as ours in which the dying are often avoided, and denial on the part of both the dying and the living is culturally supported. Such rituals must be tailored in ways sensitive to the uniqueness and readiness of the particular family and community. Like all rituals, they cannot be imposed on people who are not ready and do not wish to participate. In rituals with the terminally ill, the ill person may be burdened with guilt, with broken promises and unfinished life work. That person needs to give himself or herself permission to surrender to death, while the living offer forgiveness for being left to struggle on alone and their permission for the loved one to die. A ritual with the dying is meant to help all concerned master the task of letting go. Members of the Alternate Rituals Project of the United Methodist Church, who outline such a service, believe it should contain elements of confession and pardon, of praise and witness, and of offering and dedication.

Divorce. Divorce provides one of the clearest examples of a modern day rite of passage which has been considered idiosyncratic in the past but has now become more normative. Nevertheless, because of cultural lag there is still little social support or cultural material to enable participants to better master this transition. Since more than one out of every two marriages ends in divorce, divorce can no longer be defined as a deviant status, yet for many it becomes associated with shame or disgrace, making it a difficult transition for adults and children to master. Like any transition, divorce implies loss, readying for and incorporation of new roles and status, elements of holding on and letting go, and, perhaps for some, relief from conflict or even freedom from physical abuse or other kinds of oppression.

The divorce ritual too must symbolize holding on and letting go in a way that facilitates necessary grief work and promotes healing, defines and documents publicly the divorced person's new status, and rejoins the divorced to the wider community. Such a ceremony "enables the divorce to be recognized by all, the pain of it to be shared, the gifts of the gospel to be experienced, and the resolution to move into the future with new purpose to be an act of the entire Christian community" (Alternate Rituals Project 1976, 85). Family ministers may initiate self-help groups in which divorced people can share with others their anxieties, burdens, and strategies for surviving as singles.

Endings and Beginnings. There are many kinds of endings and beginnings in this mobile, urbanized society which involve powerful losses, loneliness, anxiety, and a need for new adaptations. Family ministry, the wider community, and families themselves may fail to recognize the toll such transitions can take and the accompanying need for conscious mastery through ritual. Many idiosyncratic transitions involve a move from one setting that is highly familiar to another that is alien. These include the young person establishing his or her first separate residence, the family who is being moved again by the large corporation, the older person who must move to a long-term care facility, the child who will be placed in residential care or a group home, the child returning to the family from foster care, the Vietnamese child adopted by a family in the community.

The church can help such families master these transitions in ways that are not isolating or demeaning. The family ministry may reach out to welcome and help connect the new person with a wider network of potential extended family and work with other institutions in considering how they might help people master the transition. On a more individualized level, family ministry can commit itself to work with particular families through the transitional period. A church-connected residential facility, whether for young or old, for example, must encourage full family participation in the entire process. Cultural differences must be recognized, understood, and wherever possible not only incorporated but celebrated, perhaps through enactments of important rituals which might include symbols, special food and dress, and shared participation in ritual activity.

Rituals of endings and beginnings, celebrated in community, should include a clear statement of purpose with opportunities for reminiscing, for consideration of the meaning of the transition, for defining the new status, for letting go and sending forth, and for remaining connected with what is left behind.

Other more idiosyncratic transitions were alluded to earlier. Many women today, for example, are choosing to have children outside of marriage through artificial insemination or adoption—often transracial adoption—creating a new set of challenges. Church, school, and family rituals assume traditional, heterosexual family organization and their rituals may exclude those family forms which are different. The children in such families may be misunderstood or even treated cruelly by others. And although the church family minister may disagree with the gay or lesbian lifestyle of some of these families, he or she will feel a responsibility to understand and aid them in their life transitions. For example, family ministry may play a significant part in recognizing the adoption of a baby or child into a same-sex or friendship family.

The Interfaith or Intercultural Family

Some churches have discouraged, prohibited, refused to perform or failed to recognize interfaith marriage; the purpose here is not to argue such proscription but to note that the position of the church can add to the strain and isolation such couples frequently experience. For some couples, their parents or other family members may also be opposed, cutting the couple off from the support and connectedness needed to nourish and strengthen the marriage. The lack of church blessing and consequent distance from the church community may enhance tension between the marital partners, especially if the church community has been significant to one or both. In some situations, if the marriage cannot be performed in the church, the church may find it possible to offer a ceremony of commitment and/or a welcoming reception for the newly forming family.

Each partner brings to marriage a history of different traditions. In the case of interfaith or intercultural traditions, these traditions may be quite different. In such couples, actions based on cultural or religious difference may be experienced by each partner as rude, hostile or stubborn behavior (McGoldrick and Preto 1984). Differences in tradition must be negotiated over a period of time as the couple, in a sense, creates its own family culture, drawing on important traditions from each of their experiences.

In family-life seminars with premarital and newly married couples, participants can explore their similarities and differences and can identify their wishes for their marriage, what they hope to preserve from the past, and what they are willing to relinquish. A useful assignment in work with not-yet-married couples —even those who have not clearly defined the nature of their commitment—is to ask them to plan their wedding in great detail. This assignment surfaces commonalities and differences in beliefs and traditions, making personal and family cultural preferences more explicit and available for the couple's assessment and negotiation. A similar kind of work needs to take place in all new families, whether formed by marriage or some other mutual commitment.

Those individuals who are unable to identify their religious and familial traditions are, interestingly, as likely to misunderstand and resent the spouse's behavior as those who are more connected and committed to their heritage. The following case, drawn from group counseling, is such a couple:

Judith, a young Jewish woman from Chicago, highly involved in her faith and passionately committed to preserving her Jewish identity and her family's ethnic and religious traditions, became engaged to Jerry. He was a young man from a rather disengaged, Midwestern family that, if asked, would identify itself as Protestant. But he had had no church affiliation since early childhood. The old adage that "opposites attract" seemed relevant here. Jerry, a quiet, gentle man, was not only attracted to Judith's vibrancy but also to the strong sense of connectedness and the richness of tradition in Judith's family. While Judith could articulate clearly her convictions and what she wanted to happen in their new family, Jerry took the position that he "had no traditions" and that it was up to Judith to bring into the marriage whatever was important to her.

The counselor and other group members were concerned that Jerry was "giving up too much" and that he might later resent Judith, blaming her for what he had lost, if the new family did not also reflect his values and his "culture." Jerry was sent, in a sense, to do an ethnography of his own family, to reconnect with family members, to talk at length with his mother and sister (his only surviving relatives from his family of origin), and to begin to identify what he cared about most deeply. Slowly, he was able to claim those parts of his heritage that he wished to preserve and to discuss them with Judith.

Family rituals express each partner's heritage and sense of coherence and continuity. Work with interfaith or intercultural premarital couples and with couples experiencing difficulty needs to include careful interviewing about their ritual life. The interview will help them surface their unrecognized differences in tradition, defusing the toxicity and rendering their family "culture" available for some renegotiation. Family ministry may also provide a context in which extended family members from both sides can be included in larger meetings to raise their concerns and to be helped to include and support the outsider.

Underritualized Families

Rituals, as was said earlier, provide order, meaning, and a sense of coherence in family life. We need them to define and value ourselves. Many families are underritualized for a variety of reasons. Material, cultural, or spiritual poverty can lead to underritualization. Some families—homeless, poor, disenfranchised, exhausted, overwhelmed, or simply depressed—may lack the resources or the energy to make order out of disorder. They may have lost their own definition or sense of coherence. Bruised through (sometimes) generations of misfortune, such families experience a sense of timelessness, forgetting the past and despairing of the future. These families can be helped to develop simple, patterned, daily rituals that strengthen their cohesion and reaffirm their pride and their sense of themselves as a family (Hartman and Laird 1983). The development of ritual with poor and underritualized families must proceed slowly and carefully and must be tailored to these families' resources, since such families need to develop a sense of mastery and competence. They do not need to experience yet another failure. For one family this may mean establishing one, small, daily ritual around a new division of labor in the household, such as parent and children sharing the meal preparation; in another family the parents may share a story from the past with their children. Another plans a special family outing.

Some families are cut off from tradition through migration or loss, while others have difficulty coming to terms with a painful past they wish to bury. Immigrant families, for example, are pressured and sometimes pressure themselves to Americanize very quickly, cutting themselves off from the wisdom of the older generations. Some, such as the Cambodians, have experienced such inexplicable horror they cannot share their pasts with their own children. Other families become underritualized as a function of the strains of intermarriage or because they are cut off either geographically or psychologically from their families of origin. Family-life seminars in the church or counseling with individual families can help them to remember and recapture some of their more important traditions. Such methods can also aid families to resolve losses through carefully constructed ritual, to restore their lives gradually, and to regain pride in their own traditions.

The Rigidly Ritualized Family

Some families develop elaborate and rigid rituals which ward off change and mask contradictions. Such rituals preserve secrets or family myths, as in the family that cooperates to hide the drug addiction of the father, a medical doctor and "pillar" of church and community. Other rituals keep particular family members in subordinate positions, scapegoat a particular family member, or simply serve to hold family members close, preventing their leaving. These families will require the help of a skilled counselor or therapist who can help them alter rigid ritual patterns, paving the way for more open communication and structural change in the family.

For example, a counselor may suggest that a woman visit her father's grave at planned intervals to tell him those things she was unable to speak of in his lifetime, helping to free her from a longstanding pattern of conflicted relationships with men. In a marriage disturbed by unfaithfulness, with the wife being unable to forget her husband's earlier affair, "punishing" him for many years, the couple may be helped to design a ritual of expiation and forgiveness, perhaps through a symbolic burial or burning of the affair. A family involved in rigid patterns of drinking, usually highly ritualized in nature, may be helped to substitute other, more healthy rituals, such as a brisk family walk or jog during what would normally be the cocktail hour.

Designing Rituals and Traditions

There are a number of essential principles in designing family rituals. The best rituals develop out of the cultural material at hand; they grow out of and build upon the family's special language—its metaphors, meanings, symbols, myth, and folklore. The ritual should be tailored to the family, not superimposed based on the therapist's or family minister's own sociocultural and religious biases. The planned ritual should be based on careful, ethnographic knowledge of the family's cultural style and patterns, gained in a positive relational context in which the family's ways are respected. While the ritual may draw upon familiar cultural material, it also must be specific to the purpose at hand, for example, to reclaim, alter, or enrich the family's ritual life, to interrupt a dysfunctional pattern, or to resolve a loss.

More specifically, the ritual should incorporate that cluster of ingredients mentioned early in this chapter as essential to the very definition of ritual.

1. *Action/performance*—Ritual enacts something; it contains both words and movement, helping the actors in the drama move from one status to another.

Such ritual action may entail a symbolic letting go of something from the past, through burial, the tearing up of old letters, flushing, burning, or perhaps an act of saying goodbye in a new and caring way, with the exchange of a poem or a gift. It may mean toasting, welcoming the new, or reclaiming in changed fashion a worn and tedious family ritual, for example, through a new pattern of preparation and design for the holiday dinner.

2. *Repetition*—While the once-enacted ritual can imply enormous potential for change, connecting the participants to a new group and a new status and reminding all concerned of their shared values, as in the wedding or the bar mitzvah, most rituals use repetition most effectively, as we know from important religious rituals. These same principles may be applied in the design of family ritual, as in the lighting of candles at dinner once a week or the weekly family meeting to take stock and negotiate differences.

3. *Stylization and Drama*—One of the reasons that rituals are powerful is the fact that they are enacted in stylized and even dramatic ways, speaking analogically to their participants. Church services, for example, even in the most modest and unhierarchical of churches, are highly stylized and often rich with dramatic impact. The decorating of a Christmas tree provides a familiar family example of stylized ritual. Each family member delights in the rediscovery of a favorite ornament, and there is often a ritualistic, mutual teasing about how others are participating, reinforcing generational and gender roles and relationships. The holiday dinner, the funeral, the sweet-sixteen party, or the taking of the driver's test are other examples of common family rituals that have their stylized and dramatic components.

In work with families, you may design rituals that alternate, in a dramatic way, holding on and letting go (I once suggested to a couple who, after seven years, could still not decide to marry but neither could they part, that they go to a local park and play for some twenty minutes on a see-saw. They were to figure out together, then, how to get off of the see-saw without jeopardizing the safety or comfort of the other. This couple soon made the decision to part as lovers but to remain friends). There can be considerable drama involved in burying an affair, shredding an old diagnostic summary, or sending a letter of resignation to the family abdicating a demeaning or outworn role.

4. *Order and Spontaneity*—While you may, with the family, design and prescribe the particular elements of the ritual and the order in which it is to occur, you may also wish to include a time for creativity and spontaneity, for planned chaos or disorder. It may happen whether you plan it or not! Few of the carefully planned therapeutic rituals I have helped families design have turned out quite as expected, for, as systems theorists tell us, when one introduces a change the entire system will respond and rearrange itself. It may be that a time is planned at a holiday dinner in which each participant will be asked to remember, in his or her own way, a family member who has died in the last year. A wife or husband may be asked to present the other with a special gift of their own choosing, to be presented at a particular time and in a particular way. Or, using a suggestion from more traditional societies and from carnival, you may prescribe a time in which

males become females for a day and vice versa, a ritual designed to unlock rigid gender roles.

5. *Time and Place*—Careful attention should be given to the choice of time and place for the ritual to occur. Sometimes the counselor's office or a church family seminar can provide a safe haven in which to rehearse and perform the ritual. The ritual enactment may be planned to take place during a support group meeting and will involve the participation of others. Sometimes the counselor might accompany the person to another setting. For example, Whiting (1988) describes his work with a woman who was an experienced trekker and wilderness leader. He and his client sat together around a campfire burning things she wished to let go of, thoughts and experiences she had collected on file cards over a period of time. Pieces of charcoal were retained as a memento of the experience. Imber-Black (1988b) describes a couple whose life seemed to be dominated by a secret they would not share with her, their therapist. She invited the couple to bury the secret on a frozen hill behind the clinic, indicating that the ritual helped to loosen the struggle both between the husband and the wife, as well as between them and the therapist.

6. *Specified Time and Place*—Not only may the ritual be repeated, but it may be performed at particular times and in a particular place. For example, a couple with marital difficulties may complain that they cannot get their children to go to bed at night, or a lonely single mother may have trouble getting her children off to school. In the former case, the children may stay awake to act as buffers or to absorb the conflict, while in the latter situation the children may be afraid mother will become despondent and lonely without them, even suicidal. Mother and father may be instructed to send the children to bed at a particular time each night, making the experience pleasant through the reading of a story, a bedtime snack, or a special time for talking. The parents may be helped to define a special time for their own relationship, separate from the children, or a time and set of rules for facing their marital conflicts without the children's help, again using repetition and a specified time and place. School-phobic children may be reassured that mother is alive and well if they are allowed to come home for lunch, or to call once in the morning and once in the afternoon. Family ministers may help connect mother to resources and supports outside of the family.

7. *Symbols and Symbolic Actions*—Careful listening to the family's special language, for their central symbols and metaphors, provides resources for designing ritual. The task to be accomplished through ritual may itself suggest special language or action. For example, one young woman may need to graduate from a child-like role in a family, or a husband may need to symbolically dispose of a set of feelings in order to let go of residual and handicapping anger at his wife for an earlier disloyalty.

Sometimes the use of household artifacts, family heirlooms, and various kinds of handmade or purchased gifts may symbolize movement to a new status or a changed set of relationships. For example, a father may hand down a special heirloom to his son, a daughter may be given her own set of keys to the family car, a husband an apron, or a wife a briefcase. Imber-Black (1988b) points out that documentation is often meaningful and reflects new commitments, since documents imply that changes are serious and are official. The making of a will, granting of a diploma, or the conferring of a medal provide examples. Such enactments and their accompanying special words, actions, and symbols mark gains and shifts, helping people move beyond the "stuckness" of present roles and relationships which may be dysfunctional.

8. *Communication*—Rituals do not just express and recreate the past; they also help to construct a new reality, a new truth. At a funeral, for example, a new story of the deceased begins to be constructed as the mourners reminisce and as choices are made about what will be remembered. These stories take shape and are altered, particularly during important family ritual times such as holiday dinners, those times when family cultural norms are expressed and missing members are remembered or carefully forgotten. The church can play an important role in providing opportunities for making central family rituals more personally meaningful and reconstructive.

While traditional funeral literature may be comforting and inspiring, many such occasions in our technological society have become distanced from personal life experience. The most moving and important part of a funeral service may be the poem read by a family friend or the structured time for the sharing of personal remembering and eulogizing. The practice of cremation, for example, or the closed casket, can mean that survivors have a more difficult time believing in and moving on from the loss.

Counselors who work extensively with mourning (e.g., Johnson 1987) argue that it is very important for mourners to view the body or a photograph of the dead person, even in cases of extreme disfigurement; these counselors help prepare survivors for that experience. In some situations the use of photographs, scrapbooks, or personal belongings can serve to communicate the meaning of the loss. Rituals can help families let go of as well as hold on to the lost person.

Conclusion

Rituals are rendered more powerful and more meaningful because they generally have a collective, shared dimension. Margaret Mead asks:

Does the ritual action enable persons, however deep their grief or confusion, however high their excitement, to reach out to the feelings of others who have experienced the same thing, and to their own previous experiences . . . ? (Cited in Alternate Rituals Project 1976, 10).

As a community, the church provides a context in which dialogue, sharing, giving to others, and meaning may take place as central tasks. Church workers, as they walk in the life space of their congregants, are in a unique position to experience the felt needs, to learn of the crises, and to mobilize support and forums for sharing. While rituals may be performed in isolation, and sometimes it is important that individuals have special ritual times for speaking to themselves, for many passages or other life experiences the collective dimension is essential, connecting the individual and family to the larger experiences of humankind, helping them make sense of their experiences.

References

Alternate Rituals Project. 1976. *Ritual in a new day: An invitation.* Nashville: Abingdon Press.

Bermann, E. 1973. *Scapegoat.* Ann Arbor: University of Michigan Press.

Byng-Hall, J. 1973. Family myths used as defense in conjoint family therapy. *British Journal of Medical Psychology* 46:239-50.

Friedman, E. 1985. *Generation to generation: Family process in church and synagogue.* New York: Guilford Press.

Hartman, A. and J. Laird. 1983. *Family-Centered social work practice.* New York: Free Press.

Imber-Black, E. 1988a. Idiosyncratic life-cycle transitions and therapeutic rituals. In *The changing family life cycle,* eds. B. Carter and M. McGoldrick, 149-62. New York: Gardner Press.

———. 1988b. Ritual themes in families and family therapy. In *Rituals in families and in family therapy,* eds. E. Imber-Black, J. Roberts, and R. Whiting, 47-83. New York: Norton.

Imber-Black, E., J. Roberts, and R. Whiting, eds. 1988. *Rituals in families and in family therapy.* New York: Norton.

Johnson, S. 1987. *After a child dies: Counseling bereaved families.* New York: Springer.

Kimball, S. 1960. Introduction to A. van Gennep, *The rites of passage.* Chicago: University of Chicago Press.

Laird, J. 1984. Shamans, sorcerers, and social workers: The use of ritual in social work practice. *Social Work* 29:123-29.

———. 1988. Women and ritual in family therapy. In *Rituals in families and in family therapy,* eds. E. Imber-Black, J. Roberts, and R. Whiting, 331-62. New York: Norton.

McGoldrick, M. and N.G. Preto. 1984. Ethnic intermarriage: Implications for therapy. *Family Process* 23:347-62.

Moore, S. and B. Myerhoff. 1977. Introduction: Secular ritual: Forms and meanings. In *Secular ritual,* eds. S. Moore and B. Myerhoff, 324. Assen/Amsterdam: Van Gorcum Press.

Reiss, D. 1981. *The family's construction of reality.* Cambridge, Mass.: Harvard University Press.

Selvini-Palazzoli, M. et al. 1977. Family rituals: A powerful tool in family therapy. *Family Process* 16:445-53.

Turner, V. 1969. *The ritual process: Structure and anti-structure.* Chicago: Aldine.

van der Hart, O. 1983. *Rituals in psychotherapy: Transition and continuity.* New York: Irvington Publishers.

van Gennep, A. [1909] 1960. *The rites of passage.* Chicago: University of Chicago Press.

Whiting, R. 1988. Guidelines for designing therapeutic rituals. In *Rituals in families and in family therapy,* eds. E. Imber-Black, J. Roberts, and R. Whiting, 84-109. New York: Norton.

Wolin, S. and L. Bennett. 1984. Family rituals. *Family Process* 23:401-20.

8

Providing Professional Services to Widows and the Bereaved

Penny Long Marler and Malcolm Marler

Widowhood is a pervasive status in the United States today, and becoming more so as our society ages. In 1980, according to the Bureau of the Census, there were 12,794,000 widowed persons in the United States. Of this number, approximately 80 percent were women. According to the Widowed Person's Service Research Center (1982), widows make up 11.9 percent of the total female population in the United States; and 68.9 percent of these are over 65. As Butler (1981) commented, "This is not only a century of old age, but also a century of older women" (3). More importantly, this is a century of older widows.

One of the most stressful life events is the death of a spouse. From an ecological perspective, widowhood represents a change in the configuration of relational space—the webs of relationships that define our living and are our recourse in our dying. So, widowhood is experienced first and foremost as a social loss—the loss of a primary relationship and the subsequent disruption of a larger, often delicately balanced, social network.

Janice was sixty-eight when her world was turned upside down. That was the year that her husband Harold, who had a brief history of heart problems, died following a heart attack and a two-week hospitalization. Janice and Harold were very close; he had looked forward to retirement. Janice had two grown daughters and four grandchildren. One of her girls lived nearby. The other was living about ten hours away in a Northeastern state.

PENNY LONG MARLER, M.S.S.W., M.Div., is faculty associate at the Center for Social and Religious Research at Hartford Theological Seminary (Conn.) and is completing her Ph.D. in the sociology of religion at Southern Baptist Theological Seminary. An experienced social worker, she is the wife of MALCOLM L. MARLER, M.Div., D.Min., church development consultant for the Western Connecticut Baptist Association and minister with singles/families at the First Church of Christ, Congregational, Glastonbury, Conn. Dr. Marler is a frequent conference leader for nursing home ministry and care of widowed persons.

Janice and Harold had been involved in their local Baptist church. When Harold died, Janice's family and church friends rallied around her; her doctor prescribed a mild tranquilizer to "help her get through it all." And her minister was attentive for the first several weeks. Overall, she thought she was doing fairly well.

Janice was really not interested in going to church after Harold died. If she went, she felt uncomfortable in the couples' class. Sitting in church alone, she always caught herself looking for Harold (and seeing him!) when the ushers filed in for the offering. The whole process was depressing. She felt that she would like to talk to someone about her loneliness and sleeplessness, but she felt silly about her inability to "handle" what had happened.

Mealtimes were particularly tough for Janice. She rarely fixed a meal or set the table to eat by herself. Mostly, she nibbled when she was hungry or got some "fast food." As a result, Janice began to gain weight. Her daughters fussed at her for her eating habits and admonished her for "not going out more often." Embarrassed by her appearance, angered by her daughters' pushiness, and hurt because her old friends rarely included her in their gatherings, she rarely went out at all. She even quit attending her neighborhood garden club.

Within a year, Janice experienced another close death, that of her father. As the executor of his estate, she managed to settle some of the financial and legal matters; but at the same time, old hospital and insurance claims from Harold's death came back to haunt her. She felt overwhelmed. After several trips to her doctor because of some nagging physical symptoms, Janice was sure that something was very wrong with her. She felt her children, her friends, her church, and particularly her beloved spouse had let her down. In what she considered a weak moment, she called her minister for help. He was surprised to hear from her; he had assumed things were going fine.

Janice's story is not unusual. In general, death is something most Westerners prefer not to think about. Although death and bereavement are inevitable, many people like Janice are ill-prepared for the stresses of the death of a spouse. Decisions about the funeral service and burial arrangements, controversy among extended family over last bequests, unresolved insurance claims, and hospital bills all complicate the initial phases of grief. Lifestyle adjustments like cooking for one, eating and sleeping alone, attending to household or other duties which the spouse usually accomplished, as well as the stress of holidays and anniversaries present continuing challenges for widowed persons struggling to overcome grief and build a new life.

Defining widowhood as a social loss creates new avenues for programing prior to, during, and after the time of immediate crisis. Such intervention is based on two factors: (1) the biblical portrait of widowed persons as both care recipients and caregivers in church communities and, (2) the ecological concept of mutually responsive support networks.

The remainder of this chapter explores the *problem* of grief and widowhood through a brief literature review. Then, biblical and theoretical *perspectives* for understanding and addressing the needs of widows and widowers are examined. Finally, a comprehensive *program* for widowed people in a church community context is reviewed.

Problem: When a Spouse Dies

Marriage provides a point of reference for identifying who we are in relation to friends, relatives, neighbors, legal institutions, and the church. The death of a partner constitutes a radical break in those webs of identity. A newly widowed, elderly man expresses it this way:

Married we were sure of who we were and what we were doing and [we were] content with it. Now uncertainty sets in; our confidence is waning. Frustration seems [to be] at every turn. We wander amid confusion unable to set a path to follow. We wait and look about for a way of life wherein we can be comfortable.

When a vital connecting relationship is severed, people suffer a double challenge: regaining social balance in the face of obvious loss and coping with behavior and thought patterns that persistently deny the fact of that loss (Marris 1977). Socially, widowed people are faced with "fitting in" as singles in largely "couple" circles; simultaneously, they have difficulty accepting a new social status themselves. This internal struggle, which is a natural process accompanying grief, is apparent in the quotation just cited. For months following the death of a spouse, self-references to "we" and "our" as opposed to "I" and "my" are common. Successful grief work, however, involves *separation* from continual thoughts and yearnings for the loved one and *reorganization* of life in the present. Oftentimes, this is difficult to accomplish alone.

The Grief Process: Common Considerations

Normally, grief progresses through stages or phases. These represent the normal physiological and psychological responses to the shock of grief (Impact)—the depression, bitterness, fear, anger, guilt, and disorganization of grief—(Recoil) and finally, the gradual reorganization, commitment, and resolution of grief (Accommodation).

A general time limit has been suggested for the successful accomplishment of grief work. According to Oates, if a bereaved person has not progressed to the final phase by the end of two years, professional assistance may be indicated. Indeed, one significant study of younger widows found that most reached the accommodation stage by the end of one year (Harvey and Bahr 1980); other studies of older widowed persons indicated significant grief resolution by the end of the second year (Marler 1983). However, the length of grieving is variable and depends on a variety of factors including: degree of attachment to the spouse, period of preparation, age and general health, financial security, vocational commitment, supportive family network, presence and affection of friends, and habitual patterns of handling crises (Hafer 1981). So, grief work could be relatively short or painfully long. Regardless of time, the principal aim is separation and growth (Cassem 1975; Smith 1975).

The loss of a loved one, though a developmental inevitability, is always painful; "almost always health suffers" (Bowlby 1980). Physical symptoms related to bereavement in the initial stages of grief include: sighing respiration, lack of strength and exhaustion, gastrointestinal distress, sleep disturbance, and a feeling of extreme tension (Arkin 1981; Hafer 1981). Also, cross-sectional and longitudinal studies reveal higher mortality rates for widowed as compared to married persons (Jacobs 1977; Susser 1981; Stroebe et al. 1982). The highest mortality risk was found during the first six months after bereavement (Rees and Lutkins 1967; Parkes et al. 1969; Helsing and Szklo 1982). Significantly, mortality from suicide is greater than expected among the widowed during the first few years of bereavement (Kapiro, Koskenvuo, and Rita 1987).

In addition to a physical health risk, grieving also presents a mental health risk for the bereaved. Psychological responses initially serve to "soften the blow" in the Impact phase of grief, but can become dysfunctional and disrupt the normal grief process (Proulx and Baker 1981). Lindemann describes one psychological disturbance which often accompanies grief as "heightened preoccupation with the emotional state of sorrow" (1979, 170). Bowlby (1980) emphasizes the pervading sense of loneliness. Reflecting on these physical and emotional changes, a widower remarked, "In losing your spouse things happen to your body and mind for which no one is prepared. You have no built-in defense or method of comprehending what happens next."

Another typical response to bereavement is social isolation or withdrawal (Switzer 1970). Marris states that "any severe loss tends to undermine the meaning of other relationships too, because they are interrelated" (1977, 23). Disturbances in social relations include: excessive hostility to others, extreme helplessness, and a general inability to interact effectively (Lindemann 1979). One widowed friend expressed it this way: "When you lose your mate you feel like you're only hitting on three cylinders. You can't function right."

The bereaved individual is using all available energy in the separation process, which is an internal endeavor (Freud 1949). As a result, outside relationships become tiring, difficult, and confusing. This is especially problematic because the support of friends and family is critical for resolution and recovery in the grief process (Lopata 1973, 1979; Keith 1981; Harvey and Bahr 1974; Arling 1976). Grief work, the normal process of psychological separation from the spouse, contributes to the disruption of supportive social networks and is also complicated by them.

A variety of associated factors may increase the chance of social isolation: loss of income, physical illness and depressive episodes, stresses related to raising children, and even the aging process itself (Lopata 1970; Palmore et al. 1979; Morgan 1976). For the typical widowed person—female and over sixty-five—the death of a spouse is merely one of many losses including retirement, the "empty nest," fixed incomes, deaths of other family members, declining health, and lowered social status in a predominantly youth-oriented Western culture (Atchley 1985).

Older Widowed vs. Younger Widowed

For the most part, research on widowhood has focused on younger widowed persons. "Younger" may be generally defined as below fifty years of age (Glick et al. 1974; Harvey and Bahr 1980). Reasons which have been given for an emphasis on younger widowed groups include: 1) an expectation that younger widows are affected to a greater degree by the experience of bereavement due to "the untimeliness of the death" (Bowlby 1980, 84); and 2) the premise that grief in old age is "a different phenomena from the grief of younger people" (Parkes 1976, 343). Goodstein (1981) suggests that studies of elderly in general are avoided by most professionals because of their inability to face thoughts of aging and dying on a personal level and Western culture's emphasis on and interest in youth.

Nudel (1986) draws distinctions between older and younger widowed persons. She indicates that older widowed persons have more support because of their sheer numbers. Nudel states that "profound losses" of health, social support or job status provide "lessons in coping" for older widowed folk that younger widowed do not share. She also points to the solace of years of memories available to the older widowed.

While there are more older than younger widowed people in the general population, this fact does not necessarily translate into increased social support. Many factors contribute to social isolation among older widowed persons. For example, many older widows either cannot drive or are reluctant to drive alone, particularly at night. Also, after many years of living as a couple, a widow has difficulty negotiating a social life as a single. Typically, the adult children do not live nearby, and while they tend to provide increased social support immediately following the death, they soon return to their normal routines. Lack of family interaction may become a significant source of dissatisfaction for older widows in the second year following bereavement *if* friendship ties are not available to replace this interaction (Marler 1983). Indeed, Ferraro (1984) found that friendship ties are of primary importance for adjustment among older widowed persons.

Yet, interaction with *widowed persons only* may be detrimental (Marler 1983). Older widows we have interviewed report that "hanging around with widows" only makes them feel "too much like a widow." They generally express a need to normalize their relationships, which includes establishing relationships with a variety of other people. The losses associated with aging do not necessarily increase the coping skills of older widowed persons. Indeed, cumulative deaths, retirement, increased incidences of acute and chronic illness, transportation difficulties, and loneliness most likely contribute to increased social isolation and poorer adjustment to widowhood (Lopata 1979). Research has shown that older widowed people have less hope for the future than younger ones (Marler 1983), and hope is a significant factor in the successful resolution of grief. Perhaps important for the needed generation of hope, involvement in religious activities is positively related to adjustment among the older widowed.

Younger widows, on the other hand, usually enjoy a wider, natural support network; yet, that network includes few people who have experienced the death of a spouse. In general, younger widows tend to receive support from family and friends through the first year of bereavement (Glick et al. 1974; Harvey and Bahr 1980). Such support is positively related to the resolution of grief. Conversely, a lack of social supports is detrimental and usually occurs because family and friends do not know how to respond to the younger widow/er. This is reinforced by the tendency of younger widows to exaggerate the inability of others to tolerate their grief (Harvey and Bahr 1980). Nevertheless, studies indicate that by the end of the first year of bereavement, most younger widows report normal aspirations for the future. The factors which account for this sense of well-being include: advance warning of the spouse's death, the presence and availability of friends, and involvement in religious activities.

According to Nudel, the presence of children is a qualitative difference between older and younger widowed persons. The younger widowed person must not only deal with his or her own grief but that of the children. There is an added economic concern if the deceased spouse was the primary breadwinner, and this concern is only heightened when other dependents are involved. Subsequently, Nudel states that the older widowed tend to be in better financial condition than younger widowed after the death of the spouse.

Although the presence of young children may result in added stress for widowed people, their presence can also provide a buffer from loneliness and a point of distraction from grief (Marler 1983). For many older widowed persons, living alone for the first time in their lives, simple, daily activities become difficult if not meaningless. Cooking for one, eating alone, and sleeping alone reinforce the fact that they are, indeed, *alone*. Further, while older widowers typically remarry and so remedy their aloneness, sheer statistics guarantee that most older widows will not.

While lack of income may not be a problem for older widowers or widows who have prepared for their retirement, for those who have not, worries over income can be a serious barrier to grief recovery. Generally, studies have found that morale is significantly related to income levels among widowed persons (Harvey and Bahr 1974; Morgan 1976; Atchley 1985). Older widows, in particular, are likely to experience a significant loss in income for several reasons: 1) obstacles to securing employment are difficult to overcome; 2) many of these women have been absent from the job market for years; and 3) discrimination against hiring women makes job prospects less encouraging (Bell 1971; Berardo 1968). Depending upon preparation for income security prior to the death, younger as well as older widowed persons are vulnerable to the added stress of inadequate incomes. Indeed, Hafer (1981) states that 40 percent of all widows are below the poverty level.

Finally, Nudel's portrayal of younger and older widowed persons betrays a common tendency to characterize one group as more needy than the other. Our own research has merely indicated that the needs are *different*. Thus, the programing implication is increased sensitivity to these differences. For all the practical differences between widowed people, they share a critical, common experience. A close death tends to suspend time and level degrees of attachment. In that moment, whether young or old, losing a loved one hurts. A journal of an elderly widower reflects the universality of loss:

> With the death of your spouse, suddenly it is apparent how short time is. It seems your marriage was over in a flash; no matter if it was ten or seventy years. . . . Our life comes to a sudden halt, yet we live on!

Widows vs. Widowers

Research on gender differences among the widowed has been limited. Most writers tend to characterize expected differences based on cultural roles and patterns of socialization. For example, some have suggested that men have more difficulty coping with the emotional and practical demands associated with widowhood (Nudel 1986). Because men are expected to be independent, stoic, and strong, they tend to cultivate fewer intimate relationships than women; and the intimate relationships they do have tend to be with their wives. In addition, 80 percent of all widowed persons are female. So, widowers have fewer available male role models for successful grief work.

Men also lead specifically role-defined lives fulfilling practical tasks like: household repairs, financial management, lawn care, and car maintenance. Thus, essential domestic roles are not a part of the traditional male repertoire. Widowers often have difficulty performing many necessary daily living tasks. A widower is more likely to grab a sandwich than cook a meal, to neglect housecleaning and attention to his appearance, or to "farm out" children to relatives or friends (Nudel 1986).

Women, however, face related stresses. Widows who have held more traditional household roles are frequently mystified by financial matters. Unfortunately, settling estates, filing insurance papers, and attending to hospital bills are not easy matters for the novice—much less a newly widowed woman still struggling with grief. Also, widows are favorite targets for con men who prey on their fears and ignorance selling everything from elaborate security systems to expensive (and often unnecessary) home repairs or improvements. Finally, a lifetime of domestic experience may guarantee necessary skills, but simple ability obscures the fact that cooking and cleaning are often done for the benefit of others. Many widows we have talked with report how difficult it is to "cook for just me."

In the area of practical deficits, both widowed women and men are affected. Generally, then, there is real value in cultivating role flexibility during marriage so that both spouses have the knowledge and skill to perform necessary household tasks.

A recent empirical study comparing the effects of bereavement provides new interpretation for the affective or emotional differences between men and women. Wister and Strain (1986) studied the well-being of older widows and widowers. Contrary to popular assumptions, they found that there was no difference between the groups on measures of depression and life satisfaction (also consistent with the findings of Lund et al. 1986). In addition, they discovered that widows have a wider social-support network than widowers.

Their analysis of these two findings is particularly enlightening. They conclude that because of the early socialization processes of males—the development of self-reliance and a "stoic approach to personal problems"—they may not require the same depth in their social relationships in order to find satisfaction with life. Normally, it seems older widows require a larger base of support to attain the same level of satisfaction as widowers. For older men, cultivating one or two relationships based on mutual interests and comradeship rather than closeness may be the best prescription for successful negotiation of widowhood (Wister and Strain 1986).

Interestingly, Wister and Strain note that recent transformations in sex roles may result in future cohorts of older people with very different socialization patterns. Future older women may be more socially independent and self-reliant, and future older men may be more dependent on a broader base of primary relationships. Nevertheless, the implication for programing for widowed persons is clear —both men and women require a base of social support to assist them in negotiating the painful processes of grief work successfully. Gender, as such, is not a good predictor of differential need among the widowed.

Perspective: Looking Through Biblical and Ecological Lenses

Having defined and described the problems of widowhood, we now turn to the issue of interpretation. What factors condition church community response? Given a social problem definition, how can ecological theory inform approaches to programing, and how does that particular theoretical perspective interface with the biblical understanding of widowhood? We believe the church has both a biblical and an historical mandate to provide support and to empower widowed people. When an individual in stress is supported in the context of a larger social network, reciprocal gains can be expected. Care recipients may become natural helpers, caregivers. Social network theory is, after all, a relationship-building perspective.

The Widow as an Altar of God

> You shall not wrong a stranger or oppress him, for you were strangers in the land of Egypt. You shall not afflict any widow or orphan. If you do afflict them, and they cry out to me, I will surely hear their cry (Exod. 22:21-23; see also Deut. 10:18; 27:19; Ps. 146:9; Is. 1:17; Jer. 7:5-6; 22:3; Zech. 7:9-10).

The term *widow* comes from an Indo-European root, *ghe*, which means "forsaken" or "empty." In the Greek, a widow (*chera*) was someone "without" or "left without" (Thurston 1985). According to Hurley (1981), the term had strong social and financial overtones more appropriate to a widow than a widower. Further, there is no biblical reference for a *widower*. The death of a spouse simply left a man unmarried. His financial condition was not affected; he could easily remarry.

Because of the social status of women, widowhood was an uncertain state. A widow could not inherit apart from her husband; at his death, the inheritor of his estate became responsible for her care. Without a spouse or an inheritance, widows were subject to levirate marriage or could be sold into slavery (Thurston 1985). Still, the Hebraic widow, like the poor remnant of Israel, looked for the fulfillment of God's promise (McKenna 1967). Her spiritual task was to wait and pray—much as Anna, the widowed prophetess (Luke 2:36–37).

Jesus rebukes those who oppress widows (Luke 20:46–47). Further, Jesus singles out widows and uses them as object lessons through the story of the widow's mite (Mark 12:41–44; Luke 21:1–4) and the parable of the unjust judge (Luke 18:1–8). As David Garland describes in chapter 2, Jesus shows sensitivity to the fragile social position of the widow of Nain by restoring her only son to life. Not only did Jesus exhibit concern for widows, they also cared for him. Widows accompanied and provided for Jesus and the disciples and even participated in the election of Judas's replacement (Luke 8:1–3; Acts 1:14; 2:4).

Thus, widows were a recognized group in the early Christian community. They had an acknowledged claim to benevolence (Acts 6:1ff) and recognized privileges and status (1 Tim. 5:3–16). Thurston (1985) notes that the story of Tabitha provides important clues regarding the status of widows. Significantly, at the death of Tabitha, a revered and charitable Christian disciple of Joppa, Peter called not only "the saints" but also the "widows" to witness her miraculous resurrection (Acts 9:32–43). Further, as no husband is mentioned in the text, it is thought that Tabitha may have been a widow herself. Indeed, Thurston further speculates that Mary in Acts 12:12, Lydia in Acts 16:14, Phoebe in Romans 16:1, Mary in Romans 16:6, Chloe in 1 Corinthians 1:11, and the daughters of Philip may all have been "forerunners of the congregation of widows" (281n).

The fact that widows become not only special recipients of care but notable caregivers is sustained in writings of early church fathers through the symbol of the widow as an altar of God. Osiek (1983) discusses the implications of such a symbol. In Polycarp, widows are referred to as "an altar"; in Tertullian, as "God's altar"; in the *Didascalia Apostolorum* as "the altar of Christ"; in Methodius as a "living altar." Osiek notes that the original basis for associating the widow and the altar is "the depositing of the gifts of the faithful upon the altar and their distribution to widows as recipients of charity" (Osiek 1983, 166).

Thurston and Osiek state that the widow as altar became a powerful symbol of the special place of service and prayer in a church community. Indeed, a special class of widows can be traced through the third century in the writings of Ignatius, Tertullian, Cyprian, and Cornelius, bishop at Rome. Thurston (1985) concludes that

widows as a distinct group declined in the fourth century as virgins took prominence in the West and deaconesses in the East, and they practically disappeared by the year 400 as monastic orders arose . . . (283).

In the early Christian community, widows served as "effective agent(s) in a spiritual transaction within the Christian community" (Thurston 1985, 288). Accordingly, this special class of widows performed two primary functions: 1) intercessory prayer for the community (sanctifying the gifts brought to them) and 2) sacrificial living as a model and remembrance of Christ's life (enacting service out of sacrifice).

In conclusion, the church needs to recover the original biblical and historical vision of widowed persons as legitimate care recipients in the church. If widowhood is defined as a social loss, then strengthening the support network of widowed persons becomes critical to adjustment and recovery. Further, as ecological theories imply, building social supports in a church community not only contributes to grief resolution but constitutes a seedbed for empowering widows and widowers to take on new and meaningful helping roles themselves. The church, however, must assist the process of caregiving by widows through restoring and blessing channels for their special service.

Widowed Persons and Helping Networks

Church communities are rich sources of social support networks for widowed people. The range of possible network interventions is wide and as varied as the needs of individuals in any setting. Warren's (1981) work on Problem-Anchored Helping Networks (PAHNs) is helpful for understanding and interpreting program possibilities in church communities. As Pancoast notes in chapter 4, a church which facilitates a supportive social environment must create a climate of encouragement, mobilize a variety of helpers, and serve as a link to outside resources and services.

Creating a Climate of Encouragement. Widowed persons are not very good at expressing their needs. The normal processes of grief sap their energy and motivation. Churches are equally ineffective in reaching out to grieving people because of the fear of saying or doing the wrong thing or ignorance about their particular needs. An active congregational program of intervention to widowed people presupposes, first, *a clear sense of mission to others* and, second, *an awareness of the problem.*

Churches must be led to consider their responsibility for people who are hurting both within and outside their fellowship. Many churches have explicit statements of mission and develop ministries that are consistent with their particular understanding of who they are as a congregation and how they relate to their larger communities. Most, however, plan ministry "reactively," depending on program ideas in current church literature or on the most pressing needs presented by vocal congregants. While ministry programs may legitimately be inspired by models from other settings and while the experienced and felt needs of members are always important to consider, *effective* ministry must be more intentional and focused. The initial vision for ministry to widowed persons in the St. Matthews area of Louisville, Kentucky, is a reflection of shared commitment and careful study.

The New Friends program at St. Matthews Baptist grew out of a broader commitment on the part of the church to channel resources intentionally to ministry efforts in the community. This commitment reflected the congregation's understanding that an evangelistic church must also be a ministering church. The congregation believed *being* and *doing* were inseparable for the caring congregation. This conviction led membership and staff to an intentional study of the church and community to discover critical needs.

St. Matthews Baptist's commitment to ministry included ecumenical cooperation and participation. The church is a member of St. Matthews Area Ministries —a community organization formed and supported by thirteen churches representing six denominations to meet the needs of people in their local area. As a part of this ministry group, the congregation was privy to several community needs assessments and analyses. A major finding of this research was the growing population of widowed people in the area. Simultaneously, ministers at St. Matthews Baptist and other area churches observed an increase in the number of widowed persons who came or were referred for counseling. All of this led to the formation of a widowed persons' task force at St. Matthews Area Ministries.

The task force was primarily responsible for sponsoring a community-wide workshop for widowed people. This one-day event was publicized by area churches and included representatives from the professional helping community. Through this workshop, over seventy-five widowed people were identified who expressed a desire for further educational or supportive events.

The churches in the community, and St. Matthews Baptist in particular, made an initial commitment to find hurting people in their area. Out of this commitment, serious study of community needs revealed a growing population-at-risk. The following persons were included in the preliminary study: local funeral home personnel, the nearby senior citizens center director, the director of the Widowed Persons' Service, the coordinator of WOW (Widows or Widowers, a support group for widowed persons sponsored by the Catholic church), local church ministers, as well as widowed people themselves. Many of these joined in planning a workshop, and workshop participants were then surveyed to assess their perception of need.

In these ways, a climate of encouragement was fostered both among churches and within congregations in the community. A general spirit of helping grew out of intentional commitments to ministry; the interest and resources for particular forms of ministry grew out of awareness of need. The needs of widowed people were not just guessed at—they were studied carefully.

A climate of encouragement can be further enhanced by creating and maintaining diverse channels of information. A series of sermons or educational workshops on death and grief which deal with the spiritual, social, emotional, and practical consequences of bereavement may be a good place to start. Also, strengthening existing networks in a preventive way might include emphases on making wills and planning funeral services as a part of preretirement workshops. Other educational seminars could address the importance of developing separate friendship networks, cultivating skills in nontraditional, gender-related tasks (such as cooking, car maintenance, and budget management) as well as expanding leisure interests and activities. Too, "uplifting" the status of the widowed and using their particular expertise and insight in education and training about bereavement issues is important. Whatever avenue is chosen, it is imperative that the church community is *aware* of the dimensions of the problem. Only awareness shapes creative vision for ministry and leads to effective response.

Mobilizing a Variety of Helpers. In chapter 4, Pancoast describes the various helping roles available in the church community setting. Recognizing and mobilizing these helpers can create numerous opportunities for meaningful intervention to strengthen the social support network of widowed people. Regardless of the size of a congregation, a network of helpers in all or some of these categories provides potential avenues of ministry.

1. *Social Intimates: Family and Friends.* Research has shown that the presence and care of family and friends are positively related to successful grief work. Therefore, strengthening relationships between widowed persons and their circle of social intimates is important. Basically, the involvement of family and friends takes one of three directions. First, the newly widowed person may have close family and/or friend relationships, but neither the widowed person nor these intimates know how to talk about the delicate issues of death and grief. So, they may choose to distance themselves from the source of their mutual pain. Eventually, family members or friends may avoid the widowed person altogether—or he or she may choose to withdraw from contact which is perceived as too painful.

   Second, newly widowed persons and their social intimates may respond by clinging to each other for support. Initially, intense emotional and practical support may be mutually comforting. However, after a few months, family and friends feel a need to return to their own independent routine. Then, constant demands to spend time talking about the deceased, visiting the cemetery, sharing meals, and attending to household and business details may be resented by children, close friends, or even the widowed person. Increased dependency usually results in a cycle of conflict and guilt.

   Third, some newly bereaved people do not have an available network of family or intimate friends. Often their spouses were also their best friends and they confided in no one else. This is particularly true, as noted before, of widowers. Others may either have no children at all or no children who live within easy driving distance. Quite a few widowed persons may have no living children or other close family members.

   In all three cases, strengthening and building social support networks is indicated. Strengthening the existent network may be accomplished through education and sensitive, open, family counseling. Family members, close friends, and the widowed themselves need to know what to expect when a spouse dies. What are the normal characteristics of grief? What can a close friend or family member do and say that will be helpful? What help might we expect from our church or from other organizations in the community?

Further, building new relationships—enlarging the social support system—may relieve the responsibility (perceived and real) of the primary caregivers. Indeed, if others are available to meet practical needs, then family and close friends may be free to provide the kind of trusting, emotional support and caring only people with long-term close relationships share. Finally, if social intimates are not available, other helpers are needed if widowhood is to be successfully negotiated.

2. *Neighbors.* Neighbors are traditional helpers in smaller communities, particularly villages and small towns. Urban, mobile lifestyles and two-career families have resulted in less informal neighboring in our society (Bellah et al. 1985). This is critical for many widowed people who once depended on neighbors for socialization, for help with household tasks, for housewatching when the family was out of town, and for emergency or temporary transportation.

Recovering the lost art of neighboring must be more intentionally addressed today to meet the needs of widowed persons. Often, the adult children of elderly widowed people or the minister of a local church may want to contract informally with neighbors to provide limited socialization, keep a watchful eye, or do some joint shopping. The very proximity of neighbors makes them ideal folk to add to the newly widowed's fragile social network. The creative minister will be aware of church members who may live near a newly widowed person and can help make needed connections.

3. *Natural Helpers.* Most ministers can identify the natural helpers in their congregations. When a loved one dies, natural helpers are those men and women who respond immediately with pies, casseroles, and advice. In smaller, rural congregations these natural helpers are essential caregivers for grieving people. In larger, urban congregations, natural helpers are more difficult to find; and in turn, it is more difficult for these helpers to find those in need.

Natural helpers tend to assist by sharing their particular skills or abilities. Not all natural helpers feel comfortable with grieving people or know what is most helpful to say or do. They know that there is grief and pain, and they must act. They usually respond by volunteering something they do comfortably well. A natural helper might offer to take the children for a couple of days, spend the night, or pick up relatives at the airport. Because they have natural energy and motivation, these helpers make excellent leaders with some training and guidance.

Natural helpers may also be willing to be put on a list and serve on an "on call" basis to give assistance when a widowed person is in need. Simply having a reliable and willing handyman or baby-sitter on hand can be very comforting for someone newly widowed. We have found that many widowed persons themselves are the best natural helpers.

4. *Role-Related Helpers.* The specialized needs of the newly widowed call for the advice and skills of role-related helpers. As has been reviewed,

complicated legal and financial matters, unexpected and unexplained physical and emotional symptoms, and other tangential worries attend the death of a spouse. Churches usually include lawyers, physicians, mental-health specialists, social workers, plumbers, contractors, accountants, and funeral home directors who can help the newly bereaved. More importantly, because these people are church members, prior ties of trust and support make help easier to give and receive.

We have used role-related helpers in a ministry to the widowed in a number of ways. First, they are excellent sources of information about the needs of widowed people because many of them are in daily contact with them. Thus, they are good at educating congregations—articulating a vision for ministry to special groups and building a climate of encouragement based on increased awareness of problems. Role-related helpers make good (and inexpensive) conference, seminar, or workshop leaders.

They also can be good referral or resource persons for individuals with particular needs. One community agency with whom we have worked has developed a directory of community services for widowed people, including names and phone numbers of key contacts. A church could easily produce such a resource booklet or file so that widowed persons could be assured of competent, caring, and in some cases, less-expensive assistance as a ministry.

5. *People with Similar Problems.* The most significant widowed persons program in the United States was initiated by Phyllis Silverman and is described in her recent book, *Widow to Widow* (1986). Her notable work is based on an ecological perspective. Silverman maintains that successful accomplishment of grief work entails building new relationships and skills, indeed, shaping a new identity. As Garland suggests in chapter 1, such identity-building is based on strengthening existing relationships and creating new ones. To this end, Silverman advocates training and utilizing widowed persons themselves as key helpers in the newly widowed person's social network.

A widow-to-widow approach focuses on a special category of helpers that Pancoast designates as those with a "similar problem." In Silverman's model, trained widowed persons provide informal counseling with the bereaved on coping with loneliness, dealing with children, handling in-laws, and making it through the holidays. They also provide referrals of trusted professionals for more complicated legal or financial matters. Such widowed aides also perform practical tasks if needed, such as providing transportation, cooking a meal, helping store clothes and other personal items belonging to the deceased, or helping write notes.

Silverman's widow-to-widow approach, however, does not exhaust the possibilities for meaningful intervention utilizing "people with similar problems." A structured or support-group approach is also a helpful medium for addressing the problems of widowhood and engaging the empathy and creativity of fellow-sufferers (Middleman 1981). Small groups are by nature more threatening than individual intervention, and we have found they are more appropriate for widowed persons who are in the Recoil to Accommodation stages of grief. As a rule of thumb, we do not encourage group work until after the third month of widowhood. In addition, groups for widowed people should be facilitated or led by skilled persons.

Utilizing Outside Resources. Silverman's widow-to-widow approach has been appropriated by a national organization called the Widowed Persons Service. Churches who have an active Widowed Persons Service in their area should acquaint themselves with this excellent resource. Staff people in this organization eagerly share knowledge and resources with interested community agencies. In addition, the Widowed Persons Service provides excellent training for widows and widowers to serve as volunteer aides to the newly bereaved.

An ecological approach incorporates not only the helping networks and resources within a congregation but also those resources in the larger community. Congregations multiply their own resources and energy and further strengthen the networks of individual widowed people in crisis when other community agencies are included in intervention strategies. (For more information on Widowed Persons Service and other national helping organizations for widows and widowers, see Appendix 2.)

Contextual Responses. Creative and responsive ministry to widowed persons might include any combination of helper-networks. The range of interventions, however, are practically limited by the size, location, and resources of a particular congregation. Smaller congregations in rural settings, closer-knit suburban neighborhoods, or urban and ethnic enclaves may emphasize: strengthening existing relationships with social intimates (intentionally educating and planning with family members and close friends); instituting a limited widow-to-widow program (pairing well-adjusted and trained widowed persons with the newly bereaved); and/or mobilizing a small network of natural helpers (keeping a referral list of interested church members and their particular skills or interests). Larger congregations or coalitions of churches may investigate more comprehensive programs of ministry like "New Friends."

Program: Networking and "New Friends"

The church is a natural setting for a ministry to the widowed persons because of the multiple opportunities for supportive relationships. Sunday School classes, women's and men's missions groups, and various professionals are all examples of the resources available to widowed persons in the local church. Additionally, many clergypersons have specialized training and experience in dealing with grief. Churches also have the opportunity of continuous relationships with the widowed persons that no other institution enjoys.

We have found, however, that the presence of resources for the widowed in the church does not mean they will be used effectively. Two stumbling blocks to a church's ministry include a reactive style of planning ministry in general and the tendency for clergy to focus on a one-on-one approach to caring. Lack of intentional organization and planning can hamper the availability and utilization of resources. Also, ministers' schedules are often crowded with crises that demand immediate attention and numerous administrative responsibilities. It is very difficult, if not impossible, for the minister to do all of the caring needed when a member's spouse dies. We believe it is the responsibility of the whole church, not just the professional ministry, to care for the widowed. Therefore, a well-planned program of intervention and support that includes ministry in groups is one way a church can respond effectively. Patricia's story gives an overview of one person's experience.

Pat Tingle is a forty-two-year-old widow whose husband died suddenly. She had just moved to a new city, did not have a job, had no children, and only one relative in town. She felt totally alone. Pat and her husband had been very involved in a church in another city but had not joined a new church since their move. After a friend told her about a widowed support ministry called New Friends at a local church, Pat called the church to get more information about the group.

Just two months after her husband died, Pat attended a Thursday night meeting and participated in one of the various groups and classes offered by New Friends. At first, she could not talk in the meeting without crying uncontrollably. She was still in shock. "What am I going to do? This was not supposed to happen to me so early in my life," she would say between her tears.

She attended a sharing group and discovered others who had similar thoughts and feelings. Eventually she registered for a seven-week structured group that helped her understand the grief process and her own pain. There she began to talk about her anger and frustration and found acceptance and caring in the group. A few months later she attended elective classes with guest speakers on topics such as "Dealing with Your Loneliness" and "Coping with Anger from a Christian Perspective."

After six months, Pat joined the church that sponsored New Friends because it had met a very important need in her life. She explains, "I don't know what I would have done without the New Friends group and this church. They understood and were patient with me when I needed it most. I was a stranger, and they loved me like one of their own. I'm still amazed at that! I tell everybody about my church."

Pat still has rough days. When needed she receives counseling from her pastor to work through temporary setbacks. But she is beginning to look forward to life once again. She attends the New Friends group only once or twice a month now and sees this as a sign of growth. She is quick to add, "It's comforting to know, however, that New Friends meets every Thursday night. A supportive group is just a few days away if I need it."

The ministry of New Friends did not just happen. It was planned carefully by a church that wanted to make a difference in the lives of the widowed community. Following is a discussion of how New Friends proceeded from a perceived need in the community to a wholistic ministry to widowed persons.

History, Organization, and Structure

St. Matthews Baptist Church averaged one new widowed person every month in its church family (an average Sunday morning attendance of seven hundred), so it saw the need to provide support and education for the widowed during the months following the death of a spouse. The church also discovered through St. Matthews Area Ministries (an ecumenical community ministry of thirteen churches) that the need was not unique to its own congregation. Since the church had a history of freely offering its ministries to the community as a part of its mission and purpose, a program was developed to reach outside (as well as inside) its membership to the widowed community.

St. Matthews Area Ministries had sponsored short-term groups for widowed persons for three years. (The format of these groups was later incorporated into the New Friends ministry and is discussed as a structured group below.) Several of the groups had continued to meet on their own for support. Many persons expressed a desire to be with other widows and widowers who had completed similar groups.

Fifteen widowed persons were invited to talk about the possibility of a weekly ministry to widowed persons in the community. A high level of interest was evident when twelve people attended. In that meeting, the people shared that they wanted to provide a weekly place where widowed people could receive help with emotional, spiritual, social, and other practical needs.

Two additional meetings were planned and a steering committee of eight persons was formed. The initial responsibilities of the steering committee included planning for: weekly registration, refreshments, a devotional period, various groups and elective classes, and a monthly dinner. A coordinator was selected to be responsible for convening each meeting, encouraging the steering committee members to carry out their responsibilities, and communicating with a staff minister about the needs of the group. Choosing a name for the ministry was an important step in group identity formation. "New Friends" was appropriate, for this group realized that one of the biggest adjustments faced by the widowed is forming a network of new friends.

The steering committee was encouraged to involve as many people as possible with small responsibilities, to build ownership and cohesiveness within the group. Publicity for the first meeting included a letter to all widowed persons of the host church and a news release to fifteen area churches. Twenty-one attended the first meeting. There, one person gave a devotional talk, and the purpose of the group was discussed. After choosing a name, participants were given a choice between a sharing group and a social group. During the first three months, the steering committee met every two weeks to evaluate the ministry and explore ways to improve it. Two other types of groups were added to meet the various needs of the participants.

Two years later, New Friends is an ecumenical, wholistic ministry for widowed persons in the Louisville community with an average attendance of forty to fifty. At least one new person comes every week; one evening, as many as eight newcomers were recorded. The ministry addresses the spiritual, emotional, social, and practical needs of widows and widowers and is open free of charge to people of all faiths through St. Matthews Baptist Church.

New Friends meets every Thursday night with the following program schedule (except on the second Thursday of the month, when dinner is served):

7:00–7:30   Large group—announcements and devotional
7:30–8:30   Choose a group: sharing, structured, social group, or elective classes
8:30–9:00   Refreshments and fellowship

Participants register as they enter each week and new guests are added to the mailing list and receive their nametags. A friend is assigned to the first-time participants to introduce them to the group and help them feel welcome. A brief orientation to the ministry is offered to newcomers during a break between the large group and small groups.

Participants may choose between a number of groups that were developed to meet the needs of both the newly widowed and those who have been widowed for many years. Ideally, a newly widowed person first attends a sharing group. It provides an informal, open forum for exchanging mutual concerns.

Then, a participant may enroll in a seven-week structured group. In this more formal setting, individuals discuss their own grief processes with the direction of a trained facilitator. After completing the structured group, a person might choose an elective class to increase knowledge and skill in an interest area, or return to the sharing group for additional support. Finally, he or she might be interested in participating in a social group for informal conversation, table games, and other kinds of light leisure activities. A more detailed explanation of each group is listed below.

Sharing Group. This is an open group that persons may attend *any* week for sharing with other persons who are widowed. Topics vary from week to week but relate directly to the problems that arise in grief. The sharing group is helpful to persons who need unconditional acceptance in sharing the grief process. Newly widowed participants usually choose this group first. A second sharing group is formed if attendance exceeds ten persons.

The sharing group is led by an experienced and trained group leader who is widowed. The facilitator's training is offered twice a year for four sessions on Thursday evenings when other groups are meeting. Some of the topics include: "How to listen for feelings," "How to ask open-ended questions," "How to handle dominant or extremely quiet participants," and other group dynamics. Prerequisites for becoming a sharing group leader are as follows: 1) successful completion of a structured group experience in order to understand the grief process; 2) demonstration of healthy growth through one's own grief process; and 3) a willingness to listen to others. Experience has taught the workers that leading a sharing group for no more than one to two months is optimal, thus avoiding emotional fatigue.

Structured Group. Advance registration is required for this group and the same persons go through the seven-week group together. The purpose of the structured group is to help people understand the grief process and to offer encouragement in adjusting to the many changes that accompany the death of a spouse. Those who have been widowed between three months and five years are encouraged to attend. However, it has been discovered that some who have been widowed as many as fifteen years or more can benefit from the group if they did not have an opportunity to work through the grief experience earlier. Size is limited to ten participants who are expected to attend all seven sessions to receive maximum benefit from the group. People sign up by calling the church office or by signing a list passed around regularly in the sharing group.

The content and format of the group is based upon a leader's and participant's manual (Gant & Marler 1983). The goals of the group are to learn new information about grief processes and widowhood, to share thoughts and feelings openly, and to express appreciation for common experiences. The program is designed so that three major components of learning—cognitive, affective, and behavioral—are tapped in each session. There is an emphasis on the integration of spiritual values and learning. Each session begins with Scripture, meditation, and prayer (spiritual). An informational lecturette (cognitive, affective) is then given with brief exercises to assimilate the material. Finally, homework assignments (cognitive, affective, and behavioral) help members to practice what has been learned or to prepare for the coming week's topic. The content of the program includes:

- Beginnings, getting to know one another
- An overview of the stages of grief and shock and numbness
- Coming out of the fog: What is reality now?
- Understanding anger and guilt
- Combating loneliness and depression
- The road to recovery, acceptance and setbacks
- New beginnings, recovery and hope.

A church staff member and widowed person usually colead the structured groups, although social workers and other professionals sometimes colead groups as well. Ideally, one professional and one widowed person work together. Leadership training sessions for the widowed are provided. After prospective widowed group leaders observe a seven-week session, they are invited to colead the next group.

A written evaluation form is completed by participants in the seventh group session. Each component of the group is rated on a scale from not helpful to very helpful. Each leader is also evaluated on performance as: "kept discussion moving," "preparedness," "demonstrated concern," "did not dominate discussion," "handled conflict well," and "took care to include everybody." Space is provided for any additional comments or suggestion. One participant wrote: "This group has been a lifesaver for me!" Another one noted: "It's helpful to know I am not the only one feeling the way I do. I thought I was going crazy. Now I understand what is happening to me in my grief." One man wrote, "This is the first time I've ever talked about my grief in the five years since my wife died. Thank you!"

Elective Classes. The purpose of an elective class is to address the practical needs of widowed persons through a short-term teaching session by local professionals on a variety of topics. The professionals donate their time and expertise.

These classes typically last from one to four consecutive evenings. A six-month calendar is published so that participants know in advance what the topics will be on a specific night.

Twice a year a survey is conducted of all who have attended New Friends. The survey seeks to determine the interests and needs of widowed persons and to plan classes to meet these needs. Recently, the elective classes have included such topics as: "Cooking ideas for one," "Financial management tips," "Dealing with loneliness," "House maintenance and handyman skills," "How to study the Bible," and "Overcoming depression."

A staff minister at St. Matthews Baptist Church and the steering committee invite professionals in the community to address the group on the selected topics. These include social workers, financial management consultants, lawyers, physicians, policemen, nutrition specialists, seminary and college professors, fitness instructors, ministers, automotive mechanics, and others. An effort is made to discover gifts and abilities within the New Friends' group as well. Outside speakers are often easier to secure for one-night engagements instead of a series of classes.

Social Group. The social group is for those who are interested in meeting new friends and being in a relaxed, enjoyable atmosphere. The participants in this group play games, cards, or just sit and visit with one another. Typically, participants in the social group have worked through most of their grief but value having a good time with others. One participant said, "This is the only time during the week I get out of the house and visit with others."

Monthly Dinner

A community dinner for single people of all ages is sponsored by New Friends on the second Thursday of each month at the church. Dinner is served and only the structured and sharing groups meet immediately following thirty minutes of musical entertainment. The program is scheduled by a volunteer each month and usually includes an individual or group from the community. Some 125 people attend, on average; the church hostess prepares the meal. A reminder card for reservations is mailed to all participants once a month.

The monthly dinner began as a way to keep many of the New Friends' group in touch with one another since many participants no longer needed to attend weekly. The dinner has become an excellent way to introduce New Friends to widowed persons in the community in a nonthreatening environment. Those who are divorced or never married are also invited to the dinner because some widowed persons indicated that they wanted to be with people who were different from them (not widowed). Although most of the attendants are widowed and over fifty years old, about 20 percent of the dinner participants are younger and either divorced or never married.

Principles of Programing

Several principles of programing enable the ministry to have maximum effectiveness. *First, a responsible lay person to serve as coordinator is crucial.* This person needs to demonstrate successful adjustment to widowhood, have a caring attitude toward others, take initiative easily, and pay attention to details. He or she needs to be open to personal growth and willing to delegate tasks to others. A one-year commitment by the coordinator to the ministry provides adequate stability and continuity.

Second, the steering committee guides the overall program. The New Friends' steering committee meets monthly to evaluate the ministry, do long-range planning and goal setting, and to take care of the details of upcoming meetings. Members need to feel they can raise any issue related to the ministry at this meeting. Too often, churches and ministers make assumptions about what is best for a specific ministry. Most of the responsibility needs to be given to widowed persons; it is their ministry.

Third, feedback is regularly asked for from participants. Time is planned in the New Friends' large group meeting at least quarterly to hear from those present. Different formats are used, such as written questionnaires and open discussion regarding overall direction and needs of the group.

Fourth, weekly responsibilities are shared with as many people as possible. The steering committee seeks to involve different people every week in some manner. Small tasks such as room set-up, registering members and guests, and leading a weekly devotional time can be shared with different members of the group. A calendar lists the responsibilities of the participants each week; it is not uncommon for ten people to have specific responsibilities on a given evening.

Fifth, a professional in the community acts as a resource person and advisor to the group. The minister of pastoral care at St. Matthews Baptist Church served in this capacity for New Friends in the first two years. Several persons in the community could serve as a resource/consultant. The resource person(s) can lead a group occasionally, teach an elective class, meet with the steering committee, or recruit other professionals to lead groups or classes through his or her contacts.

Re-Strategizing for the Future

New Friends is expanding its services to meet emerging needs of the widowed. Many participants report that mealtimes are the loneliest times in their week. Because of this, a dinner club is now being planned. New elective classes on practical subjects are being scheduled with the option of advanced registration. A group for younger widows and widowers will be offered to address single-parenting issues. A quarterly newsletter is being planned to improve communications within the group. Recently, a public relations committee has been formed and a brochure created to spread the word about New Friends in the community. A more comprehensive leadership training program is being developed along with detailed descriptions for every volunteer job.

The primary mission of New Friends is to create *family* for widowed people in the Louisville metropolitan area in the name of Christ. The ministry supports men and women in their grief, challenges them to grow as individuals, and helps them reach out to others. Hopefully, New Friends can serve as a model for other churches to enable the widowed to discover a new wholeness in their lives following the death of a spouse.

A past coordinator of New Friends has given a precious gift. Following his wife's death, this elderly widower recorded his thoughts and feelings in a journal. One particularly poignant entry reflects the pain and potential inherent in grief:

> Love is something within that you apply. If there is no object or person at hand to love, what is the point? This is the quandary of bereavement. Your love is there, but she is missing. We *must* find a common connection to each other.

Death does not expunge the energy of love, of being connected. The experience of bereavement does disrupt a very tangible—very vital—social bond.

For widowed persons, interventions which include the emotional and practical network support of a variety of helpers are crucial. Indeed, mobilizing the love and care of family, friends, natural helpers, interested professionals, and other widowed persons help the bereaved find common connections to others.

Perhaps the most significant outcome of ecological approaches is the empowerment of the widowed. With support and time, the energy of love may be redirected in new relational channels. Once hurting care recipients become effective caregivers. The symbol of the widow as an altar of God reflects this spiritual and social evolution from the pain of sacrifice (death) to offerings of love (support) to personal commitment (service). The challenge for professionals and laity in church settings is to understand the pain, provide offerings of love and support, and, finally, open avenues for service.

References

Arkin, A. M. 1981. Emotional care of the bereaved. In *Acute grief,* eds. Margolis et al. New York: Columbia University Press.

Arling, G. 1976. The elderly widow and her family, neighbors, and friends. *Journal of Marriage and the Family* 38:757–68.

Atchley, R. C. 1985. *Social forces and aging: An introduction to social gerontology.* 4th ed. Belmont, Calif.: Wadsworth Publishing.

Bell, R. 1971. *Marriage and family interaction.* 3d ed. Homewood, Ill.: Dorsey Press.

Bellah, Robert N., et al. 1985. *Habits of the heart: Individualism and commitment in American life.* New York: Harper and Row.

Berardo, F. M. 1968. Widowhood status in the United States: Perspective on a neglected aspect of the family life-cycle. *The Family Coordinator* 17:191–201.

Bowlby, J. 1980. *Attachment and loss.* Vol. 3. New York: Basic Books.

Butler, R. 1981. Overview on aging: Some biomedical, social, and behavioral perspectives. In *Aging,* eds. Kiesler et al. New York: Academic Press.

Cassem, N. H. 1975. Bereavement as indispensable for growth. In *Bereavement: Its psychosocial aspects,* ed. B. Schenberg. New York: Columbia University Press.

Ferraro, K. F. 1984. Widowhood and social participation in later life. *Research on Aging* 6:451–68.

Freud, S. 1949. *Collected papers.* Vol. 4. London: The Hogarth Press.

Gant, L., and P. Marler. 1983. *Synthesis: The struggle toward new wholeness.* Louisville: St. Matthews Area Ministries.

Glick, I. et al. 1974. *The first year of bereavement.* New York: John Wiley and Sons.

Goodstein, R. K. 1981. Inextricable interaction: Social, psychologic, and biologic stresses facing the elderly. *American Journal of Orthopsychiatry* 51:219-29.

Hafer, K. 1981. *Coping with bereavement from death or divorce.* Englewood Cliffs, N.J.: Prentice-Hall.

Harvey, C., and H. Bahr. 1974. Widowhood, morale, and affiliation. *Journal of Marriage and the Family,* February, 97-106.

―――. 1980. *The sunshine widows.* Lexington: Lexington Books.

Helsing, K., and M. Szklo. 1981. Mortality after bereavement. *American Journal of Epidemiology* 114:41-52.

Hurley, J. B. 1981. *Man and woman in biblical perspective.* Grand Rapids: Zondervan.

Jacobs, S. 1977. An epidemiological review of the mortality of bereavement. *Psychosomatic Medicine* 39:344-57.

Kaprio, J., M. Koskenvuo, and H. Rita. 1987. Mortality after bereavement. *American Journal of Public Health* 77:283-87.

Keith, L. 1981. Acute grief and survivor expectations. In *Acute grief,* eds. Margolis et al. New York: Columbia University Press.

Lindemann, E. 1979. *Beyond grief.* New York: Jason Aronson.

Lopata, H. 1970. The social involvement of American widows. *American Behavioral Scientist* 14:41-57.

―――. 1973. *Widowhood in an American city.* Cambridge, Mass.: Schenkman Publishing Company.

―――. 1979. *Women as widows.* New York: Elsevier.

Lund, D. A., et al. 1986. Gender differences through two years of bereavement among the elderly. *The Gerontologist* 26:314-20.

Marler, P. 1983. Bereavement, aging, and widowhood: A survey of the effects of bereavement on older widows. Master's thesis, Raymond A. Kent School of Social Work, University of Louisville, Louisville, Kentucky.

Marris, P. 1977. In *Understanding bereavement and grief,* ed. N. Linzer. New York: Yeshiva University Press.

McKenna, M. L. 1967. *Women of the church: Role and renewal.* New York: Kennedy.

Middleman, R. 1981. The pursuit of competence through involvement in structured groups. In *Promoting competence in clients: A new/old approach to social work practice,* ed. A. Maluccio. London: The Free Press.

Morgan, L. A. 1976. A re-examination of widowhood and morale. *Journal of Gerontology* 31:687-95.

Mosley, G. R. 1972. Coping with bereavement. In *Religion and bereavement,* eds. A. Kutscher and L. Kutscher. New York: Health Sciences Publishing Corporation.

Nudel, A. R. 1986. *Starting over: Help for young widows and widowers.* New York: Dodd, Mead and Company.

Osiek, D. 1983. The widow as altar: The rise and fall of a symbol. *Second Century* 3:159-69.

Palmore, E., et al. 1979. Stress and adaptation in later life. *Journal of Gerontology* 31:841-51.

Parkes, C. M. 1976. The broken heart. In *Death: Current perspectives,* ed. C. S. Schneidman. Mountain View, Calif.: Mayfield Publishing Company.

Parkes, C. M., B. Benjamin, and R. G. Fitzgerald. 1969. Broken heart: A statistical study of increased mortality among widowers. *British Medical Journal* 1:740–43.

Proulx, J. K., and P. D. Baker. 1981. Grief, grieving, and bereavement: A look at the BASICS. In *Acute grief*, eds. Margolis et al. New York: Columbia University Press.

Rees, W. D. and S. G. Lutkins. 1967. Mortality of bereavement. *British Medical Journal* 4:13–16.

Silverman, P. 1981. *Helping women cope with grief.* Beverly Hills: Sage Publications.

————. 1986. *Widow to widow.* New York: Springer.

Smith, J. 1975. On the work of mourning. In *Bereavement: Its psychosocial aspects*, ed. B. Schenberg. New York: Columbia University Press.

Stroebe, W. et al. 1982. The effects of bereavement on mortality: A social psychological analysis. In *Social psychology and behavioral medicine*, ed. J. R. Eiser. New York: John Wiley and Sons.

Susser, M. 1981. Widowhood: A situational life stress or a stressful life event. *American Journal of Public Health* 71:793–95.

Switzer, D. K. 1970. *The dynamics of grief.* Nashville: Abingdon Press.

Thurston, B. 1985. The widow as the "altar of God." *Society of Biblical Literature* 24:279–98.

Warren, D. 1981. *Helping networks: How people cope with problems in the urban community.* Notre Dame: University of Notre Dame Press.

Widowed Persons Service. 1982. American Association of Retired Persons, 1909 K Street, Washington, D.C. 20049.

Wister, A., and L. Strain. 1986. Social support and well-being: A comparison of older widows and widowers. *Canadian Journal on Aging* 5:205–18.

9

Serving Children and Families Through Agency Consultation

Laura Dean Ford Friedrich

© 1989 *Laura D. F. Friedrich*

Important experiences sometimes begin in small ways. A spur-of-the-moment visit between college friends was such a beginning in Wilmington, Illinois. They talked first of college days and mutual friends and then moved on to their respective families and current careers. They discovered that they were both in helping professions: he, a pastor at the United Methodist Church in town, and she, a caseworker with the Illinois Department of Children and Family Services.

She was in town investigating a report of child abuse. "Did you know that the incidence of child abuse and neglect is higher in southern Will County than the rest of Illinois?" she asked.

Her startling news intruded on his work over the next few days. Finally, he took this troubling information to his church's Council on Ministries. A long discussion ensued, including accounts of personal knowledge of child abuse and neglect in the community. The prevailing question of the evening was, "Is there something the church should be doing about this?"

A laywoman repeated the question the next morning when she called the executive director of ChildServ, a child welfare agency serving metropolitan Chicago and adjacent counties. The response came quickly, "Yes, the church should be working to reduce and prevent child abuse. One of our church consultants will work with you."

Much has happened since those initial conversations and the resulting consultation relationship between the First United Methodist Church of Wilmington and ChildServ. The story of the ministry that has developed out of that partnership

LAURA DEAN FORD FRIEDRICH, M.Ed., is the director of church/community consultation services at ChildServ in Park Ridge, Illinois. The author of articles on child care ministries, she prepared the *Guidelines for Leading Your Church 1989-92: Family Ministries* for the United Methodist Church. She has worked as the director of a child care program for working families.

illustrates how families can be served through collaboration between a church-related agency and a local congregation. ChildServ's Church/Community Consultation Services provides a significant model of how agencies can stimulate local congregations to develop services for the families of their communities. Families have intense needs, and churches have great capacity for responding to those needs. Church-related agencies can help bring those two groups together.

ChildServ: A Church-Related Agency Serving Families

Established in 1894 as the Methodist Deaconess Orphanage, ChildServ has a long history of distinguished services to children and their families. It was initially organized to care for parentless, homeless children roaming the streets of Chicago. The orphanage later became the Lake Bluff Children's Home, caring for neglected and dependent children, and eventually provided residential treatment for emotionally disturbed children as Lake Bluff/Chicago Homes for Children. In the 1970s, convinced that institutional living was not the best care for children, the agency began serving children and families through community-based programs of prevention, early intervention, and child advocacy. Foster care services remained as the only remnant of the substantial residential program that had included a large campus facility as well as group homes located throughout the Chicago metropolitan area and adjacent Lake County.

Now known as ChildServ, the agency continues to address the unmet needs of children in their own neighborhoods and with their own families. The agency focuses on the development of nurturing family relationships, the prevention of problems in children and families, and early intervention where problems do exist. Through its services, ChildServ strives to support and strengthen families, foster stability within family units, and prevent the removal of children from their homes of origin.

Mission

ChildServ's motivation for services to children and families finds its roots in the challenge of the gospel to serve human need and in the example of Christ of self-giving service. The agency believes that every child is a person of worth, entitled to God's gift of wholeness of life. It strives to respond to the needs of children and families on a nonsectarian basis. The agency's affiliation with the Northern Illinois Conference of the United Methodist Church supports and shapes its commitment to ministry with children and families.

Within this framework and tradition, ChildServ functions with two mission priorities in mind:

1. *Prevention/Early Intervention/Advocacy.* ChildServ becomes involved in the lives of children at an early age in order to prevent problems from intensifying and disrupting family life. Intervention with children while they are still living with their families of origin and when their problems are in the earliest stages is a direct corollary to prevention. ChildServ works with children and

families in local neighborhoods through community-based offices located in the Chicago metropolitan area and through local churches that request its consultation services in Northern Illinois communities.

ChildServ believes that child advocacy is one of the most effective ways to promote the support systems necessary for positive family development. Since children have no voice or vote, ChildServ speaks on their behalf to educate and stimulate the church, the public, and elected officials to understand better and to act on the problems and needs of children.

2. *Placement.* ChildServ views placement of children in foster homes as a last recourse when all resources have been exhausted in keeping a child with the biological family. For these children, ChildServ's commitment is reunification of the foster child with the family of origin. When long-term problems in the biological family are severe and prevent reunification, other permanent plans, such as adoption or independent living, are alternatives.

Focus on Community Services

Believing that local communities are the best places to care for children, ChildServ provides direct services to children and families in several neighborhoods in metropolitan Chicago as well as in communities adjacent to Chicago. Advisory councils work with staff in each community to help them understand community needs and resources and design effective programs to address gaps in service delivery. ChildServ networks with other community organizations to foster cooperation and coordination of services for children and families.

Poverty, child abuse and neglect, homelessness, illiteracy, teen-age pregnancy and parenting, and lack of quality child care all adversely affect the quality of family life. ChildServ addresses these issues through the implementation of programs that work with and support families:

- shelter services and transitional living programs
- family home day care for the infants and toddlers of teen-age parents
- school-based tutoring and counseling programs
- drop-in centers and parent-aide programs for parents at-risk of abuse or neglect
- therapy programs for parents and children
- family counseling, parent workshops, and support groups for young parents
- family-life education programs
- drop-in centers for elementary-age children
- foster care for those children for whom early intervention is too late or not enough.

Whenever possible, services involve significant participation of volunteers with training and support provided by professional staff. Most agency programs can be replicated in other places at relatively low cost by involving community people.

ChildServ sometimes consults through its community-based services with other child-serving agencies to help them develop programs, i.e., a school-based tutoring program or a shelter for the homeless. Most often, however, the

Church/Community Consultation Services department serves as the catalyst for assisting local groups to focus their energies and resources on community needs. ChildServ recognizes that congregations have great potential for serving children and families in their own communities and provides consultation as the way of developing congregational resources in a systematic manner.

Church/Community Consultation Services

The Church/Community Consultation Services staff works with local churches to improve the quality of family life for children and families by:
- determining the needs of children and families in the community
- identifying the resources of the congregation
- developing skills to respond to those community needs
- implementing programs that serve children and families

The Consultation Service offers four types of consultation to local churches:

1. *Technical Assistance.* Technical assistance involves work with an existing church-based program, a child care program or a food pantry. This consultation is usually focused on a specific issue of program management, i.e., skill development of a board of directors or training in grant writing for funding proposals, and extends over a period of six to nine months.

2. *Program Development.* Program development consultation enables a congregation to understand the needs of children and families and plan new services to respond to those needs. A child care center and an enrichment program for teen-age girls exemplify the projects that have developed out of such consultation. Program development usually requires twelve to eighteen months, and occasionally extends over two years.

3. *Workshops.* Workshops provide in-depth discussions of specific issues related to the well-being of children and families and include skill building for parents as well as laypersons and pastors. Consultants do workshops on parenting issues, child abuse and neglect, needs assessment, child care ministries, and other family concerns. Workshops are most often one-time events but can be a series when that meets a local church's interest.

4. *Presentations.* Presentations offer an overview of issues that have an impact on children and families, often in the form of a sermon at a worship service or a program for a group in the congregation. Information about what individuals and congregations can do to serve children and families is an important component of all presentations done by the Consultation Services.

Consultation Services approaches each local situation as unique and utilizes the consultation process as the means through which to develop the program best suited to the needs of the community and the resources of the church. Most of the work of Church/Community Consultation Services focuses on a wide range of child care programs and on child abuse prevention, but some projects address issues of teen pregnancy, alternatives to gang activity for young adolescents, and the need for parent support and education.

The consultation process provides the support and direction essential for group members to accept responsibility for the work to be done. The consultant suggests strategies to accomplish goals, offers ideas about the next steps, recommends assignments for the next tasks, and guides the identification of community resources. He or she provides an important model for working with a group and trains all members of the group to be more capable leaders (General Board of Discipleship 1989).

The consultation process involves five distinct stages:

Determining Needs and Resources. The consultant helps the local church group examine carefully the life situations of the children and families in the congregation and in the wider community. The group reflects on the church's understanding of mission and the ways in which the church already ministers with children and families. It identifies the resources within the church appropriate for ministering with families.

In some situations, the committee may decide to do a comprehensive needs assessment. At other times, the group may choose a more focused study of needs, i.e., surveying child care concerns of families or issues related to single parents. Door-to-door surveys, questionnaires, interviews, and studies of demographic and census records are options available to help churches assess needs. Visits to police and fire departments, schools, public social service departments, private agencies and hospitals determine what resources are available to children and families. Problems with service delivery and gaps in needed services also show up in the process (Miller and Wilson 1985; Schur and Smith 1980; Stockwell 1985).

Regardless of the scope of the needs assessment, the consultant always helps the group to set a clear timeline that outlines the different groups within the community that it plans to survey and the target dates for completion. The consultant stays in close touch with those persons working on the survey, offering encouragement, suggesting alternative strategies when they encounter difficulties, and reminding them of their commitments and time frames.

Establishing Priorities. The consultant enables the group to study the concerns identified in the assessment and understand the correlations among those concerns. For example, single parents usually have intense need for child care and low-cost recreational opportunities for their families. Child abuse may not show up as a specific concern, but several of the risk factors for abuse do, i.e., isolation, stress, alcoholism. Aging communities into which a growing number of young families are moving may benefit from intergenerational experiences.

One or two needs sometime emerge clearly and the group can proceed easily. Often, however, the church identifies so many concerns that people become overwhelmed. The consultant urges the group to set priorities rather than undertake every issue identified. He or she invites the group to list ways in which the church can respond to the top concerns identified in the needs survey. Then, the consultant facilitates the group's choice of the program suggestion which they believe is best and on which they are willing to work. With its priorities clearly established, the group moves on to the planning stage (Sheek 1985).

Developing Plans. The consultant helps group members develop a complete action plan which addresses all aspects of program development, including articulating a service plan; forming a governing body or relating the program to a board or committee of the church; recruiting and training volunteers; developing employment practices and hiring staff, if appropriate; organizing a fund-raising strategy; locating suitable space; and networking with resources in the wider community (Flanagan 1981; General Board of Discipleship 1989; Freeman 1987).

Throughout this phase, the consultant provides guidance and expertise, helping the congregation to focus and develop its own ideas. He or she works carefully to cultivate abilities within the group and to foster policies for the program so that it can function autonomously with local leadership. The group's ownership of the program grows during this stage of the consultation process. That sense of ownership is crucial to the program's ultimate success.

Implementing Programs. Both the consultant and the congregation often experience turning plans into action as the most challenging phase of the consultation process. The consultant works closely with the group during this time, monitoring timelines and reminding members of their responsibilities. He or she also offers support when it seems appropriate, but remains in the background when people are managing well on their own.

Occasionally, the consultant recognizes that a project is running into serious difficulties, i.e., a funding grant does not come through, volunteer recruitment is not going well, or unanticipated resistance emerges within the congregation. In any situation that threatens the implementation of the group's plans, the consultant provides guidance to help the group review its work and make essential adjustments. The consultant's ability to reflect and to analyze the group's experience often makes the difference between successful implementation of a new program and plans that never come to fulfillment (Heusser 1980; Schaller 1971; Wilson 1983).

Evaluating Outcomes. Evaluation incorporates responses from three groups: (1) participants in the program, (2) staff, volunteers, and speakers who work with the program, and (3) the planning group from the church. The consultant helps the group review feedback it has received from program participants, reflect on its work, and plan the next steps by focusing the discussion on some of the following areas: goals of the project, accomplishments of the program, ways the program fell short of its goals, suggestions for improvements, other concerns expressed by families, and next steps the group needs to plan (General Board of Discipleship 1989).

Celebration is an essential part of the evaluation phase of consultation. Both the consultant and the local church group reflect on the accomplishments of the project and celebrate the development of a new service to children and families in its community. Often, the group holds a dedication service or a social event that shares the new program with the congregation and the wider community. In addition, the consultant suggests the group submit an article on its work to a community newspaper as well as the denominational periodical and urges the group to make a formal report to the annual meeting of the congregation.

The evaluation phase of consultation is the time to encourage the group to call occasionally with updates on the program or with questions that arise. Thus, local churches know they have continuing support from the Church/Community Consultation Services, and the consultants know that they have had a role in enabling a group of committed volunteers to reach out and serve the children and families of the community in a new way.

Wilmington: A Church's Ministry in Child-Abuse Prevention

The First United Methodist Church of Wilmington was founded in 1857. Today its membership numbers nearly five hundred and has an annual budget of about $125,000. From its beginning, the congregation has opened itself to the community, evidenced today by its outreach ministries to senior citizens, its nurture ministries of Christian education, its music programs, and a shepherding program which responds to special needs of persons within the congregation. The church building provides space to community groups such as Alcoholics Anonymous, 4-H, and Girl Scouts.

Located fifty miles southwest of Chicago, Wilmington is a blue-collar community of approximately five thousand residents. Many people commute to work in nearby towns and metropolitan Chicago. Wilmington has a mobile population because of the construction of a nearby power plant, chemical plants, and oil refineries. According to 1980 census figures, 16 percent of the families in the Wilmington community were living at or below the poverty line. Both the reporting rate and the incidence rate of child abuse and neglect in Will County increased steadily during the 1980s, leading to a significant increase in investigations by caseworkers from the state's Department of Children and Family Services.

A consultant from the Church/Community Consultation Services at ChildServ traveled to Wilmington for the first time in July 1986 following the church's initial call to the agency, and discussed with church leaders several ways in which congregations can address child abuse and neglect. The consultant indicated that, should the congregation become involved, the work ahead would be difficult, the pastor's support crucial, and the participation of a committed group of people essential. The consultant assured the leaders of ChildServ's commitment to support their efforts through ongoing consultation.

At the next meeting of the Council on Ministries, the pastor indicated his strong interest; Council members organized a task force. At the next two worship services, the pastor invited members of the church to join the Child Abuse Prevention Task Force. Responses came quickly, and fourteen people attended the first meeting in August.

Resource Identification

The group accepted as its first task the identification of all the services and resources available to families in the Wilmington area. Members of the task force spent two months gathering this information, using a one-page questionnaire the consultant helped them develop. They found agency personnel pleased to talk with them and interested to find a church concerned about child abuse and neglect. They learned that the agencies also wanted to know more about services available to families; almost everyone interviewed wanted a copy of the report the task force planned to compile.

The task force incorporated the survey information into a resource directory, *Family Help Directory*. No longer a document designed only for the church's use, the directory included the names and addresses of all agencies in the area, days and hours of service, specific services provided, eligibility requirements, and fees charged. The church distributed the directory to all the churches, schools, hospitals, and social-service and municipal agencies in the community and surrounding area. Professionals and community residents applauded the directory and asked for additional copies.

The task force developed a one-page flyer containing information about the most important services for children and families, i.e., the child abuse hotline, the hospital with social workers on duty twenty-four hours a day, the shelter for battered women, and agencies providing family counseling and emergency services. They distributed the flyer to the membership of the church through the monthly newsletter and followed a few weeks later with a second flyer, containing the suggestion: "Share this with the family next door."

Education

In October 1986, the task force, along with the pastor and the worship committee, planned a series of worship services focusing on the needs of children and closing the series with a call to action on behalf of children. Bulletin inserts and articles in the church newsletter also called attention to the child abuse crisis in the Wilmington community. A member of the task force wrote a series of articles for the local newspaper focusing on abuse and neglect.

The task force held a community-wide workshop on child abuse and neglect in November, drawing individuals from four churches in addition to the United Methodist congregation. Several issues generated intense discussion among the participants: the implications of reporting suspected abuse and neglect, the reticence of some school officials to abide by the Illinois reporting law, the need to support adults who were victims of abuse when they were young, and the anguish people felt for children suffering now.

Workshop participants expressed strong interest in learning more, and the task force responded by sponsoring a four-session study on child abuse and neglect in January and February 1987, using a book written specifically for local church audiences (Kent 1985). At the conclusion of the study, participants acknowledged a new understanding of the complexity of child abuse and neglect and articulated a strong commitment to addressing the issue. One woman spoke for the entire group when she said, "I don't want to study any more. I want to do something about all these families that are hurting."

Family Support/Intervention

Responding to that urgency, the task force worked over the spring and summer months to develop a program called T.L.C. for Children, expressed in the motto, "Everyone needs tender loving care, especially children." T.L.C. encompasses three components to serve families that experience unusual amounts of stress and who may be at risk of abusing or neglecting their child(ren): Family Care, Parents' Day Out, and Parent-to-Parent.

Organized in August 1987, Family Care provides short-term support for families at times of intense stress. Volunteers recruited by the church have responded to a variety of family needs. They provided transportation to Chicago for a family with a chronically ill child who needed medical tests and treatments. For another family, coping with a new baby and the death of the mother's parents and the father's long commute to work, Family Care volunteers ran errands, cooked meals, cared for the four-year-old bewildered by all the turmoil, and called regularly to see how things were going. To a family with a new baby, a home-cooked meal is delivered along with a coupon for some Family Care services. Brochures describing Family Care services have been distributed throughout the community, and articles about the program appear regularly in local newspapers. The church office receives the calls for services, and the secretary notifies the volunteer coordinator of the requests.

Parents' Day Out, launched a few months after Family Care, offers respite child care and enrichment for parents at home with young children. An average of twenty-five children and twenty-two parents participate in the six-hour weekly program. Volunteer coordinators plan activities for the children and manage the program. Parents work in the classrooms on a rotating basis, and church volunteers also help in the classroom. Separate meetings for parents—scheduled once a quarter—provide opportunities for exploring parenting issues together and participating in enrichment activities.

Parents' Day Out was a special blessing for a mother with a very active three-year-old. Having recently moved to Wilmington from out of state, she did not know many people in the community and felt overwhelmed by her wonderful, but very demanding, son. When she brought her child to the program, she often greeted the coordinators by saying, "You're really going to earn your 'money' today!" She's grateful for the break Parents' Day Out gives her and her son, and she appreciates the new friends both she and her son are making through the program.

An illness forced one Parents' Day Out mother to remain in bed for the last two months of her difficult pregnancy. She knew her two preschoolers would miss the program and appreciated the coordinators' insistence that they continue attending even though she could not. Later, she thanked them profusely because Parents' Day Out had provided a much-needed break for her mother who came to care for the family during that difficult time.

Both Family Care and Parents' Day Out provide support and reduce isolation for community families. More importantly, these two programs enable parents to develop mutual support networks with each other and with caring individuals from the congregation. Such networks are essential in strengthening parents' ability to care for their children and in reducing the risk of family disintegration.

Parent-to-Parent emerged as the volunteer coordinators realized that some families had needs that demanded a more comprehensive service plan than Family Care and Parents' Day Out could offer. One of these families was a twenty-year-old single mother with a newborn. They needed a place to live as well as food and clothing for the baby. The Family Care coordinator referred the mother to a community pantry and recruited a volunteer willing to provide a temporary home for the family. Both the mother and the baby became ill, and Family Care volunteers drove them to doctor's appointments on several occasions. Volunteers also took care of the baby so that the mother could rest and recover her strength. The mother eventually located housing for herself and her infant son, and, with the help of Family Care volunteers, arranged some basic financial support for her family through the Illinois Department of Public Assistance.

Family Care gave significant help to this family, and yet, the coordinator knew that this family needed much more. The family needed a more stable living situation, adequate financial resources, ongoing support from caring individuals, and training in parenting skills. Family Care, unfortunately, was not equipped to deal with such long-term needs.

Another family, composed of two parents and three children, had chronic health problems and serious financial difficulties. Although both parents had jobs, they were often on the brink of eviction due to failure to pay their rent, and they were hard-pressed to cover their extensive medical bills. One child with severe behavior problems required long-term treatment, and the family could manage neither the transportation to the therapist nor the cost of the treatment. Family Care volunteers provided transportation for members of the family and connected them with the community food pantry, but they knew their help was simply not enough. This family also needed more.

Parent-to-Parent serves families such as these by linking trained, professionally supervised parent-aides, one-on-one, with parents who experience unusual difficulty with parenting. Parent-aides visit weekly with these parents to offer support and friendship and to be a positive role model. Parent-aides focus nonjudgmentally on the parents and work to: strengthen parenting and individual coping skills, increase understanding of normal child development, improve problem solving and communication skills, expand social contacts and reduce isolation, enhance home management skills, and promote utilization of community resources. As supportive and caring individuals, parent-aides try to meet some of the parents' needs so that the parents can respond more appropriately to their children's needs and demands.

The church has established a partnership with the Exchange Club Center for the Prevention of Child Abuse at Guardian Angel Home, a child welfare agency in nearby Joliet, for the development and implementation of Parent-to-Parent. Guardian Angel already has a parent-aide program; its coordinator will provide training, support and supervision to the parent-aide volunteers recruited by the church. Both Guardian Angel and the church affirm their new relationship and their service to parents who need friendship and support in order to manage the demands of parenting.

The joint effort of the Child Abuse Prevention Task Force and Church/Community Consultation Services at ChildServ has led the people of the congregation on a journey that has changed the church's life. The congregation has a new understanding of the ministry of the laity as laypersons have experienced the power and presence of God moving in their lives and motivating their decisions (Fenhagen 1977). They have developed leadership skills and accepted new roles. Many of these persons were once primarily involved in the organizational life of the church; now they have accepted responsibilities for the outreach ministry of the church and have a new sense of what it means to be people of faith and disciples in the world.

The church is also having a significant impact on the life of the broader community as it works actively to prevent child abuse and neglect through its family support programs, Family Care and Parents' Day Out, and its intervention program, Parent-to-Parent. Staffed entirely by church volunteers, these programs have provided nearly one thousand units of service to approximately two hundred children and parents in their two-year history.

As impressive as this figure is, it is important to note that the Child Abuse Prevention Task Force, now the T.L.C. Council, has made an impact in other aspects of Wilmington's life. There appears to be a correlation between the congregation's work and community trends and developments, although the task force has not conducted systematic research to determine the extent of the relationship. Evidence of a new awareness of and concern for the welfare of children and families include the following:

1. Other churches are exploring ways that they can address the needs of children.
2. Agencies and schools continue to welcome additional copies of the *Family Help Directory* and are happy to distribute brochures for the T.L.C. programs.
3. Nineteen people from the congregation have volunteered to work on a regular basis in a shelter program in Joliet.
4. Wilmington is the only community out of eleven southern Will County towns to pass a school referendum in the November 1988 election.

When they began their work, few persons on the task force understood that they were becoming child advocates. Yet, they have become advocates in the best sense of the term; they speak on behalf of children, they serve children and families, they actively support legislation that benefits children, and they influence others in the congregation and community to respond to the needs of children (Carlson 1980; Freeman 1986).

Ingredients for Success—Areas for Growth

A fruitful consultation project begins with people who respond to God's call to ministry and who follow Jesus' example of ministry with the hurting people of the world. They accept responsibility for the welfare of their community and claim a vision of hope and healing for those around them. They respond in faith with the expectation that the guidance of the Spirit will inform their decisions and bless their endeavors.

A recognition of need among children and families urges church people to action. They may have specific knowledge or more general concerns, but, in all cases, they have experienced the needs of children, directly or indirectly, and long for an opportunity to make a difference in their lives.

A sense of ownership contributes to a productive consultation relationship. Because people have usually come together in response to a perceived need rather than by election to a particular committee, members of the group have a strong connection to the project. They can influence how the project proceeds and develops, and they have the opportunity to make decisions, develop policies and shape programs.

At the same time, members of the group must also be able to share their work with others. They must be open to involving new people so that the group is continually renewed and expanded with new energy and new ideas. The work must not be bound by local church interests, but must encompass families from all segments of the community. Involving other churches in the program is particularly important.

The leadership of the pastor sets the tone for the participation of the congregation, and laypeople depend on the spiritual support of the pastor in all aspects of their involvement in the project. The pastor need not be an active member of the task force or committee, but the laity must feel his or her encouragement. The pastor in Wilmington says, "Sometimes the pastor just has to get out of the way and let the laypeople be the ministers they're called to be." The pastor must be committed to the ministry of the laity.

Finally, a successful consultation project remains focused and proceeds in a step-by-step manner. Concerned people are easily overwhelmed by the diverse and intense needs of their neighbors, and many good ideas get lost in efforts to address all issues at once. Consultation enables a group to consider one thing at a time, insuring success at each point of the process and taking time for affirmation for every accomplishment. Such recognition of a group's commitment usually spurs the members on to the next task.

The Church/Community Consultation Services at ChildServ faces two major concerns at this point in its development, that of serving churches in resource-diminished communities and evaluation/research.

Serving Churches in Resource-Diminished Communities

While the Consultation Services serves churches in middle class and more affluent communities with relative ease, churches in poor or transitional communities find it considerably more difficult to utilize the services of the consultants. The needs of congregations in those areas are intense and numerous while resources are few, and these churches find it difficult to involve themselves in family ministries beyond their own congregations. They are often struggling for their own survival as churches and have limited energies to focus on community needs. It may be hard for the churches to see how consultation might be helpful in their situations.

These churches need funding for personnel, program supplies, and building expenses if they are to develop new ministries to serve children and families. ChildServ's Consultation budget does not include resources for grants to local churches, and significant fund development is difficult for churches in resource-diminished areas.

The consultants find that the point of entry into such churches is often different from that of other churches. These congregations may request services that do not fit into the central purpose of the Consultation Services, or they have difficulty focusing their consultation requests because there are so many needs in the church and in the community. Sometimes a pastor enlists a consultant to help in mobilizing the church members to implement a new program for which the pastor has already done the visioning and planning. Such consultation projects are difficult because the laity often resent being left out of the planning process and feel little investment in the project. Laypersons may also want to focus their energies on an entirely different issue than the one addressed in the program proposal.

Strategies emerging through the consultants' work with churches in resource-diminished situations include at least six possibilities.

1. Investing significant time in marketing the consultation services and in developing consultation relationships with those churches. A congregation may need to hear about consultation several times before such a relationship seems appropriate or useful.

2. Meeting the short-term needs of a congregation by responding to requests for assistance with specific activities or events, i.e., Sunday School enhancement, a planning retreat, or leadership training. These activities are usually related to the nurture ministries of the congregation and provide opportunities for church groups to become comfortable working with the consultant.

3. Incorporating the broader perspective on the needs of children and the church's potential for ministry with families as part of these less-typical presentations or short-term consultations provided to congregations. The specific content for the event may be spiritual growth; the consultant helps people consider how their faith relates to community issues.

4. Providing assistance in developing grant proposals and researching fundraising resources, such as a denominational fund for new and emerging ministries or a community-wide charitable organization, like the United Way.

5. Helping local church groups resolve conflicts about which needs they should address first. The pastor may be concerned about developing outreach ministries while the education committee is worried about recruiting Sunday School teachers. The consultant can help groups understand that these concerns are often components of a broader issue on which they have agreement. Then, the church can develop a plan that incorporates both short-term and long-term goals.

6. Recruiting seminary students to work in the churches and fulfill some of the staff responsibilities often carried out by volunteers in other churches.

Evaluation and Research

The Church/Community Consultation Services is also concerned about the long-term evaluation of the services provided to churches. Project-by-project evaluation constitutes one of the stages of the consultation process, but ChildServ has not yet developed a review tool that would generate systematic data. Questions for which ChildServ needs more information include: How many children and families receive services as a result of the program developed with the support and facilitation of the Consultation Service? How effective are these services? How stable are programs offered by local churches? What particular management issues surface when the consultant is no longer working with a group in the church? What impact did the consultation process have on the overall mission and ministry of the congregation? What kind of after-care services would be useful to support the continuation of local church programs? What are other collaboration models that may help congregations serve children and families in their communities?

Other Consultation Models

Other church-related agencies are collaborating with congregations to develop services to children and families and are listed at the end of this chapter. Through its Education and Consultation Outreach Department, Deaconess Children's Services in the state of Washington consults with local churches on a wide range of children's issues, offers workshops on parenting issues, and is organizing a state-wide network of child advocates in local churches. Barnardo's Church and Community Project in Glasgow, Scotland, focuses its consultation services specifically on congregations in resource-diminished neighborhoods and usually works with adolescent issues. Fund raising comprises one of the phases of this agency's services, and its consultation usually engages a cluster of churches in the specific project. The Children's Home, Inc., in Winston-Salem, North Carolina, implemented its consultation program in 1988 with most of its work focusing on child care ministries in local churches and parenting workshops as a strategy for prevention services. One Church, One Child in Illinois is a collaborative project of black churches and the Department of Children and Family Services designed to promote adoptions of black children among members of black congregations throughout the state.

The Church/Community Consultation Services of ChildServ is a unique service of a child welfare agency to local churches and communities. Its intent and practice is to work with local churches in developing ministries to children and to involve more people in meeting the needs of children and families through service and advocacy.

Local churches with their myriad of gifts and resources and their many connections in the communities are well-suited to ministries of nurture, support, and intervention among families. Church-related agencies have knowledge in children's issues and expertise in program development required to facilitate a congregation's focusing its concerns and embarking on a new ministry to children and families. Through collaboration, congregations and agencies can provide significant services to community children and families.

References

Carlson, Rick. 1980. *A handbook for the child advocate.* Park Ridge, Ill.: United Voices for Children.

Fenhagen, James C. 1977. *Mutual ministry: New vitality for the local church.* New York: The Seabury Press.

Flanagan, Joan. 1981. *The successful volunteer organization: Getting started and getting results in nonprofit, charitable grass roots, and community groups.* Chicago: Contemporary Books, Inc.

Freeman, Margery. 1986. *Called to act: Stories of child care advocacy in our churches.* New York: All Union Press.

Freeman, Margery, ed. 1987. *Helping churches mind the children: A guide for church-housed child day care programs.* New York: National Council of the Churches of Christ in the United States of America.

General Board of Discipleship of the United Methodist Church. 1989. *Guidelines for leading your church 1989–1992: Family ministries.* Nashville: Abingdon Press.

Heusser, D.B. 1980. *Helping church workers succeed: The enlistment and support of volunteers.* Valley Forge, Penn.: Judson Press.

Kent, Virginia Reese. 1985. *We can break the cycle of child abuse: An adult study.* Nashville: Discipleship Resources.

Miller, Kenneth R., and Mary Elizabeth Wilson. 1985. *The church that cares: Identifying and responding to needs in your community.* Valley Forge, Penn.: Judson Press.

Schaller, Lyle E. 1971. *Parish planning: How to get things done in your church.* Nashville: Abingdon Press.

Schur, Janet L., and Paul V. Smith. 1980. *Where do you look? Whom do you ask? How do you know?* Washington: Children's Defense Fund.

Sheek, G. William 1985. *The word on families: A biblical guide to family well-being.* Nashville: Abingdon Press.

Stockwell, Clinton E. 1985. *Urban research project: A handbook for urban ministry.* Chicago: Midwest Baptist Conference.

Wilson, Marlene. 1983. *How to mobilize church volunteers.* Minneapolis: Augsburg Publishing House.

Church Consultation Models

Barnardo's
Church and Community Project
c/o Jordanhill College of Education
76 Southbrae Drive
Glasgow G13 1PP Scotland

ChildServ
Church/Community Consultation Services
1580 N. Northwest Highway
Park Ridge, IL 60068

Deaconess Children's Services
Education and Consultation Outreach
4708 Dogwood Drive
Everett, WA 98203

One Church, One Child
Department of Children and Family Services
100 West Randolph
Chicago, IL 60601

The Children's Home, Inc.
Outreach Program: Local Church Child Care
1001 Reynolda Road
Winston-Salem, NC 27104

10

Building Multigenerational Support Networks

Diane L. Pancoast and Kathy A. Bobula

Every morning at 9:00 the children begin their morning vigil at the window of the day care center. They are watching for Grandma Mary to arrive as she has for over eight years. In the next classroom Grandma Lois is already on the spot. A great conversationalist, she keeps tabs on the five other grandmas in the building, greets everyone by name, and helps the student teachers plan and carry out activities.

In the early-intervention P.R.I.D.E. program for infants and toddlers with Down's syndrome, Grandma Martha worked with the children and parents until her death this winter. In fact, it was the staff of the program who noticed her sudden loss of ability and notified her family, as they had often done in the past whenever there was any concern about her health or welfare.

Bill, a teen-ager, participated in a program which provided chore services for isolated elderly persons. He was encouraged to develop a relationship as well as perform needed jobs. He was surprised to discover that he and his "client" were both skiing enthusiasts. The fourteen-year-old and the woman past ninety enjoyed talking about the sport, as it was in the early days and as it is now, and the ski resorts they had been to.

Janine, another teen-ager, has developed a relationship with two older women through the same program. Both women were experiencing a number of physical and family-related problems. One of the women was very depressed and pessimistic while the other seemed to meet her problems with fortitude and did not let them get her down. Janine decided that she wanted to be like the positive

DIANE L. PANCOAST, M.S.W., Ph.D., is a consultant and trainer on informal social support systems. A former professor at the Portland State School of Social Work (Ore.), Dr. Pancoast has authored and coauthored books and articles on social support and natural helping networks. KATHY A. BOBULA, M.S., is a professor and the coordinator of early childhood education at Clark College, Vancouver, Washington. She is currently a doctoral student in the School of Urban Affairs, Portland State University.

woman when she got older and that she could start now to develop the attitudes that would contribute to good mental health in old age.[1]

These are four examples of relationships created by cross-age programs, programs which intentionally mix persons of different ages. Although the benefits may be originally intended to flow in one direction, these examples show that all participants can benefit, often in ways that were not anticipated by anyone.

What Are Cross-Age Programs?

For the purposes of this chapter, we are defining cross-age programs as those that involve the interaction of at least two age groups for their *mutual* benefit. These age groups might be linked together programatically: very young children, school-aged children, teen-agers, single young adults, families with young children, middle-aged folk and families, active retired persons (the young-old), and the frail elderly. So far, for reasons that will be discussed later, relatively few programs have attempted to meet the mutual needs of two or more of these groups by planning activities that involve several generations. Such programs are badly needed in our society, and churches are in an excellent position to provide them.

The most extensive development of cross-age programing has occurred between the very old and the very young. In these programs, retired, older persons help young children, and older children help frail, elderly people. These are often described as intergenerational programs, defined as "human contacts, formal or informal, between members of different generations who are about thirty years apart in age" (Cohon 1985). This definition is in accordance with the accepted notion of a generation as the length of time separating parent and child, around thirty years. Actually, however, most programs described in the intergenerational literature involve contacts between adults and children who are at least two generations apart. Also, while Cohon includes informal contacts, these are envisioned as occurring in programs which have intentionally brought the generations together even if the specific interactions are spontaneous.

We have decided to use the more awkward-sounding term *cross-age* because we do not intend to limit the focus of this chapter only to programs for the very young and the very old. We feel that, while such links are badly needed in our society, we have become so age-segregated in our daily lives that connections between *all* generations and, indeed, between those who are only decades apart are badly needed if we are to reestablish a sense of community. In order to buck the social currents of age segregation, deliberately planned encounters, in the form of organized programs and activities, are clearly required and a number of programatic suggestions will be offered here. But, in keeping with the emphasis in other chapters on creating a general milieu in a church setting which encourages the

---

[1] The first two examples are taken from the personal experience of Kathy Bobula. The third and fourth examples are based on information in a paper by Meyerhoff, Reeves and Chapman (1986).

spontaneous development of social-support networks—truly informal contacts—we will also discuss how such a milieu can be developed which encourages the inclusion of people of all ages in informal support networks.

The Trend Toward Age Segregation

We live in an increasingly age-segregated society. It is possible for a young student or worker to go for weeks without seeing a baby or an elderly person, much less being responsible for assisting them in any way. Middle-class retired people, living in special housing, may see children only around the swimming pool for a few, carefully regulated hours. Suburban housing often produces age-homogeneous neighborhoods (Riley 1981). The rapid social change that our society is experiencing at the present time can sharpen differences between age groups and can contribute to a sense of uniqueness among members of each age group. The elderly are more likely to fear contacts with teen-agers than to welcome them. Families, too, are more likely to teach their young children to mistrust the friendly overtures of other adults than to respond to them. These restrictions are born of legitimate fears and daily examples in the media of violent attacks, but they tend to permeate relationships even between neighbors and others who might potentially become valued members of a social network.

Structural forces reinforce the psychological tendencies toward increasing segregation. As a consequence of our smaller families with few children, close in age, many children do not have older or younger siblings nor experience the more varied social networks that a wider age span brings. The uniformity extends across families. Their cousins, if they see them, are also likely to be close to them in age as are the children in the families of their parents' friends. In small families, the opportunities for intergenerational as well as cross-age contacts are diminished. As James Garbarino has noted, " . . . whether one's parents will ever become grandparents, and one's brothers and sisters uncles and aunts, depends upon one's own childbearing . . . In China, under the One Child Policy, the roles of cousin, aunt, and uncle may be eclipsed in the next generation if the policy is fully implemented" (p. 61).

Blended families provide opportunities for stepbrother and stepsister relationships as well as other kin ties. Perhaps stepparents are the new aunts and uncles and stepsiblings the new cousins. However, these relationships seem rather thin and tentative.

Obviously, people do not develop relationships with their age peers only because they are thrown together. Most people value and seek out relationships with others of about the same age because they have much in common. However, the development of strong ties among age mates or cohorts may produce double-edged consequences. On the one hand, these ties may be "beneficial to the individuals involved. Age peers have long been recognized as easing the transition from childhood to adulthood; and they may perhaps aid adjustment in old age and at other points of transition in the life course as well" (Riley 1981, 140).

Most research on the housing preferences of retired elderly indicates that older people tend to prefer age-segregated housing and, in this environment, seem to be more active, have higher morale, and greater neighborhood mobility. In addition, most parents prefer not to live with their adult children, but will accept it if forced by circumstances (Regnier 1983; Rapoport, Rapoport, and Strelitz 1980; Okraku 1987).

On the other hand, if age peers increasingly turn to each other for aid and comfort, detriments to relationships between age groups may occur with the possibility for conflict between age groups and avoidance of contact with each other. We have already mentioned how fear of victimization restricts informal contact at the neighborhood level. Many people appear to feel safer when surrounded by people of the same age and therefore much new housing is restricted to people without children or over a certain age. Retired people who can afford it move for part or all of the year to warmer parts of the country where they concentrate in neighborhoods of fellow "snow birds," leaving their home communities bereft of their lifetime of accumulated community experience and contacts.

Ironically, even as the elderly are expressing their preferences for age-segregated housing, social planners are trying to plan for "service delivery" to the home to allow more elderly to *age in place* in their own homes. As the "baby boom" generation reaches sixty-five, there will not be nearly enough age-segregated housing for seniors to meet the size of the aging population. In-home services, if they are not to be cost-prohibitive, must be supplemented by volunteers and neighbors who are able to assist with routine chores such as shopping, minor house repairs, and yard maintenance.

Policy makers are also worried that political organizations based on age, such as the American Association of Retired Persons, while advocating very successfully for benefits for their age group, may heighten antagonisms between the young and the old and create resentments among the younger wage earners who must support the benefit programs (Kingson, Hirshorn, and Harootyan n.d.).

Children, busy in activities with their age peers or confined to the house by working parents who are concerned about their safety, do not go out in the neighborhood to have informal encounters on the sidewalks or in the stores with children and adults of all ages. They miss the opportunity to interact with adults in their work roles and to exercise growing independence under the watchful eyes of people who know their parents. They have few opportunities to become acquainted with elderly people in their communities.

The institutions in which we spend our time compound the decreased opportunities for casual, cross-age contact in our families and neighborhoods. In many cases, the age range in these institutions continues to narrow. Schools went from one-room affairs to graded classrooms long ago. More recently, elementary schools have been broken up to deal more flexibly with busing requirements or changes in population so that only three or four grades are housed together. Very young children now spend much of their time in preschools, grouped closely by age. Early retirement policies and patterns of hiring and promotion have narrowed the age range at the workplace so much that some companies are beginning to establish mentoring programs in order to try to engineer relationships between older and younger employees and build cross-age contact back into the work environment.

Many of our recreational and social-service programs accelerate this trend, using age as a criterion to determine eligibility for participation. Funding sources reward this focus on a narrow age group. Obviously, different age groups have different and unique needs, but, when we organize and fund services primarily by age, we are insuring that only these unique needs are addressed. There is little incentive to develop programs which might meet the mutual needs of two or more age groups. Such programs don't fit anywhere. Workers are trained as gerontologists or child-development specialists. Facilities develop an organizational climate that subtly discourages all but a narrow age range from participating. The active, retired people that use a senior center may make it clear that older, frailer elderly persons are not welcome. Attending a program for teen-agers may be "cool" for twelve- and thirteen-year-olds and out of the question for fifteen-year-olds.

Because of these trends and forces we now have a society in which few institutions offer the opportunity for a broad range of participation. The church is one of the major ones which still welcomes people of all ages. Although many of its activities are age-segregated, they take place in a common facility, under the aegis of persons who are not narrowly trained specialists, and under a general rubric of serving the needs of people of all ages. Baptism and confirmation are two rituals which specifically involve the acceptance of responsibility of one generation for another. Informal mingling at many church-sponsored events provides opportunities for spontaneous cross-age contacts. Specific programs can also be implemented to enhance these relationships.

Advantages of Cross-age Contact

Social impoverishment results from a lack of contact with different age groups in at least the following ways:

Expression of Caring

Anyone who has watched little boys and girls playing with their baby dolls or teddy bears knows that children attempt to rehearse caregiving responsibilities. But playing is not enough. They also need to see role models of older children and adults engaged in caring activities; as well, they need opportunities to practice caregiving skills themselves in real-life situations. Children who share a home with frail, elderly relatives or are in frequent contact with much older persons acquire an understanding of their physical limitations—why they cannot romp and play or may not hear or see very well. They learn to make themselves useful by providing a shoulder to rest a hand on or a pair of legs to fetch things. However, it is not very common anymore for children to have these experiences in their own homes. Likewise, they have to attend baby-sitting classes to learn how to care for infants because they do not observe their mothers or other relatives caring for small children.

Caregiving opportunities offer the satisfaction of making another person happier or more comfortable, and they also give a realistic appraisal of the burdens and sacrifices involved. Teen-agers who have had to care for small children may be less eager to take on parental responsibilities at a very young age. The great reluctance of some elderly people to "be a burden" on their children may stem from experiences they had or saw their parents have of caring at home for an elderly relative without any supportive services.

It was common in traditional, agrarian societies for the older people to take care of young children while the younger adults were engaged in productive work. In some societies, such as China, this pattern has persisted in spite of urbanization and modernization. This gives the elderly a vital role in the family. Grandparents and grandchildren often feel close bonds that are different from those between parent and child.

Opportunities for grandparents to feel useful or to establish bonds with their grandchildren are less common in modern society. Although "Dear Abby" frequently runs letters from grandparents who do not want to be tied down or taken advantage of by their grown children as baby-sitters, one suspects that many other grandparents would love to be needed by their children in this way and thereby be respected by their grandchildren as important caregivers. And if their own children are far away, they might welcome invitations to develop fictive-kin relationships, *adopting* an almost grandchild in the family of a friend or neighboring household.

The Foster Grandparent program, for example, is highly successful at formalizing this adoption process. Funded by the federal government, it pays low-income elderly a modest wage for volunteering in a program for children, including children with special needs up to and beyond the age of twenty-one. The sole responsibility of the foster grandparent is to give tender, loving care to a child who is in special need of individual attention on an ongoing basis. This program has proven extremely beneficial for children, foster grandparents, and program staff and teachers as well (Rich and Baum 1984; Saltz 1985). Young and middle-aged adults, too, may be looking for opportunities to practice caregiving skills before becoming parents or in anticipation of having eventually to care for an elderly parent.

It is important for the whole society that caregiving be seen as a meaningful, intrinsically satisfying, and socially esteemed activity. We will always need caregivers, both paid and unpaid. We have recently experienced a period in which such skills have been devalued in favor of self-fulfillment and the pursuit of lucrative careers in business and the professions, increasingly for women as well as men. Health-care workers, child-care workers, and teachers are beginning to be in short supply. Ideally, caregiving should not be an imposed burden, shouldered by one who feels resentful and trapped in the role. But many people in today's world are not being given the opportunity to explore such roles to discover whether or not they would find them satisfying.

Continuity

Margaret Mead has said, "The continuity of all cultures depends on the living presence of at least three generations" (quoted in Seefeldt 1985, 30). One needs to learn how to be a child, a parent, and an elder in a particular cultural context. One generation learns by interacting with the others as well as by interacting with age mates. If one generation is missing, the cultural context is not complete and cultural values and practices are not likely to be expressed or continued.

The presence of other generations is deeply reassuring, especially in troubled and rapidly changing times. Older people gain a sense of having lived a meaningful life when they see that younger generations are profiting from what they have learned and accomplished. Through close acquaintance, they can feel that younger generations are not so different from them instead of feeling estranged and displaced.

Children can learn about history by hearing about the way it has affected the lives of those around them. They may take comfort in knowing that others have survived crises and disasters. Perhaps the fears of nuclear war that are said to haunt today's children are, in part, a projection outward of their internal sense of dislocation and lack of personal knowledge of older people who have coped with wars, depressions, and personal tragedies. It may be reassuring to a teen-ager who is very uncertain of what his or her future holds to hear the life story of an elderly person who immigrated, held many jobs, or changed careers several times.

Contacts with other generations also help us visualize the future. We are concerned about what our society will be like in the years to come because we want our children and grandchildren to have good lives. This interest in the future is less likely to be felt by someone who cannot visualize it in terms of the impact of events on young people they know and care about.

Values

Habits of the Heart (Bellah et al. 1985) describes and analyzes the pervasive sense of emptiness that seems to lie at the end of the road for many Americans who thought they were pursuing the good life. The authors note that the history of our country has been one of increasing separation and individuation. They ask, "How can we find again a sense of meaning and coherence in communal life?" The authors further point out that our common identity as a people rests on "communities of memory" based on republican and biblical traditions. Far from enforcing narrow conformity, these traditions provide the collective identity that allows for a pluralistic society that nonetheless strives for the common good.

Traditions and collective memories cannot be passed along solely through institutions such as schools, churches, and the media. Intergenerational contacts provide the opportunity to make them live. The young need to hear from the old about the struggles of an earlier time—hardships in the old country or on the farm, labor disputes, civil rights, participation in the armed forces. They need to be able to challenge the decisions and actions of their elders in order to define for themselves their own values.

The other powerful way to pass along values is by example. Children and youth need to see older people participating responsibly in their social roles. They need to see adults making hard moral choices and dealing with the consequences. Television situation comedies are full of examples of adults and children dealing with everyday crises, and children are fascinated by them. But these playlets cannot have as great an impact as being involved with adults they care about who are deciding how to act in the world.

Cross-age contacts can benefit all participants and the society in general by giving people opportunities and practice in giving care and being cared for, by providing reassurance of the continuity of life, and by helping to define and inculcate values. There are also economic benefits to be obtained by meeting the needs of two or more groups at the same time.

Economic Benefits

Meeting mutual needs uses program resources efficiently. For instance, the professional can serve two groups at once, and the use of expensive space or equipment can be maximized. Moreover, the program can be built on the contributions that each group has to make to the other. The professional can be a facilitator rather than a direct provider, a role which is usually more time-consuming and can address the needs of fewer persons. For example, one program neatly meets the needs of three age groups by having retired craftsmen teach home-repair skills to teen-agers who then practice these skills by doing repairs for the frail elderly (Murphey 1984). The teen-agers could have been taught by professionals or the retirees could have done the repairs themselves, but the chosen approach uses the fewest paid resources while meeting the most needs.

This approach also makes optimal use of the diverse social networks that the participants bring. In the previous example, the retired craftsman might know of a paid job for a teen-age protégé through his network of former workmates, or the teen-ager might have a friend who could perform regular chores for the elderly person.

Specialized institutions may be able to do a good deal more with just a little more money if they also serve another age group. For example, a high school decided that it could respond to a community need for a senior center by offering an unused room in the school. The seniors benefit from the library, shop, and athletic facilities. They also take high school classes, providing many opportunities for role modeling and forming friendships with high school students. In addition, the seniors offer help with homework and teach craft classes. Some nursing homes have begun to offer day care for young children on the same premises, taking advantage of the skilled staff and well-appointed facility (Fogel 1985). Elderly residents can participate if they want to and are at least afforded the opportunity to see and hear young children. Sometimes the families of the day care children "adopt" one of the elderly residents as a grandparent.

Some churches might want to consider whether such uses are possible in nursing homes, day care centers, schools, or other facilities or programs that they may sponsor. The rest of this chapter will focus on ideas for cross-age programing that would be possible in the ordinary church setting.

Programing Along an Age Continuum

If churches begin to think intergenerationally and review their programs and activities systematically to see whether they provide opportunities and encouragement for intergenerational contact, they will probably see that existing programs can be modified in many ways to increase such contacts. Also, many new program ideas could be adapted to the needs of a specific congregation.

First, the congregation might need to be sensitized to the importance of cross-age contacts. Then it might be useful for a church worker or committee to review existing programs to see how much cross-age contact is provided and whether or not there is potential for increasing it. The decision of whether or not to involve two or more age groups should be based on the needs the program is trying to meet.

Specific needs or requirements of particular age groups justify age-segregated programs. Some Sunday School activities, for example, may be designed for three- or four-year-olds while others are intended to appeal to preteens. A youth choir might be another example.

In other cases, the needs of two or more age groups might dovetail. Ten-year-olds might profit by an opportunity to read or teach songs to younger children. Some older persons in the congregation whose grandchildren live far away would enjoy working with teen-agers on cooking, gardening, or maintenance projects around the church.

Finally, if the activities are intended to meet universal needs for fellowship or worship, they may be open to a wide variety of age groups. Churches are quite used to providing such opportunities in the form of potlucks, retreats, worship services, and other gatherings of the whole community.

While this breakdown might seem simple and obvious, it is possible that a church which analyzed its programs in this way would find that, through the passage of time or the development of unspoken understandings, activities which could meet universal or matched needs have become rather narrowly age-segregated. Sunday School teachers may have grown comfortable being responsible for one age group and do not spend time planning joint activities with other classes. Certain activities, intended to be universal, may be organized in such a way that some age groups cannot participate in them. In chapter 11, Ellor and Tobin describe a Bible study class that was located in church in a place that was inaccessible to handicapped, elderly congregants. Planners of church retreats may think they have taken the needs of young children into consideration if day care is provided, but they may not plan any activities in which they can participate with everyone else.

Even activities which were originally intended to meet the needs of a specific age group may have evolved over time to the point where they no longer fulfill their original purpose. A choir for young adults may have "aged in place" so that now the members are middle-aged. There is nothing wrong with having a middle-aged choir, but the church is fooling itself if it thinks that it still has one for young adults.

Undertaking an assessment of existing programs is likely to suggest many ways in which these programs can be revitalized by addressing once again the needs of the age groups for which they were originally intended, by reaching out to meet the needs of another age group, or by designing them so it is truly feasible for all to participate.

Examples of Cross-age Programs

In addition to modifying existing programs and traditional activities, churches can also increase their cross-age programing by importing and adapting methods which have been successfully implemented in other settings. The handbooks cited in the bibliography at the end of this book provide a wealth of examples, but this short list offers a number of starting points:

1. A church-run preschool can serve as a support, resource, and catalyst for family day care provided by parents in the neighborhood. The preschool can be a source of enrichment for the children in family day care as well as give respite to the parents who provide day care in their homes. Teachers in the preschool can recruit new home caregivers from the congregation and other contacts in the neighborhood and act as matchmakers between parents needing day care and family day care providers.

2. Day care for children and the elderly can be combined, especially for special needs or niches, such as before- or after-school care, summer care, and infant care. A church-based preschool might consider looking after an elderly person for several hours to give the primary caretaker a break.

3. Churches could become homework centers, staffed by older tutors. Many children come home to an empty house where there is no one to help them with their homework and see that they get it done. A group of older persons could offer to provide a snack and homework assistance, perhaps only a day or two a week, at the church.

4. Sunday School can be organized in "family pods" where children of different ages are clustered in "family" groups for lessons, parties, and other activities. The family idea could be extended to others in the congregation. Perhaps each family pod could have a grandparent.

5. It is fairly common for young mothers to find other young mothers with whom they can form support networks. They may be less likely to have contact with older women who have been through the experience of raising children and can provide the perspective that this brings. A church could devise a program that allowed for maternal mentoring relationships to form. Young mothers often need nurturing, as well as their children.

6. Youth-elderly service exchanges can be set up so that the elderly can get needed chores done and teen-agers can provide services and learn some skills at the same time (Meyerhoff, Reeves & Chapman 1986).

7. Isolated or single-parent families can adopt a grandparent from the congregation to include in family holidays. The Jewish Community Center in Portland, Oregon, has such a program. The younger adults and families agree to include the grandparent in holiday celebrations and to provide transportation. In exchange, they want the elderly person to pass along his or her memories and stories from the past as well as religious traditions.

8. Outings or other activities for a particular age group could be specially planned to include someone from another generation. Each child in Sunday School could invite one elderly person to a play or on a field trip. A group for seniors could include a teen-age or young adult group in a dance or picnic.

9. Many churches hold camps or retreats for the congregation. One could be planned with an intergenerational focus. Cross-age core discussion groups could meet throughout the retreat to discuss topics highlighting the different perspectives each age group could bring.

10. Oral histories of the church can be produced by youth groups who interview elderly members. Such histories are more interesting to read and to collect, if they focus on anecdotes and stories, rather than just "the facts." Teen-agers can learn how to elicit these stories.

11. Churches can sponsor folk art, cooking, craft, or music workshops or fairs where older people can teach skills to younger adults and children.

Any one of these programs could have quite far-reaching impact in helping people to get to know others of different ages. Out of the more structured contacts, people have an opportunity to add to their personal networks and ecological families.

Principles of Cross-age Programing

A successful cross-age activity that meets the needs of the participants begins slowly, without grandiose expectations, and is closely monitored so that alterations can be made. The literature on such programs suggests that following a few basic principles will help ensure success.

- The prestige and self-worth of all participants should be protected. The emphasis should be on mutual benefits. There should not be a distinction between the "doing" and the "done for."
- Program activities should be well-organized so the purpose is clear and participants do not feel they are wasting their time.
- Activities should be meaningful and produce concrete results (even though many of the benefits may be less tangible).
- Contact between persons of different ages should be personalized, intimate, and of sufficient duration to allow relationships to form.

Program Design Considerations

Many cross-age programs have found that the facilitator role is crucial. There should be one person, volunteer or paid, who is both highly committed to the purpose of the program and flexible as to means. If one approach to developing cross-age relationships is not working, the facilitator must be willing to try something else.

Programs work best when they are built on natural connections of acquaintance, proximity, or interaction at church. These relationships will be easier to sustain because they are likely to contain an element of duty or obligation and because it will be easy for the participants to have contact with one another. Many cross-age programs are more a matter of deepening and enriching relationships rather than creating new ones.

Program developers cannot assume that participants have the necessary social or helping skills. An older person may have been a successful parent but may not have the skills to teach small children or know how discipline situations are usually handled in a preschool. A teen-ager who has volunteered to do yard work may not know a weed from a flower. A cross-age program must be prepared to provide training. In some cases, this training may be the most valuable part of the program to the participants.

It is not necessary to set goals too high. Long-term relationships are not likely to result from very many of the contacts. However, one good experience could result in a basic attitude change for a participant which would have many ramifications outside the program.

Next Steps

While cross-age programs are still not common and encouragement for them, in the form of funding, training, and program guidelines, is only beginning to coalesce, a number of resources are available to anyone who is looking for ideas. We have provided an introduction to them in Appendix 3. New cross-age programs are an effective way of highlighting an issue and recruiting new energy, but some of the most effective cross-age relationships can be fostered informally in the daily interactions in a church setting.

References

Bellah, R. N. et al. 1985. *Habits of the heart.* New York: Harper and Row.

Cohon, J. D. 1985. Survey research as the initial step in developing intergenerational projects. In *Growing together: An intergenerational sourcebook*, eds. K. A. Struntz and S. Reville. Washington: American Association of Retired Persons.

Fogel, L. 1985. Keeping in step with the very young and the very old. In *Growing together: An intergenerational sourcebook*, eds. K. A. Struntz and S. Reville. Washington: American Association of Retired Persons.

Garbarino, James. 1988. *The future as if it really mattered.* Longmont, Colo.: Bookmakers Guild, Inc.

Kingson, E. R., B. A. Hirshorn, and L. K. Harootyan. n.d. *The common stake: The interdependence of generations.* Washington: The Gerontological Society of America.

Meyerhoff, J., L. Reeves, and N. Chapman. 1986. Elderly-youth exchange: Problems and prospects. Paper presented at the meetings of the Gerontological Society of America, Chicago.

Murphey, M. B. 1984. *A guide to intergenerational programs.* Washington: National Association of State Units on Aging.

Okraku, I. O. 1987. Age and attitudes toward multigenerational residence, 1973 to 1983. *Journal of Gerontology* 42:280–87.

Rapoport, R., R. N. Rapoport, and Z. Strelitz. 1980. *Fathers, mothers and society: Perspectives on parenting.* New York: Vintage Books.

Regnier, V. 1983. Housing and environment. In *Aging: Scientific perspectives and social issues.* 2d ed., eds. Woodruff and Birren. Monterey, Calif.: Brooks/Cole.

Rich, B. M. and M. Baum. 1984. *The aging: A guide to public policy.* Pittsburg, Pa.: University of Pittsburg Press.

Riley, M. 1981. Social gerontology and the age stratification of society. In *Aging in America: Readings in social gerontology.* 2d ed., eds. C. S. Kart and B. B. Manard. Sherman Oaks, Calif.: Alfred Publishing.

Saltz, R. 1985. We help each other: The U. S. foster grandparent program. In *Growing together: An intergenerational sourcebook,* eds. K. A. Struntz and S. Reville. Washington: American Association of Retired Persons.

Seefeldt, C. 1985. The question of contact. In *Growing together: An intergenerational sourcebook,* eds. K. A. Struntz and S. Reville. Washington: American Association of Retired Persons.

11

Serving the Older Person: The Church's Role

James W. Ellor and Sheldon S. Tobin

"You shall rise up before the hoary head, and honor the face of an old man, and you shall fear your God: I am the Lord"

(Lev. 19:32).

Churches and synagogues have been answering requests for help from members of their communities for thousands of years. One of the significant influences on the response of churches has been the availability of assistance from secular governments. Tobriner (1985) notes that in sixteenth-century England, almshouses were begun as extensions of monastic service. However, later in that era, under the influence of shifting priorities of the church and the introduction of the "poor laws," administration of these facilities moved to secular government. These institutions primarily served people over fifty; they are some of the earliest models of housing for the elderly.

This century has seen a similar transition in the United States. Before the 1930s, churches and religious groups were the primary providers of services for the poor and elderly. Since President Roosevelt's New Deal and President Johnson's Great Society, federal legislation has taken up some of the gap in services. The role of the church has changed in the last fifty years. However, it is far from obsolete. Most churches remain actively involved in serving older adults. This chapter will examine family ministries in the context of serving seniors within

JAMES W. ELLOR, M.A., D.Min., is an associate professor in the Department of Human Services at National-Louis University, Lombard, Illinois. Currently he is cochairperson of the editorial board and chair elect of the steering committee of the Forum on Religion and Aging of the American Society on Aging. SHELDON S. TOBIN, Ph.D., is director of Ringel Institute of Gerontology and professor in the School of Social Welfare at the State University of New York-Albany. Formerly the editor of *The Gerontologist*, he authored (with James Ellor and Susan Anderson-Ray) *Enabling the Elderly: Religious Institutions with the Community Service System.*

congregational and community settings. One approach, "The Community Advocacy Model," will be presented as a strategy that has been tested and is available for churches wishing to address the needs of seniors.

Lucy Steinitz (1981), in her study of all the churches and synagogues in one suburban community, found that some churches function as surrogate family for their older members. The literature is unclear, however, regarding how to characterize churches as family surrogates, whether to refer to the congregation as a whole or to specific functions assumed by clergy and congregants. No matter how it is conceived, churches do indeed assume family roles with older adults. For example, some pastors become legal guardians for individual older members. Churches also supply home support services for older adults in many communities. At least in these instances, the church has become a surrogate family to provide for its older members.

Yet, older adults, particularly those who are single, may be difficult to conceptualize within the context of a family ministry. For example, Mrs. Smith, a founding member of the congregation, is now widowed and alone. Her family has moved out of town and she has developed high blood pressure and is hard of hearing. Is she a single adult? Is she a part of a family that simply is not living in the local community? In many churches, even if adult children live in the community, the seniors will be counted separately as a family of one.

Garland (1985) has noted that the classical sociological definition of families has emphasized *physical dependence* on a specific group of persons who are genetically linked. In chapter 1, however, she discusses an alternative approach in which a family is defined by the *functional linkage* of its members rather than their genetic or physical connection. For those seniors whose families no longer live in the local community, the church may become a "functional" family unit. For such persons, the church provides a connection to tradition, a supportive group of persons, and facilitates meaning in their lives.

Before 1930, churches were frequently the only possible providers of human services in many communities. However, in the current environment of social services, the basic programs and support systems that are necessary for the individual to live and survive are available in most communities. The congregation's response to human needs would now seem to be motivated by a sense of serving older adults as members of the church family. Churches provide many of the services that are provided by extended family members. Transportation to the doctor, meals, visitation, and even assistance in selecting a nursing home are all tasks that churches assume to assist members of the congregation. At times, churches recognize that a service is needed by more than a few seniors and may elect to formalize the service. However, a majority of activities that churches are engaged in to support the elderly are more of an informal nature. For example, Mrs. Smith needs a ride to the doctor. She calls Reverend Jones who contacts Mr. Brown who gives Mrs. Smith a ride. Case records are not kept and transportation services are not advertised in the church bulletin as being available. Yet, parishioners know that they can count on their church family for help when it is needed.

The Elderly in the Church

Seniors are important to the church and the church is important to seniors. In a recent survey, two thousand people were asked a series of questions about their religious faith (Better Homes 1988). The results of this study are consistent with earlier studies by Louis Harris (Harris and Associates 1975) and numerous other studies. When asked, "Are you involved in spiritual/religious matters primarily?" 75 percent of those over the age of 55 noted involvement for "moral guidance and strength"; 74 percent responded, "to deal with everyday life." Studies have repeatedly shown that persons over the age of 55 are the most likely, when compared to other age groups, to attend church or synagogue on a regular basis and most likely to seek support from their faith in times of crisis (Tobin et al. 1986).[1]

In a study of the alumni of a specific seminary related to the United Church of Christ, Ellor and Coates (1986) found that churches in this sample reported that 31 percent of their members were over the age of 65. Of this group, an average of 34 percent of the congregation was found to be above age 65 in the churches served by only one paid staff member while in the larger churches served by a multiple staff, 25 percent of the congregation was of senior-citizen age.

In the past ten years, most churches have found that they have larger percentages of seniors and more human needs to be concerned about. Seniors have become accustomed to being able to turn to the church at times of need. As one pastor said, "We do not think of ourselves as a social service agency. We think of ourselves as a family." However, as church families experience more elderly with needs, a more formal or systematic approach to their needs is necessary.

Roles and Services of Churches

Churches provide services to persons who request assistance. These services usually are not formal social work services but can be conceptualized into four groups:

- religious programs: Bible studies, worship services, etc.
- pastoral programs: pastoral counseling, homebound visitation
- the church as host: rental of church property for functions benefiting the elderly
- the church as service provider: creation and running of a formal social service agency (Ellor, Anderson-Ray and Tobin 1986)

This study and others have suggested that churches tend to develop programs and services to fill gaps. Thus if they identify a need that is not fulfilled, they will create a program in response. We have also observed that the more formal the service (such as counseling services or emergency shelter for children), the more likely the church is to develop this resource as an independent entity from the church and eventually spin it off to complete independence. A gap may be defined

---

[1] For a review of this material see, Tobin, S.S., J.W. Ellor, S.M. Anderson-Ray, *Enabling the Elderly* (New York: State University of New York Press, 1986).

differently by various groups. An individual congregation may conceive of a gap as the philosophy and theology behind the program and not just the lack of a specific service. Thus a Bible study previously existing in a given community does not mean that a second one will not be developed based on an alternative theology. In other cases, gap filling refers to the provision of services where previously no service exists.

Values for Program Development

Some of the considerations that are important in developing programs for working with seniors are (1) a wholistic approach, (2) advocacy, (3) involving seniors in every aspect of planning, and (4) networking with other congregations and local social services agencies.

A wholistic approach

As a church considers the needs of older adults, it should understand that seniors are more likely to have multiple chronic illnesses as well as a variety of acute infirmities that plague other age groups. But older adults not only have concerns for their physical well-being. They also have emotional and social needs which often are inseparable from physical needs. For example, although Alzheimer's disease does not afflict all older people, fear of the disease is common among seniors.

Concurrently, senior adults also have significant spiritual needs. The National Interfaith Coalition on Aging noted that the "spiritual is not one dimension among many in life; rather, it permeates and gives meaning to all life." (Thorson & Cook 1980, xiii). One important contribution of such scholars as Alfred Adler and Granger Westberg (including Westberg's addition of the spiritual dimension) has been the concept that while each person has five dimensions—physical, emotional, social, intellectual, and spiritual—it is not possible to separate them into distinct areas (Tubesing 1979). Indeed, it is not advisable to try to do so. Each man or woman is a significant, whole person who is unique and should be treated with the respect that he or she deserves.

Churches must also consider programs that meet the diversity of needs of older individuals in the congregation. Thus, a church might provide transportation to help seniors see their doctors, or get to the hospital for treatment, or take part in recreational activities, counseling services, Bible studies, and other spiritually-focused programs. In most communities, transportation services, meal programs, and even counseling services can be found in local social service agencies. However, most of these agencies, if they receive funding from the government, will not provide for spiritual needs. Thus churches may be able to refer seniors to those agencies for certain services while reserving to themselves the role of dealing with the spiritual dimension of life. Where these services do not exist, or where the waiting list is so long that all who need help cannot get it, the church may choose to develop transportation and meal programs.

Advocacy

One common factor of all the various patterns of church roles is the concept that the congregation should be an advocate for its members. Coates and Ellor (1984) have noted that advocacy involves three levels of intervention in any community: (1) Intervention to meet the needs of individual clients, (2) intervention aimed at the needs of all seniors in the community, and, (3) intervention in which the church attempts to address the needs of all older people through state or federal legislation.

In each case, the church is working with a broad group with diverse needs. As the church addresses the needs of each person, the concern needs to reflect all seniors within the congregation. If the congregation can transcend the needs of individual seniors, they can gain a perspective on the needs of the elderly in the entire community. They may find that so many people need transportation services or home-delivered meals that a group approach is warranted. They may also find it is helpful to work with other churches and social agencies to provide for the needs. In other cases, the church may find that the only way to address an issue like senior abuse is to obtain legislation. They may work with other groups to promote laws to address this issue.

Involving Seniors in Every Aspect of Planning

For centuries, traditional missionary groups in local churches have worked to share the Christian faith with people in other lands. These efforts have made significant contributions to the church's mission worldwide.

However, such a method—people in one country planning something for people in a different country—is not a useful one for working with older adults in local congregations. Too often the elderly are perceived as a frail group of individuals for whom ministries are needed. Clingan (1980) notes that when working with older adults, we should work *with* them to identify their needs and formulate ministry. Seniors should be involved in planning any ministry that benefits older adults. A few individuals cannot know the opinions or needs of all seniors. Thus, surveys of seniors and their families are important avenues of involvement of the elderly in ministry.

Networking with Other Congregations and
Local Social Service Agencies

In today's service environment, individual congregations are never alone in their concern for older adults. Since the Social Security and Older Americans acts, the federal government has been extremely involved in providing services to elderly Americans. The entire United States has been partitioned into state and area agencies on aging. These are governmental agencies that channel funding and provide programs. They vary in effectiveness and availability in any given community, however, they should be consulted and invited to be involved in at least an advisory capacity in any program of ministry with the aged. These agencies can be of great help to congregations in understanding the gaps that exist in services and what work can be most effective.

Churches may also wish to establish or work with an existing interfaith network of services for the aged. These community networks are often available to help individual congregations. They can help the congregation reach out to more persons in need and expand the effectiveness of their work. Lewis (1989), in her study with Msgr. Fahey, found that "community connectedness"—an interreligious component—is an element in successful programing.

The Community Advocacy Model

Older adults frequently present unique challenges to family ministries within a congregation. Most churches have some type of visitation ministry to the homebound or hospitalized elderly, while some congregations have also developed Bible studies and other programs for older members. Frequently, as their memberships have aged, clubs and groups not originally designed for older adults have evolved into senior-adult services. Less common is the church that has developed an intentional ministry with older adults. The Community Advocacy Model provides such an approach. This model has four steps:

1. Bring together a planning group to steer the ministry's development.
2. Develop ways to assess the needs and concerns of seniors within the congregation and community.
3. Based on the needs-assessment, design the approach to ministry.
4. Evaluate the program periodically to determine its effectiveness.

Getting started with any program that addresses needs begins with the individual or a group of persons who are aware of a need. Unfortunately, these "sparks of interest" do not always get past a modest inquiry. In a recent survey of six communities, the authors found two problems in the initiation of services in churches: *insufficient need* to warrant response and *a lack of lay leadership*. Many churches, particularly small churches under two hundred members, are aware of the needs of a few members but do not feel they have the resources to respond. For example, members in a small Protestant church were aware of two couples who were struggling with the problems of older family members afflicted with Alzheimer's disease. One member suggested a family caregivers' support group. Upon consideration, this was rejected because there did not seem to be enough congregants to warrant constituting a group. An interfaith effort would have been perfectly appropriate. While any individual church may have only one or two families who need the services a group could provide, other neighborhood churches and temples would surely supply enough to justify the organizing of a group. In this way, a facilitator may also be found. The National Federation of Interfaith Caregivers,[2] founded by a network of Interfaith Caregiver groups with

---

[2] National Federation of Interfaith Caregivers, Inc., P.O. Box 1929, Kingston, New York 12401, (914) 331-1198.

funding by the Robert Wood Johnston Foundation, has offered numerous exam-ples of people working together in a community to address the needs of seniors.

In another instance, a survey revealed a very young church with few seniors, none of whom seemed to need anything that the church could provide. In this case the problem was with the survey, which was directed only at seniors. When this congregation did a broader survey of general needs, they found a significant group of middle-aged persons—adult children—who were trying to cope with the concerns of their elderly parents. In this case, the seniors in need were not members of the church and often did not live in the same state as the church members. However, the adult children did need support and assistance.

Leadership is also a matter of concern in most congregations. The pastor and staff cannot do everything in the average church. Lay leaders, particularly leaders with specific expertise, are a precious commodity. Some congregations are fortu-nate enough to have a ready supply of natural leaders. Most, however, need to nurture and develop leadership among the members. Rewarding these persons for their efforts, supporting them when they are confused, and facilitating their growth through workshops and reading material are methods that have been found to be successful.

The first step in the model, then, is to bring together a planning group. If this group is from within the church, this step may not be a big one. However, it is extremely important to involve diverse groups from within the church to be sure of reaching a common understanding of goals, particularly for defining the recipi-ents of services in a manner consistent with the needs of the entire congregation.

The second step of the model entails two surveys. The first is a survey of the needs of the target group. Whether the planning committee is targeting seniors or adult children of seniors or both, input should be solicited systematically from the target population as to the needs that exist and who should provide them. Ques-tions should inform the committee about the demographic characteristics of those filling out the survey. For purposes of confidentiality, the respondents' names are generally not solicited. What is requested, usually, are age, gender, location within the community, availability of family, and availability of transportation. These questions allow the committee to compare the profile of the respondents to that of the parish or church area. This may help identify groups of people who may not have responded, such as homebound seniors. Also the committee can cross-tabulate the information to determine if specific subgroups of persons are request-ing a special type of service. Questions should also ask about the needs of seniors: Bible study, personal spiritual resources, worship, transportation, food, house-keeping, and others.

The second survey is of people who can provide for the needs that are identi-fied. One source is the formal social service agencies in the community. Local municipal or county governments in the United States, or a state office on aging, can put the committee in touch with such groups. Often, the Area Agency on Aging (A.A.A.) has already compiled a list of local social services that can be useful to the committee.

The second group is somewhat more difficult to find. These are the informal, voluntary providers of service—nurses, recreation leaders, and others who do not have any formal training. A more complete discussion of these "natural" helpers is found in chapter 13.

The third step is to determine what programs make the most sense in light of the needs and available resources. This should be done only after the formal and informal resources have been assessed and the needs of seniors have been solicited.

The fourth and final step in the model is evaluation of the program. Programs need to be assessed at six-month to one-year intervals to be sure they are providing the intended services. This can be accomplished by the planning committee. However, it is preferable to have the evaluation done by someone from outside of the planning group who can objectively examine the program.

The Community Advocacy Model can be used effectively by a single congregation or by bringing congregations together to form a network. For example, one Baptist church found in a general survey of the congregation that 60 percent of the congregation, over 200 members, were retired. This congregation had a history of a successful Sunday School and social club activities that included older adults. The church had even hired a retired minister to provide visitation for seniors in their homes. However, no one person or group was responsible for bringing together the various efforts for seniors and their families.

The pastor began by calling a meeting with the pastor of visitation, as well as the chairpersons of the women's and men's organizations and the director of adult Christian education. This group discussed the various activities currently available for older members and concluded that a single council within the congregation could monitor the available programs as well as develop new programs to address unfulfilled needs. This group developed a list of nine people who would be willing to serve on this new council.

The first activity of the new planning group was to design two surveys. The initial survey involved all the adult members of the congregation. The survey's goals were to discover the programs and services that were currently available to seniors and their families, and to determine what might be important to add to those programs. The second survey, conducted by three church members, sought to determine what social services were available in the community. This group began by contacting the local A.A.A. Then the committee contacted each agency listed in the A.A.A. directory and asked questions about the services each provided. The committee also asked the agency contact person to identify needs that were not adequately addressed by either the formal or informal (families, other religious congregations, or friends) service providers in the community.

Data from the two surveys revealed some surprising gaps.

The church was proud of numerous Bible studies that were available. Unfortunately, the Bible studies were held at night, in a library that was only accessible by way of a winding set of stairs which seniors found difficult to climb. The seniors requested more daytime Bible studies, in more accessible places.

The survey also revealed a critical need for someone to provide meals and other supportive services for those who had just returned home after hospitalization. Seniors who were on waiting lists for community agencies were of particular importance. With patients being sent home from hospitals so quickly in recent years, it was found that many seniors went home sicker than in the past. In addition, the gap between discharge and the first visit of a doctor or nurse has widened. Services that appear to be available may not be adequately funded, causing long waits for the infirm.

The committee then worked with the Sunday School director to schedule a Bible study during the daytime, in an accessible location. They also developed a short-term home help committee led by a retired nurse who was able to help the older church members with home services. She organized groups to bring meals and set up a system to ensure the availability of appropriate community agencies for each senior.

In the process of planning this project, the committee found that the church needed to provide telephone contact with seniors. They were able to find homebound seniors who were willing to do some telephoning and they also found that those served by the program could be successfully encouraged to become partners of the committee in providing services after they had recovered from their own acute illnesses. Thus this church program not only responded to the needs of its senior members; it did so in such a way that social networks were formed and supported.

In a second example, a small evangelical congregation found that four or five members were concerned about their older parents. This church was in a community of predominantly older people. When the pastor talked to other clergy in the community, he found that members in their congregations had similar concerns. With this information he formed a committee representing four of the local churches which created a support group for adult children of older adults. From this beginning, the committee engaged in a more formal process of needs evaluation and designed an entire network of services to be provided by the various congregations.

The Community Advocacy Model helps churches listen to the elderly and involve them in the seniors ministry. Churches work with other congregations as well as local social services and their work is constantly examined for quality and sensitivity to changing conditions.

The Community Advocacy Model provides an approach that can be adapted by any church to address the needs of seniors. If used successfully, four kinds of service programs can be developed: religious, pastoral, programs in which the church serves as host, and those in which the church is the direct service provider (Tobin, Ellor, and Anderson-Ray 1986). In turn, Msgr. Fahey's (1988) four roles can be fulfilled: the removal of barriers, enrichment of life, networking for the frail, and serving the disabled. Success, however, will only be assured by including *a wholistic approach*, incorporating *advocacy* into programing, *involving seniors* in every aspect of planning, and *networking with other congregations* as well as local social service agencies. Progress will be made if older adults are perceived as an important, essential part of the congregational family and, in turn, if the church as extended or surrogate family provides support for the wholeness of each of its elderly congregants.

References

Clingan, D. F. 1980. *Aging persons in the community of faith.* St. Louis: Christian Board of Publications.

Coates, R. B., and J. W. Ellor. 1984. Enhancing the church as service provider to the elderly through curriculum development. Manuscript.

Ellor, J. W., S. M. Anderson-Ray, and S. S. Tobin. 1983. The role of the church in services to the elderly, *Interdisciplinary Topics in Gerontology* 17:119–31.

Ellor, J. W., and R. B. Coates. 1986. Examining the role of the church in the aging network. In *The role of the church in aging,* ed. M. C. Hendrickson, 99–116. New York: The Haworth Press.

Fahey, C. May 1988. (Personal communication).

Garland, D. S. R. 1985. Family life education, family ministry, and church social work: Suggested relationships. *Social Work and Christianity* 12(2):14–25.

Harris, L., and associates. 1975. *The myth and reality of aging in America.* Washington: National Council on the Aging, Inc.

Lewis, M. A. 1989. *Religious congregations and the informal supports of the frail elderly.* New York: Third Age Center of Fordham University.

Religion, spirituality, and American families. 1988. *Better Homes and Gardens,* New York: Meredith Corp.

Steinitz, L. Y. 1981. The local church as support for the elderly. *Journal of Gerontological Social Work* 4(2):43–53.

Thorson, J. A. and T. C. Cook. 1980. *Spiritual well-being of the elderly.* Springfield, Ill.: Charles C. Thomas.

Tobin, S. S., J. W. Ellor, and S. M. Anderson-Ray. 1986. *Enabling the elderly.* New York: State University of New York Press.

Tobriner, Alice. 1985. Almshouses in sixteenth-century England: Housing for the poor elderly. *Journal of Religion and Aging* 1(4):13–41.

Tubesing, Donald A. 1979. *Wholistic health.* New York: Human Sciences Press.

12

Delivering Service in
Black Churches

Robert Joseph Taylor, Irene Luckey, and
Jacqueline Marie Smith

Throughout the history of blacks in the United States, religion and churches have been vital to the development and maintenance of black communities (Frazier 1966; Lewis 1955; Mays and Nicholson 1933; Smith 1986). It is well-known that the church in the early twentieth century was the "communication" center of the black community (DuBois 1967). At least as late as a generation ago the vast majority of blacks maintained an association with churches in their communities (Lewis 1955). It has been argued that the church in rural Southern black communities functions as a semi-involuntary communal association (Nelsen, Yokley, and Nelsen 1971).

Black churches are a unique and distinctive institution because, in addition to addressing the universal social and psychological needs of their members, they also alleviate and buffer the hardships and difficulties resulting from racial discrimination and prejudice (Roberts 1980; Jennings 1983). A recent investigation of black Americans' perceptions of the role of black churches revealed the positive and multifaceted functions of religious institutions (Taylor, Thornton, and Chatters 1987). The majority of respondents endorsed the view that the

The preparation of this manuscript was supported in part by grants from the National Institute of Mental Health, The Ford Foundation, and a First Independent Research Support and Transition (FIRST) Award (R29 AG06856), Robert Joseph Taylor, principal investigator. The authors would like to thank Linda Chatters and other members of the Program for Research on Black Americans for comments on earlier versions of this paper.
ROBERT JOSEPH TAYLOR, M.S.W., Ph.D., is assistant professor in the School of Social Work and a faculty associate at the Institute for Social Research at the University of Michigan. IRENE LUCKEY, M.A., D.S.W., is assistant professor of social welfare and a faculty associate with the Ringel Institute on Gerontology at the State University of New York-Albany. She earned the doctorate in social welfare from the City University of New York. JACQUELINE MARIE SMITH, M.A., M.S.W., Ph.D., is assistant professor at the School of Social Work at Howard University, Washington, D.C.

church has helped the condition of blacks by: (1) providing spiritual assistance, (2) exerting a sustaining and strengthening influence, (3) giving personal assistance, (4) providing guidelines for moral behavior, (5) acting as a source of unity, (6) serving as a community gathering place, and (7) being a vehicle for attaining social progress for blacks. Due to the pervasive influence of religion and churches in the lives of black Americans, churches are an ideal setting in which to provide social services.

This chapter will examine the findings of recent research on religious participation and church membership as a source of informal social support and discuss strategies churches can use to deliver services in black communities.

Characteristics of Black Churches

Major characteristics of black churches include their communal nature, denominational hegemony, and the evangelical content of worship practices. Traditional communal or folk practices characterize the religious participation and observances of black Americans. Intimate face-to-face primary group interaction characterized the religious practices of enslaved blacks (Raboteau 1980) and, more recently, the storefront churches of blacks residing in urban areas (Fauset 1944). Regardless of denominational affiliation, urban-rural setting, or regional differences, the notions of church fellowship and a sense of community have retained special significance and remained consistent themes in the life of the black church (DuBois 1967; Lincoln 1984).

One of the most significant features of the organized religious experiences of black Americans is that the organizational roots of the black church are derived principally from two denominations—Baptist and Methodist. This pattern of denominational hegemony dates back to slavery (DuBois 1967) and persists to the present day. Important intradenominational differences exist between blacks and whites in religious doctrine and in the form and content of religious service. As compared to other denominations, black Baptists and some black Methodist subdenominations manifest greater evangelical content in their form of worship. As a religious movement of the eighteenth century, evangelicalism was clearly an interdenominational effort, but Methodist and Baptist churches made relatively greater use of evangelical techniques (Bassett 1980). Evangelicalism is characterized by an emphasis on the conversion experience (i.e., being born again), religious proselytism, New Testament Bible studies, and salvation solely by faith (Bassett 1980).

Empirical studies have demonstrated an association between denomination, race, and some aspects of evangelicalism. Denominational differences in evangelicalism were noted by Glock and Stark (1967) who found that 24 percent of Congregationalists, 57 percent of Roman Catholics, and 97 percent of Southern Baptists reported high levels of evangelical religious experience. Further, racial differences in data from a 1980 Gallup Poll indicated that blacks were more likely than whites to have had a born-again experience and to encourage others to believe in Jesus Christ. Due to the fact that blacks are more likely to belong to a Baptist church than any other denomination, it is unclear as to whether the noted black-white differences in religious practices and evangelical experiences are actually based on race or denomination. The denominational hegemony of Baptists and Methodists and the evangelical content are characteristic of the religious practice of both blacks and Southerners more generally. The parallels between these two groups are not surprising considering that between 1870 and 1940 approximately 80 percent to 90 percent of the black population lived in the South and presently about 50 percent of blacks still reside there (Taylor 1986a). Because of the confounding influences of race, denomination, and region, future research into religious participation needs to disentangle these factors.

Religious Participation

Americans report a greater degree of confidence in the church than in any other formal institution. Sixty-five percent of respondents surveyed in 1979 indicated that they had a lot of confidence in the church or organized religion. In contrast, a third of respondents reported a "great deal" of confidence in business, labor unions, the Court, and Congress. Three out of four Americans characterized their religious beliefs as being "important" to them. Yet for the majority of Americans, church participation, as reflected in frequency of attendance, has declined from 1950 levels (Gallup 1981). For the average week in 1955, 49 percent of the U.S. population attended church or synagogue whereas, by 1975, only 40 percent did so (Carroll, Johnson, and Marty 1979).

In contrast, for the period 1966–1973, black Americans were the only racial group for whom rates of church attendance increased (Glenn and Gotard 1977). The General Social Surveys of the early 1970s demonstrate that black church attendance substantially exceeded that of whites. Similarly, a multivariate analysis found that controlling for the effects of age, gender, income, education, occupation, and denomination failed to alter the relationship between race and church attendance, with blacks having a higher frequency of attendance than whites (Sasaki 1979).

Findings from the National Survey of Black Americans

One of the major limitations of the empirical literature on religious participation is that the findings cannot be generalized to blacks and other minority groups because of sampling procedures which either exclude blacks entirely or include very small numbers of black respondents. For example, one study which found that deprivation in family relationships is associated with involvement in church activities, was based on responses from a national survey of white Episcopalians (Glock, Ringer, and Babbie 1967). Only 2.8 percent of respondents in a 1980 study of 2,775 members of Protestant denominations were black Americans. Due to the small numbers of blacks included in these studies and in the majority of cross-sectional surveys of the general population,

National Survey of Black Americans

Church Attendance

Nearly everyday	4.5
At least once a week	35.5
A few times a month	30.6
A few times a year	19.4
Less than once a year	10.0
	100.0% (1,922)

Church Membership

Yes	67.6
No	32.4
	100.0% (1,922)

Frequency of Reading Religious Materials

Nearly everyday	27.0
At least once a week	23.5
A few times a month	23.9
A few times a year	18.8
Less than once a year	6.9
	100.0% (2,098)

Frequency of Watching and Listening to Religious Programs

Nearly everyday	21.0
At least once a week	46.8
A few times a month	14.4
A few times a year	9.8
Less than once a year	8.0
	100.0% (2,097)

Frequency of Prayer

Nearly everyday	78.0
At least once a week	8.3
A few times a month	6.4
A few times a year	4.2
Less than once a year	3.1
	100.0% (1,922)

Frequency of Requesting Prayer

Nearly everyday	13.6
At least once a week	17.9
A few times a month	19.1
A few times a year	20.8
Less than once a year	28.5
	100.0% (2,089)

Degree of Subjective Religiosity

Very religious	34.1
Fairly religious	49.5
Not too religious	13.3
Not religious at all	3.1
	100.0% (2,091)

Univariate Distribution of Religious Variables
Table 12-1

197

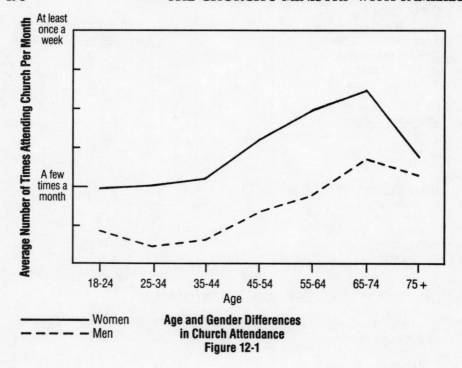

**Age and Gender Differences
in Church Attendance
Figure 12-1**

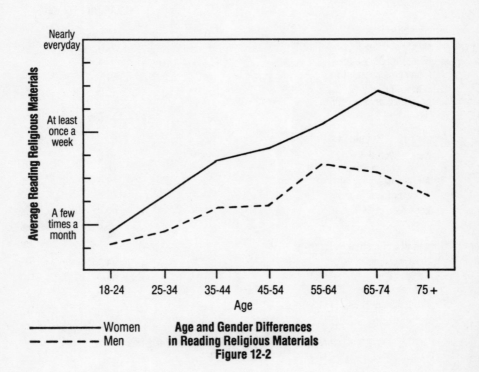

**Age and Gender Differences
in Reading Religious Materials
Figure 12-2**

it is not possible to perform analyses which differentiate among important subgroups within the black population. As a consequence, this literature gives the mistaken impression that black Americans as a group are essentially similar in their religious beliefs and behaviors.

A major advantage of the analyses presented in this chapter is that the data is from the National Survey of Black Americans (NSBA). The NSBA sample is the first nationally representative cross-section of the adult (eighteen years and older) black population living in the continental United States. This sampling procedure resulted in 2,107 completed interviews collected in 1979 and 1980, representing a response rate of nearly 70 percent.

Religious Participation of Adult Blacks. A percentage distribution of selected indicators of religious participation among the NSBA sample is presented in Table 12-1. Almost 5 percent of respondents reported that they attended religious services nearly every day, 35.5 percent reported that they attended weekly, 30.6 percent a few times a month, 19.4 percent a few times a year, and 10 percent less than once a year. Two out of three respondents indicated that they were members of a church or other place of worship.

A general profile of participation in nonorganizational religious activities revealed that 78 percent said that they prayed nearly everyday. Similarly, 27 percent indicated reading religious books daily, 21 percent indicated watching or listening to religious programs on television or radio daily, and 13 percent reported asking someone to pray for them on a daily basis. Eight out of ten blacks reported being "religious."

Multivariate analyses of these indicators reveal significant demographic variability in the degree of religious participation among blacks. Age and gender exhibit the strongest associations with the level of religious participation. Across each indicator women are more religious than men and older blacks are more religious than younger blacks. Region and marital status also display fairly consistent relationships with religious participation: southern and married blacks report higher levels of religious participation than their counterparts. Collectively, these findings demonstrate the centrality and heterogeneity of religious participation among black Americans (see Taylor 1988a, 1988b and Taylor, Thornton, and Chatters 1987 for a more in-depth discussion of this work).

The information provided in figures 12-1 through 12-4 presents a detailed examination of age and gender differences in four critical indicators of religiosity: frequency of church attendance, frequency of reading religious materials, frequency of watching or listening to religious programing, and frequency of prayer. The values of the religious variables are as follows: 5 = nearly everyday; 4 = at least once a week; 3 = a few times a month; 2 = a few times a year, and 1 = less than once a year.

Both age and gender differences are evident in each of the figures. The gender relationship, however, is more pronounced with women displaying a higher degree of religiosity than men. Although the age differences are generally positive, there is some decrease in church attendance (figure 12-1) and reading

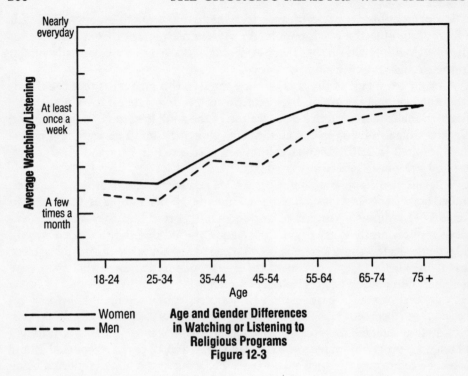

Age and Gender Differences
in Watching or Listening to
Religious Programs
Figure 12-3

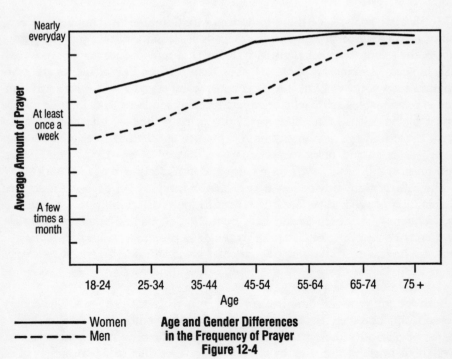

Age and Gender Differences
in the Frequency of Prayer
Figure 12-4

religious materials (figure 12-2) among very old respondents. The decrease in church attendance among older respondents can probably be attributed to health impairments and transportation difficulties. The decrease in reading religious materials among this same population is probably a cohort effect as opposed to an aging effect; this cohort of older blacks had limited educational opportunities and only a few years of formal education. Consequently, they were less likely than younger blacks to be able to read.[1]

Religious Participation of Elderly Blacks. Analyses of the NSBA data also indicate that elderly blacks display a high degree of religious involvement (Taylor 1986b). They attend religious services on a frequent basis, are likely to be official members of a church or other place of worship, and describe themselves as being religious. Religious participation varied by gender, marital status, age and urbanicity. As might be expected, elderly women attended religious services more frequently, were more likely to be church members, and reported a higher degree of religiosity than did elderly men.

In comparison to married people, divorced and widowed respondents attended religious services less frequently and reported lower levels of subjective religiosity. Divorced respondents were also less likely to be church members. Elderly blacks residing in rural areas were more involved in church activities than their urban counterparts. In addition, age was positively associated with degree of subjective religiosity.

Implications of Religious-Participation Findings

Marital-status differences in religious participation among blacks has important implications for ministers and church groups. Divorced and widowed respondents were found to attend religious services less frequently and were less likely to be church members. From a ministerial viewpoint, it is important to ensure continued church participation following the loss of a spouse (through death or divorce). Ensuring regular participation in religious services and church activities is particularly crucial for widows, considering the reduction in social relationships which occurs after the loss of a spouse. Since divorced couples may not want to maintain membership in the same church, ministers may need to help facilitate the involvement of one of the spouses in another church. Similarly, if a church has fairly strict informal sanctions against divorce, neither the man or woman may feel comfortable in associating with their church and with fellow church members. Under these circumstances, ministers may want to assist both parties to become members of other churches. Ministers may also serve as advocates in behalf of the divorced in their own church communities.

---

[1] This collection of findings is significant because they confirm assumptions regarding religious participation among black adults and describe the behavior of important subgroups of that population.

Black Churches as Sources of Informal Social Support

Historical and present-day evidence suggests that black churches are extensively involved in the provision of support to their members. Although it is generally accepted that church members are important sources of assistance to blacks, this issue has received surprisingly little systematic attention and scrutiny. Recent analysis of NSBA data has examined the role of church members as a source of informal support to elderly black adults (Taylor and Chatters 1986a, 1986b) and blacks across the life course (Taylor and Chatters 1988).

Church Members as a Source of Support to Black Adults

Taylor and Chatters (1988) examined sociodemographic and religious factors as predictors of the receipt of support from church members and found that for two out of three respondents (64.2 percent) church members provided some level of support. Church attendance, church membership, subjective religiosity, and religious affiliation were all significantly related to the receipt of support. Research on informal support networks concurs. Demographic differences indicated that men and younger respondents were more likely, while divorced respondents were less likely to receive support. Catholics were less likely to receive support from church members than were Baptists. The limited amount of research on black Catholics indicates that Catholicism is characterized by predominantly white congregations and less communal, more formal forms of religious practice. Conceivably, these circumstances do not facilitate the transfer of assistance among church members. In addition, higher incomes and residency in rural areas were associated with never needing assistance from church members.

The Role of Church Members in the
Support Networks of Aged Black Adults

In another analysis, three indicators of church support were examined: frequency, amount, and type of support received from church members among elderly blacks (Taylor and Chatters 1986a). Frequency of church attendance, as a form of public commitment, was a critical indicator of both the frequency of receiving assistance and the amount of aid provided.

Respondents' subjective assessments of the importance of attending religious services were also positively associated with frequency of receiving support. Among the demographic factors, an interaction between age and the presence of adult children was found. For those elderly people with children, advanced age was associated with more frequent assistance from church members. However, among childless elderly, advanced age was associated with dramatic decreases in the frequency of such support. This finding suggests that adult children may function to facilitate linkages to church support networks on behalf of their elderly parents.

Regardless of age, elderly persons who were church members received roughly comparable levels of assistance. For elderly respondents who were not members of a church, however, age was an important moderator of levels of support. Oldest respondents (75+) who were not church members received significantly more support than did their relatively younger counterparts (55–64). In providing assistance to others outside of the church, age may be a particularly critical factor in the allocation of support resources. Age of recipient likely acts as an indicator of greater need for assistance to which church members respond. In this regard black churches are to be commended for providing assistance to very old blacks who are not members of their churches. In addition, regional differences revealed that North Central residents receive more assistance from church members than Southerners.

Taylor and Chatters examined whether elderly blacks received concomitant support from family, friends, and church members, and if so, the type of assistance provided (1986b). Descriptively, eight out of ten respondents received support from either a best or close friend, roughly six out of ten received support from church members, and over half received support from extended family members. Only a minority of respondents were socially isolated in the sense that they did not have a best or close friend and failed to receive support from either family or church members.

Analysis of the type of support received from friends, family, and church members indicated that these groups may differentially provide particular types of aid. Respondents were more likely to receive either total or instrumental assistance (i.e., goods and services, financial assistance, and transportation) from family members; from their friends they would receive companionship. Similarly, there was a greater chance of respondents receiving advice and encouragement, help during sickness, and prayer from church members. In addition, individual support sources were distinctive in the assistance they provided to elderly blacks.

These findings indicate that the type of support received by elderly blacks may not be governed by hierarchical or task-specific constraints. While these data indicate a general tendency to receive a particular type of assistance from one support group, there was considerable overlap in the type of support provided. In addition, although respondents were more likely to receive total support from family, over 5 percent of respondents who received assistance from friends and church members reported that they received total support from these sources. For certain groups of elderly blacks, friends and church members may be of greater importance than has been previously thought.

Implications of Findings on Church
Members as a Source of Informal Support

The findings that childless elderly receive assistance from church members on a less frequent basis has important implications for family ministry. Research has shown that among both blacks and whites, the elderly with children have larger and stronger supportive networks than childless elderly. Adult children and spouses are viewed as primary sources of assistance in fulfilling the caregiving and support needs of their elderly parents. As discussed earlier, among blacks, adult children also facilitate the receipt of support from church members for their elderly parents. Consequently, childless elderly are in double jeopardy in that they have a lower likelihood of receiving help from both their family and church members. For this group of individuals the role of church outreach programs cannot be underestimated. Ministers and church officials should visit, on a regular and frequent basis, elderly church members who are in poor health. They should also encourage other church members to provide fellowship with this group.

Service Delivery

The effectiveness of public social service systems has frequently been criticized because of failure to reach target populations with high levels of need. The defense offered by system advocates is that such populations are hard to locate, and if located are transient or sporadic users of service. Service providers imply that individual or select groups of users fail to meet their own level of need even when presented with resources by the service delivery system. Through their actions, bureaucratic service delivery systems may alienate many individuals who are in severe need. Through the use of informal social support networks, churches may be in a unique position to provide services to those who have "fallen through the cracks" of the formal social service delivery system.

Historically, churches have had a strong tradition of responding to the social welfare needs of their members. Demonstrated high rates of church attendance among blacks ensure regular contact and provide churches the unique opportunity to respond to the needs of the black community. The complexities of the problems confronting impoverished blacks, coupled with an increasingly restricted governmental role and limited social resources, confront churches and other community agencies. Issues of program goals and objectives, needs assessment, resource allocation, outreach efforts, program access, and service delivery strategies should be addressed so that services may be rendered effectively.

Goals and Objectives of Service Delivery

The goals for providing services to black clients should be to *reinforce the strengths of families and individuals* and *enhance the capacity to formulate and implement solutions to problems.* In accordance with these broader goals, specific program objectives should be structured and administered in a manner which strengthens existing informal support networks, enhances self-esteem, and promotes family functioning.

Program Design

Organizational procedures for service delivery should maximize available opportunities for clients. These procedures should reduce perceptions of powerlessness and actively counteract negative evaluations of blacks which are often fostered by large, bureaucratic organizations (Solomon 1976). The centrality of religious institutions suggests that churches may be an appropriate service delivery setting for those who are seeking help with problems, yet are reluctant to utilize formal agencies. Familiarity with churches and their functions makes outreach efforts somewhat more successful than large social agencies may experience.

Site location is a major issue in designing service delivery; it has a direct impact on the level of service utilization. Careful consideration should be given to identifying the optimal location for reaching the targeted population, determining the site's accessibility via public transportation. If such access is impossible, some other form of transportation can be easily provided.

Because previous experiences affect the utilization of programs (Dancy 1977; Solomon 1976), services should be located in facilities which, for the benefactors, are not associated with perceptions of alienation and poor response.

Service Array

A wide variety of services can be provided by churches which address the needs of black adults. Services can be grouped into two major categories—*information/ referral* (e.g., employment assistance, housing, financial management, emotional support, and access to health care) and *direct service delivery* (e.g., marital counseling, child-parent relationship problems, transportation, substance abuse, and homemaker assistance). Although the informal support system is instrumental in coping with these problems, in many instances intervention by the formal network is essential.

Information and referral is a crucial service which churches can provide. By participating in the problem-solving process, clients learn important skills for negotiating in bureaucratic agencies. Clients need to know where to go, what services are available, and program eligibility requirements in order to obtain appropriate help. Research suggests that for many blacks, information concerning programs and services is limited (Luckey and Nathan, forthcoming). Churches can be instrumental in developing a file of available programs and services. To facilitate the effectiveness of the information and referral process, churches should identify resource persons who maintain contact with agencies and programs. Resource persons can screen out programs which are unresponsive to diverse ethnic and racial groups. This approach sustains the goal of providing services that are sensitive to ethnic-racial diversity at both the entry level and throughout the help-seeking process.

In providing information and referral services, it may be necessary for the resource person to facilitate entry into the formal system. This person or a member of his or her informal network (a relative or friend) might accompany him or her to the agency for the first visit. Follow-up determines if services were provided and the disposition of those contacts.

The church may provide direct, individual or group assistance including marital counseling, help with parent-child relationship problems, emotional and moral support, and assistance with transportation problems. Blacks have traditionally turned to the church for assistance in these areas. Programs designed to address these needs must have service providers who are sensitive to the interplay of individual, family, and environment (Germain and Gitterman 1980).

Ethnic Sensitivity

Effective service provision for blacks involves understanding the history, culture, community, and informal networks of this population. A historical perspective on blacks which addresses their coping and survival skills provides the basis for an ecological approach to the help-seeking process. This perspective aids in recognizing the systemic nature of barriers and constraints facing the group, as well as their strengths and resources. (For an in-depth presentation of blacks and the helping tradition, see Martin and Martin 1985.) Further, understanding the history and culture of blacks is useful in assessing the present situation of those seeking help and the influences of family, culture, and environment upon the situation. Particular attention must be paid to how ethnicity and social class contribute to individual and group identity, dispositions toward basic life tasks, coping styles, and the types of problems which are likely to be encountered (Devore and Schlesinger 1987).

Role of Providers

Service providers function in many roles to assure that clients receive needed assistance. These roles include acting as a broker of services and resources, educator, mediator, counselor, and social action advocate. Several of these roles are utilized in helping with a single problem. As a broker, the service provider helps individuals identify and secure resources (Solomon 1976). In the initial contact with programs, those who perform information and referral functions may also play an active role in securing needed service. To foster self-sufficiency in managing problems, however, efforts must be made to provide clients with the skills to utilize community resources. Consequently, the role of broker involves both securing resources and empowering clients to independently secure services.

The role of educator focuses on providing information and skills regarding specific situations or problem areas. For example, those providing assistance to families who have parent-child problems should provide specific parenting skills and information (e.g., encouraging the child to express concerns to parents, as opposed to generalized parenting lectures).

Counseling is one of the major roles of both clergy and laypersons. However, the provision of counseling services by laypeople may be problematic. Issues of confidentiality, even if properly respected by those providing the services, may be viewed by counselees with some degree of uneasiness. As a consequence, they may not totally disclose the information necessary to assess a situation properly. If church members are to provide counseling services, consideration should be given to what areas counseling will be provided for, when people should be referred to others, and who is best suited to provide the services.

The role of mediator involves the amelioration and/or resolution of inter- and intrasystem conflict (Connaway and Gentry 1988). The service provider as a mediator may be instrumental by suggesting a creative settlement or by helping parties to reach amicable solutions.

Situations for which the focus is environmental or systemic require structural rather than individual change. Advocacy and social action are functions which both workers and churches could perform. Advocacy is designed to protect existing rights or entitlements, whereas social action establishes new entitlements (Connaway and Gentry 1988). Advocacy may be on behalf of an individual or group problem (e.g., the discontinuation of disability benefits without a change in the person's medical, financial, or other eligibility criteria).

A Case Example

The Shiloh Baptist Church of Washington, D. C., provides an example of the types of services and activities that churches can maintain in black communities. This large church, located in the heart of a low-income black community, has a membership that spans every socioeconomic level. Through over two hundred clubs and organizations, Shiloh Baptist Church attempts to address its members' spiritual, psychological, and material needs. The clubs and organizations are housed in the facilities of the Family Life Center (gym, banquet hall, meeting rooms, etc.). Some innovative programs offered in the center include the prison ministry, Senior Center for the Deaf-Impaired, Male Youth Enhancement Program, Parent Aid Program, Adopt-a-Family Program, Successful Single Club, and Investment Club.

The prison ministry addresses the needs of black men who are incarcerated. In addition to providing spiritual assistance, this ministry provides social services and transportation to prisoners and their families. The deaf ministry and Senior Center for the Deaf-Impaired assist individuals who have developed hearing problems with the onset of old age, providing transportation, social activities, and case advocacy for elderly blacks with hearing impairments. The Male Youth Enhancement Program provides positive role models for black youth. It challenges youth and older black males to pursue goals of enhancing self-esteem and fostering leadership skills. A Parent Aid Program assists parents with issues of child rearing. The Adopt-a-Family program creatively provides a surrogate extended family to single parents and young families. The Successful Single Club provides Christian fellowship, social activities, professional counseling, recreational trips, and coping strategies for single black men and women. In addition, members of an Investment Club meet and discuss financial management and entrepreneurship.

Many churches have extremely limited resources and small memberships and as such cannot provide the broad array of services and programs offered by Shiloh Baptist Church. These programs illustrate the types of activities that churches may want to adapt to their own situation as they strive to strengthen families.

This chapter has discussed the degree of religious participation of black adults, the informal helping networks of members of black churches, and strategies of using churches as outlets for social service delivery. Because black adults exhibit a high degree of religious participation and church members are an integral component of black adults' informal social support networks, churches can become a conducive mechanism for providing social services. Church-based programs, by filling existing gaps and rendering services in a personalized and culturally sensitive manner, can be a crucial source of assistance because they are in a unique position to provide services to those who are reluctant to seek help from large formal institutions.

References

Bassett, P. 1980. Evangelicalism. In *Academic American encyclopedia*. Danbury, Conn.: Grolier Inc.

Carroll, J. W., D. W. Johnson, and M. E. Marty. 1979. *Religion in America. 1950 to the present*. San Francisco: Harper and Row.

Connaway, R. S., and M. E. Gentry. 1988. *Social work practice*. Englewood Cliffs, N. J.: Prentice Hall.

Dancy, Jr., J. 1977. *The black elderly: A guide for practitioners*. Ann Arbor, Mich.: The Institute of Gerontology, The University of Michigan-Wayne State University.

Devore, W., and E. G. Schlesinger. 1987. *Ethnic-sensitive social work practice*, 2d ed. Columbus, Ohio: Merrill.

DuBois, W. E. B. 1967. *The Philadelphia negro: A social study*. New York: Schocken Press.

Fauset, A. 1944. *Black gods of the metropolis*. Philadelphia: University of Pennsylvania Press.

Frazier, E. F. 1966. *The black church*. Chicago: University of Chicago Press.

Gallup Report. 1984. *Religion in America*.

Germain, C. B., and A. Gitterman. 1980. *The life model of social work practice*. New York: Columbia University Press.

Glenn, N., and E. Gotard. 1977. The religion of blacks in the United States: Some recent trends and current characteristics. *American Journal of Sociology* 63:443–51.

Glock, C. Y., B. B. Ringer, and E. R. Babbie. 1967. *To comfort and to challenge: A dilemma of the contemporary church*. Berkeley: University of California Press.

Glock, C. Y., and R. Stark. 1967. *Religion and society in tension*. Chicago: Rand McNally.

Jennings, R. M. 1983. Intrinsic religious motivation and psychological adjustment among black Americans. Ph.D. diss., University of Michigan.

Lewis, H. 1955. *Blackways of Kent*. New Haven: Connecticut College and University Press.

Lincoln, C. E. 1984. *Race, religion, and the continuing American dilemma*. New York: Hill and Wang.

Luckey, I., and M. E. Nathan. (n.d.). *Human services in the rural environment*.

Martin, J. M., and E. P. Martin. 1985. *The helping tradition in the black family and community*. Silver Spring, Md.: National Association of Social Workers, Inc.

Mays, B., and Nicholson. 1933. *The Negro's church*. New York: Arno Press.

Nelsen, H. M., R. L. Yokley, and A. Nelsen. 1971. *The black church in America*. New York: Basic Books.

Raboteau, A. J. 1980. *Slave religion.* Oxford: Oxford University Press.

Roberts, J. D. 1980. *Roots of a black future: Family and church.* Philadelphia: Westminster.

Sasaki, M. S. 1979. Status inconsistency and religious commitment. In *The religious dimension: New directions in quantitative research,* ed. R. Wuthnow. New York: Academic Press.

Smith, J. M. 1986. Church participation and morale of the rural, southern black aged. Ph.D. diss., University of Michigan.

Solomon, B. B. 1976. *Black empowerment: Social work in oppressed communities.* New York: Columbia University Press.

Taylor, R. J. 1986a. Receipt of support from family among black Americans: Demographic and familial differences. *Journal of Marriage and the Family* 48:67–77.

———. 1986b. Religious participation among elderly blacks. *The Gerontologist* 26:630–36.

———. 1988a. Correlates of religious non-involvement among black Americans. *Review of Religious Research* 30:126–39.

———. 1988b. Structural determinants of religious participation among black Americans. *Review of Religious Research* 30:114–25.

Taylor, R. J., and L. M. Chatters. 1986a. Church-based informal support among elderly blacks. *The Gerontologist* 26:637–42.

———. 1986b. Patterns of informal support to elderly black adults: Family, friends, and church members. *Social Work* 31:432–38.

———. 1988. Church members as a source of informal social support. *Review of Religious Research* 30:193–203.

Taylor, R. J., M. C. Thornton, and L. M. Chatters. 1987. Black Americans' perception of the socio-historical role of the church. *Journal of Black Studies* 18:123–38.

13

Helping Natural Helpers

Diane L. Pancoast

In chapter 4, we discussed a number of intervention possibilities based on understanding the linkages in a network: creating a climate which encourages network building, creating opportunities for people to build new ties, intervening in dysfunctional networks, helping a network coalesce and function smoothly in a crisis, and recognizing and facilitating various helping roles. This chapter will discuss methods of identifying certain key figures, or natural helpers, in networks and supporting, indirectly, their efforts on behalf of members of their networks.

The examples of networks we presented in chapter 4 were highly simplified. On an ongoing basis, no one can monitor all the ties in a congregation. Even if it were possible, making people so highly aware of their interactions with each other would be counterproductive.

There is a way, however, that church leaders can keep their fingers on the pulse of the congregation. In our diagram in chapter 4 some individuals were called nexus persons, natural helpers, and role-related helpers; these all had a large number of ties to others in the network. Most church leaders learn this early in their careers, sometimes unpleasantly, by running afoul of these people. By identifying these central figures and key links and staying in regular contact with them, leaders can be aware of emerging problems in the wider congregation and strengthen the key figures at the same time.

Identifying Natural Helpers

In a bounded setting like a church congregation, the identification of key figures should be relatively easy once one begins to look for them and to appreciate the roles they are playing. Some will be central because they have personal charisma or access to resources. Others have many relationships because they are naturally gregarious and like to spend their time in direct or telephone contact with many other people. Still others may be the center of network "stars" because they learned early in life, perhaps as the children of dysfunctional parents, that taking care of others and solving their problems could provide an identity and sense of purpose (Beattie 1987).

Church leaders will want to know who these people are. Those with charisma and access to resources are likely to be in leadership roles or should be recruited to leadership positions. The gregarious ones are the "grapevine" of the congregation; it is important that their role is recognized and that they are supplied with accurate information. They may also be encouraged to reach out to include new or isolated members of the congregation in their communication networks. Those who are central because of dysfunctional patterns, learned early in life, are likely to get in over their heads, plunging into helping situations without considering either the consequences of creating dependency or the impact of these relationships on other parts of their networks. Church leaders can help them to set limits and be available if they "crash". They can also decide that such people need help in determining how to meet their own needs and how to achieve a balance between caring and being cared for. An awareness of the networks in the church can help to identify each of these types of key figures.

Characteristics of Natural Helpers

However, none of these key figures are our focus in this chapter. Our definition of "natural helper" is narrower than that used by many other authors, including Bowman, who has contributed an excellent chapter on training natural helpers for lay ministry (chapter 14). While he and many others would include peer helping (friend-to-friend) and volunteers in structured programs, in this chapter we will focus on persons who are offering substantial assistance to several people outside of any organized program. They may describe those they help as friends, neighbors or relatives, but the helping is not truly reciprocal. They may feel that such helping balances out over the long run, but at the time that they are perceived to be natural helpers, they are clearly *offering* more help than they are *receiving*. These natural helpers are perceived by members of their networks and communities as persons who are extraordinarily helpful. In fact, researchers identify natural helpers by this criterion: that they are nominated as a helping person by at least three people who know them (Patterson 1984).

Sometimes natural helpers hold leadership positions (Todd and Armstrong 1984; Norton, Morales, and Andrews 1980). But they are less likely to be in the front of the room when a meeting is held, leading the group, than in the back, being sure that latecomers find seats and the coffee is made. Church leaders who are new to a congregation may be surprised to hear their names come up when members of the congregation are talking about the stalwarts of the congregation because they have not appeared to be prominent, but then the leaders will remember that these are the people who have called to let them know about someone who is sick, who have dropped a quiet word about a family in turmoil, or who have driven several widows to a church potluck.

If the activities of natural helpers are noticed and commented upon, the helpers are likely to say that they don't do anything special, just what any person would do in a similar situation. A woman who single-handedly feeds 130 migrant workers every day says, "I think [other] people would be willing to help if they only knew about the situation." Others around such people, however, are very aware that they do far more than most people. Often other members of their personal networks are proud, but not always supportive, of their efforts. A frequently heard comment is "my friends and relatives think I'm crazy to do all this, but I enjoy it" (Kelley and Kelley 1985, 362). The daughter of a woman who is a key helping figure in a mobile home park for retired people reacted strongly when her mother's good works were praised by a visitor to the park, "You should be her daughter," she sputtered. "She never has time for me."

If they do acknowledge their helping role, natural helpers often say that they are carrying on a tradition they learned in their family or that they are paying back past kindnesses done to them. Kelley and Kelley (1985, 362) cite these comments from natural helpers they interviewed.

> When I was a child I carried meals from our kitchen across the backyard to my aunt and uncle who were stone broke.

> My father was active in organizing farmers during the depression. He was always involved in caring for people. It was the Christian thing to do.

> People helped me when I needed it, so what I have, I'll give.

The woman who feeds the migrants says, "I know how it is when food runs out." As a young girl in Germany after World War II she would walk for miles in search of food only to find that it had run out just before she arrived. Surveys have found that lower-income groups are proportionately more generous in their charitable giving than the more affluent.

Religious faith is frequently cited as a motivator by natural helpers. A natural helper interviewed by Patterson (1984, i) said, "What I give her is moral support . . . . I think to be more exact, in my case, she gives me a sense of a deeply religious faith." Patterson found that more than 80 percent of the eighty natural helpers she interviewed viewed themselves as being part of a religious community of faith.

Natural helpers are not more likely to be found in one social class or another or in rural or urban settings. Natural helpers are teen-agers, grandmothers, and middle-aged businessmen. They live in public housing projects, welfare hotels, suburban neighborhoods, Indian reservations, small towns, and big cities. They work as postmasters, garage mechanics, waitresses at truck stops, pharmacists, cafeteria cooks, school janitors, and taxi drivers, to name but a few. A number of them are homemakers; some are retired. Some people who have a paid helping role (e.g., nurse or social worker) are as engaged in helping people when they are off duty as when they are at work.

Examples of Natural Helpers

Probably the best way to begin to think about natural helpers is to have a good mental picture of such a person. Generally, it is possible to think of someone from one's own life or from professional experience who would fit the criteria we have outlined above. The following examples are drawn from the experiences of workers in Eldercare, a program of home care for frail elderly persons in Washington state.

Rose. Rose is seventy-nine years old, a widow with no relatives, who lives in her own home in a small town. She participates regularly in several organizations and walks her small dog through the neighborhood twice a day. Some years ago, after her husband died, she decided to avoid loneliness and feel useful by finding other people she could help. The children in her neighborhood know that on Saturday afternoons, Rose will give them ice cream. This is her way of staying in touch with the local youngsters.

Most of her helping efforts, however, are devoted to several elderly people she visits on her daily walks. She sees one old woman out in her garden every day, dressed in a dirty old raincoat and rubber boots. Her own yard is full of weeds, but this woman is always weeding her neighbor's garden, putting the weeds in boxes in front of her own house. At this point, Rose only stops for a brief chat with this woman, but this is very significant for her, since all of the other neighbors think she is very strange and do not speak to her.

On her walk, Rose stops in to talk with another elderly widow whom she met in a club they both belonged to. Now she is too frail to go out, so Rose stops in to see her every day and have a cup of coffee.

Currently, the person Rose is helping the most is Mary, a woman with Alzheimer's disease, who lives alone in her own house. Rose comes every morning to be sure Mary gets up. Rose makes her breakfast and takes out the garbage. Later in the day, if she finds Mary outside trying to mow the grass, a task which is too much for her, or purposelessly raking the rocks in a nearby parking lot, Rose gently leads her back into the house. If Mary has locked herself out, Rose climbs in the window. In the late afternoon, Rose checks on Mary again to make sure she is settled for the night.

Mr. and Mrs. Jones. Two other natural helpers live in a trailer court. The Joneses formerly directed a retirement home. When they retired themselves, they decided that they would like to devote a lot of their time to helping others. They chose their trailer court for the opportunities it offered to help residents older than themselves and deliberately picked a location for their trailer near the entrance of the court where they could watch the comings and goings of the other residents and be accessible in case anyone needed them.

They have started a club for social activities and send cards to anyone who has a birthday or is in the hospital. This club provides a way of monitoring needs of the residents: neighbors feel they need to tell the Joneses if someone is going to the hospital. Birthday parties are an occasion for contact and seeing if other needs are not being met, since the Joneses take the birthday card around for signatures.

They have also started a walking group for exercise. This gives them another opportunity to call on people and to encourage isolated persons to engage in an activity. They always invite people who are new to the court to join the walking group or take part in social activities. When they have potluck suppers, the Joneses offer to make food for someone to bring if they can't make it themselves.

This couple has developed well-defined limits for their helping activities. They reach out to a new person several times, but if their efforts are discouraged, they withdraw, waiting to see if they will be needed at another time. After some encouragement, they expect people to be able to participate in activities on their own without help or encouragement. They do take on more extensive responsibilities for persons who are ill or not taking good care of themselves: fixing meals, transporting to appointments, helping pay bills, washing clothes. They realize that they can only provide this level of assistance to one or two people, so, if they see more need, they try to find other helpers in the trailer court who would be willing to get involved by bringing in some meals, making repairs or checking every day on the person who is ill.

Mr. and Mrs. Smith. The Smiths are both involved in helping their friends and neighbors. They are a middle-aged couple who live in a remote and scattered mountain community. The tavern is the main social center of this community and the Smiths, like most of their neighbors, are fairly heavy drinkers. Mr. Smith works at logging and construction jobs when he can find them and cuts firewood when he can't.

The Eldercare staff met Mr. Smith when he called the office at five o'clock on a Friday afternoon looking for help for two old bachelor friends. These men lived together in a cabin in the woods and one of them was bedridden. The other old man had fallen and injured himself when he went down to the river to fish that day. Now they both needed help. Trying to find formal services over a weekend for someone who lives fifty miles away in the mountains is very difficult. After trying every possible source and coming up empty handed, the Eldercare worker called Mr. Smith again and asked him whether he would be willing to organize some informal services from friends and neighbors to help the men through the weekend, promising to send a nurse on Monday. He agreed.

When the nurse went out she found the Smiths taking care of the men as best they could but the situation was very bad. The cabin was filthy and the disabled man, whose clothes had not been changed for a year, was tied to the bed to keep him from falling out. The nurse helped the Smiths make arrangements to send him to the hospital.

The Smiths continued to look after the other old man until he was on his feet again. They cleaned and repaired his cabin. During the period when the old man needed a great deal of care, the Eldercare program paid the Smiths and they moved their trailer onto his property so they could be close to him. When there was no longer a need for this level of care, the Smiths moved back to their own land and stopped receiving payment. However, the Smiths continue to take the old man meals and take him into the tavern.

Eldercare has subsequently learned that the Smiths help many other people for no payment. Sometimes they use the tavern kitchen to make meals to take out to people who are sick. Because the tavern owner is an alcoholic, the Smiths take care of her and run the tavern for her when she is too sick to do it herself. They bring firewood to people who have no heat.

Problems of Natural Helpers

It is not uncommon for helping professionals, when they get to know natural helpers, to be uncertain that they have anything to offer them in the way of assistance. The natural helpers are providing such an impressive amount of assistance, so skillfully and cheerfully, that the professional feels somewhat in awe. Ongoing contact usually reveals, however, that the natural helpers do have problems and make mistakes and that they can benefit from the experience and perspective of a professional. Natural helpers' problems fall into the following categories.

Lack of Knowledge

Natural helpers may not understand certain kinds of behavior, particularly if they have not encountered it before. Sometimes the natural helpers do not recognize serious mental or physical conditions such as Alzheimer's disease, addiction, or depression. They may be baffled by changes in their friends' behavior or think that negative aspects of that behavior are directed at them personally. For example, a natural helper thought that a woman who was too depressed to come to the door was angry at her.

Natural helpers sometimes lack knowledge about medical conditions and treatments and may interfere with medical care if they do not understand its purpose. They may not be aware of services that friends are eligible for or have negative opinions about the service based on previous experience or hearsay. For example, Rose may not have been aware that the old lady she spoke with every day on her walks could have received an assessment and inhome services.

Sometimes the natural helpers do not know about other parts of the "client's" network. They may not be aware that there are interested and concerned family members. One natural helper thought that her friend's granddaughter was unconcerned. Her friend was too confused to be able to tell her that the granddaughter visited three evenings a week, after work. Neither was the granddaughter aware that the natural helper stopped by in the mornings.

Less often, it is not lack of knowledge but inappropriate attitudes that make the natural helper less effective when working with some situations. Like the Smiths and their friend the tavern keeper, a helper may tolerate heavy drinking or misuse of medications when these practices have become a serious health hazard. On the other hand, another helper might strongly condemn the moderate amount of drinking that occurs when the Smiths' elderly friend visits the tavern and fail to see that it may be a necessary accompaniment to the socialization that such visits provide.

Natural helpers may go too far in making decisions for the client, particularly when handling money. One helper, for example, bought a new chair for a confused elderly woman when the woman really wanted to use the money for a new winter coat. Applying our criteria, someone who was seriously and deliberately exploiting a client would not be considered a natural helper and we have found no such cases among people who meet these criteria. The problems have been minor and based on misunderstandings.

Role Confusion

Since there are no clear cultural prescriptions for natural helpers, it is not surprising that the natural helpers are sometimes uncertain about what they are doing. They do not know whether or not it is valued or appropriate. Sometimes they feel unappreciated by their friend or by family members. Depressed and alcoholic people tend to be erratic, grateful for help one day and angry the next. Persons confused by mental illness or Alzheimer's disease may not be aware of what others are doing for them. People struggling with difficult problems may be getting advice from a variety of sources and may act in ways that the natural helper does not approve.

Natural helpers must carefully consider how much responsibility to take in handling their friends' affairs. They sometimes become involved in handling their money, paying bills, and even selling their house or furniture if they go into a nursing home or die, if there are no relatives. They step in because they see a need but they worry about whether they are going too far, whether they will be criticized by other friends or formal authorities or a distant relative of whom they are not aware. The natural helper may take on more responsibility because he or she wants to "protect" the friend who may not want relatives or formal agencies to know of increasing incapacitation.

Setting Limits

Natural helpers are usually good at limiting their helping activities. The Joneses are an example of a couple that carefully monitors their involvement. Jerome Guay found that natural helpers who were assisting severely mentally ill persons in Quebec were better able to direct their efforts to those persons who could make the best use of them than were the professionals (Guay 1984). However, like professionals, natural helpers sometimes do have difficulty setting limits and become too heavily involved in helping others. This can occasionally even be dangerous. In an incident reported in the newspaper, a natural helper who had been helping an alcoholic woman neighbor for some time was shot by the neighbor and lost an eye. The neighbor had called this person in the middle of the night because she was having hallucinations and thought someone was breaking into her house. When the helper went over to calm her, the woman mistook her for an intruder and shot her. Overinvolvement seldom has such tragic consequences but is a significant problem for natural helpers and may cause them to withdraw completely from helping, once formal services are introduced, or to be reluctant to help another person.

Relationships with Formal Services

A final area of difficulty for natural helpers is interfacing with formal services. For example, the Eldercare program eventually provided a chore worker to assist a woman with Alzheimer's disease whom Rose, the natural helper, was looking after. He came in at noon, made her meal, and stayed until evening. Soon after he started helping the elderly client, Rose came by and saw that the old lady was washing the dishes. She called the agency to complain that the chore worker should have been washing the dishes, since he was being paid to do this work. The agency worker explained that the chore worker was supposed to encourage the client to remain active and do as much for herself as she could. Because the agency had established a relationship with Rose, she called and the misunderstanding was straightened out.

But often the natural helpers do not have access to the formal services and are left to draw their own conclusions about the effectiveness of the services.

Sometimes natural helpers feel unneeded when a formal service is introduced; they may even feel that the service is an implicit criticism of their efforts. On occasion, this criticism has actually been explicit; an overeager or insecure worker can make the natural helper feel unwelcome. Unless the formal service staff knows about the natural helper, they may not even be aware that he or she is withdrawing.

Services are often complex, confusing, and inefficient. So, it is not surprising that the natural helpers have problems with them. Communication among various service providers may be poor. Some critics have looked upon the informal caregiving system as less stable than the formal one, but often the situation is the opposite. Employees of social service agencies come and go more frequently than natural helpers. Eligibility rules for services change frequently and funding levels ebb and flow.

The Role of Church Leaders with Natural Helpers

Church leaders who recognize natural helpers in their congregations and see the value of supporting and enhancing their efforts can serve as a major source of aid and comfort for them. They can help them in at least the following ways.

Spiritual Enrichment

Perhaps the most significant way that churches can support natural helpers is simply to be what the church *is*. We have already noted the important role religion plays in many of their lives. Natural helpers who are members of a congregation may be seeking no more than spiritual renewal when they attend. It is the absence of demands and the opportunity to reflect on spiritual matters that they value in the church. Effective helpers, exhibiting freedom from drain (Collins and Pancoast 1976), do not get burned out by helping others and do not use their helping activities to escape from their own problems or meet their own needs. However, their emotional wells can run dry, too, and they may turn to the church for comfort and personal affirmation.

From time to time, church leaders might want to recognize more explicitly the important contributions natural helpers make. This can send a message to members of the helpers' personal networks, as well as to the helpers themselves, that their efforts are valuable and appreciated. Informal helpers can be encouraged and supported in their ministry, which is just as significant to the life of the church as volunteer ministries such as teaching in church school or serving on church committees. The recognition must be low key, however, respecting the wish of many natural helpers to remain unobtrusive.

Linking Informal Helpers: The Leader as Facilitator

The church setting can offer natural helpers many opportunities to talk with other natural helpers if they choose to do so. A church leader can introduce one helper to another or suggest that a helper contact another member of the congregation about a specific problem. A woman who is informally counseling several troubled teen-age friends of her son may appreciate being able to compare notes with someone else who is involved with teen-agers. In addition to sharing experiences, the natural helpers can inform each other about resources in the community. Sometimes helpers form support groups, but a great deal of effective linking occurs in an unstructured way, if the opportunities are there.

Access to Information and Advice: The Church Leader as Consultant

There will be times when the natural helper feels overwhelmed or puzzled as to where to turn for additional assistance. In other situations, the church leader may sense that the helper is not being effective, even though the helper does not realize this. If the church leader has established a relationship of trust and mutual respect with the natural helper, he or she will be able to offer suggestions of additional resources or approaches which would be outside the experience of the helper. In this way, the problem-solving network can be enriched.

The goal of the church leader should be to increase the competence of the natural helper as well as to solve the immediate problem. Therefore, whenever possible, the church leader should not intervene directly either to solve the problem or to make a referral but, instead, should consult with the natural helper. If the leader is successful, the helper should not have to turn to him or her again when a similar problem presents itself.

While the church leader should always be ready to offer advice or information when it is requested and to create situations where it would be easy and comfortable for a natural helper to ask for assistance, natural helpers should never feel that their activities are being monitored or that they are expected to follow up on any advice or information they may be given. The church leader is in no way a supervisor of their activities. If natural helpers feel that they will be questioned about how a particular piece of advice worked out, or asked to do something they are not comfortable with doing, further requests for assistance will not be forthcoming and the church leader will lose an important link into the network. It is much better for the church leader to show interest and concern by simply being available if and when natural helpers want to report how things are going.

Potential Source of Respite or Substitute Care: The Leader as Program Developer

Natural helpers, key figures in the networks of the congregation, are in an excellent position to identify emerging needs in the church family. While every effort should be made to enhance the effectiveness of the informal helping system, needs and problems will arise with which the informal system cannot cope, either because expertise is required beyond that of the network or because the helpers are forced to step out of the roles in which they are comfortable. In other instances, if helpers could count on occasional respite, they might be able to continue to provide help.

When a problem of this type is identified, an organized response is justified. Todd and Armstrong (1984) describe how a group of natural helpers in a small New England town organized a support group to discuss the problems they encountered in caring for elderly relatives and neighbors. This group eventually became active in securing new senior housing for the town.

The church leader can help develop smooth referral processes, develop more organized programs to meet needs that the informal system is not comfortable with, and find ways to provide relief and respite to overburdened helpers. For example, a support group for widows might be organized to help them share their grief in ways that might not be acceptable in their own personal networks and to widen their circles of acquaintances. Sex or drug-education programs can be organized for teen-agers. Members of the congregation who are caring for elderly parents might develop a list of people who would be willing to come in and provide care on a temporary basis.

What Are the Issues for Church Leaders?

A number of programs have been set up in various parts of the United States and in other countries to offer the sorts of assistance to natural helpers that we have been discussing (Froland et al. 1981; Gottlieb 1983; Whittaker and Garbarino 1983; Pilisuk and Parks 1986). It is likely that most church leaders are involved in such activities, with varying degrees of commitment and conscious awareness, as they go about their daily interactions with members of the congregation. A number of the chapters in this book describe efforts which are at the highly organized end of the continuum. It has been the intention of this chapter to show that much good work can be done to strengthen informal helping networks in less formalized ways, if these networks are understood and appreciated and if the church leader makes the most of the opportunities to enhance them provided by the ordinary contacts of church life.

It is likely that any church leader who does so will encounter some of the same difficulties and challenges as those who have done this kind of work in other settings. We can draw upon their experiences to help anticipate what some of these difficulties might be.

Evaluation

It can be very difficult to evaluate the effectiveness of interventions in the informal system. Just as the work of natural helpers is often unobtrusive, efforts to assist them will also often be subtle. In many cases, if the assistance is skillfully provided, the natural helpers will feel that they solved the problem themselves.

The church leader is likely to have plenty of direct feedback, positive and negative, about the effectiveness of his or her assistance, but more formal evaluations, or even descriptive reports, will be very difficult to produce.

Real Work

Church leaders may be used to being seen as problem-solvers and authority figures. Without even being aware of it, they may expect their interviews with congregation members to be businesslike and problem-focused. In order to establish relationships of trust with key helping figures, the church leader may have to spend time with them in ways that seem more like socializing than work. The church leader cannot force an agenda or a timetable without distorting the relationship. This may be less of a problem in a church context than in some others, such as mental health clinics or human service agencies, but it still may cause some anxiety for a church leader who is insecure about his or her role in the congregation. As the natural helpers come to trust a professional and to learn what sorts of help may be expected, they will become more efficient in using the church leader's time, but a level of informality will always characterize the interactions.

Contacts with many of the helpers will be very rewarding since these people are the proverbial "salt of the earth" and are quite used to making those around them feel welcomed and appreciated. They often like to express this friendly attitude by offering food or small gifts. Again, this may not be as much of a problem in a church context as in some others where taking gifts is suspect or prohibited, but, even so, the church leader may enjoy the natural helpers' company so much that he or she may have some anxiety from time to time about who is benefiting from the relationship—self or helper.

Overformalization

The church leader must constantly resist internal pressures and external suggestions to organize more formal programs and procedures around the informal helping activities. Sometimes this pressure may even come from the helpers themselves, who may think that the church leader wants to organize a program and will go along with it in order to please him or her. We have discussed a number of possibilities for more organized approaches and Ted Bowman has a sensitive and very useful chapter in this volume on the same themes. But in this chapter we continue to stress that the ongoing, less structured support is the bread and butter of effective assistance to natural helpers.

Natural helpers may request training in counseling techniques or personal care skills. Training must be carefully handled or it can have the negative result of making natural helpers feel less confident of their innate abilities. If they compare their usual practices to those the trainer is recommending or those recounted by other members of the class (an activity which is inevitable) and quietly decide that they have been doing things wrong, they may conclude that a more prudent course of action is to back away from giving help or may adopt practices that seem more professional but are less successful because they are artificial. Kenkel (1986) warns that, "a sudden shift in the role or conduct of a central support person can be noticed and felt throughout the community. If natural caregivers associate too closely with mental health professionals, townspeople soon learn of it and become wary of them" (470).

We need more evaluations of various interventions with natural helpers so that we know what will be effective. The reports of two projects show us how much can be learned through experimentation and evaluation. Wolf (1985) describes a project called Elderly Neighbors which recruited, trained, and paid small monthly stipends to older women in a black neighborhood to provide various forms of assistance to their elderly neighbors. "The unintended consequences of the strategy transformed volunteers into workers and neighbors into clients" (Wolf 1985, 424). Eight block workers were trained and employed by the project. Three of them were highly resistant to the attempts of the project staff to professionalize their interactions with their friends and neighbors, to reach out to others on their block whom they did not like or approve of, and to keep records of their contacts. They eventually resigned from the project.

From the description of their helping activities, it would seem that these three block workers fit most closely the definition of natural helpers we have used in this chapter. They had always been involved in helping others. They were part of the project, but had many more contacts and performed many more personal services than the workers who accepted the professionalized role. When they resigned, these workers told the project staff that they would continue to help people, at their discretion, on their own schedule, and without keeping records. There is much to learn from this project and we can hope that others like it will be described as honestly. It appears that the project was not helpful to the natural helpers but that it did no lasting harm. The natural helpers were confident enough about their chosen lifestyle to reject any attempts to change it.

The Elder Support Project described by Todd and Armstrong (1984) seems to have produced more favorable results, including "a higher level of mutual support for caregivers and natural helpers, resulting in greater support for elders, and greater satisfaction and less stress for the helpers; increased collaboration between organized groups serving the elderly; and an increased ability to use and secure additional resources from outside the community" (89). In this project, the natural helpers were not trained or supervised, and there was no expectation that they would change their helping activities. Instead, they were offered the services of a mental health consultant who offered them a variety of forms of assistance, all at their request.

Multiple and Vague Role Demands

As we have seen, meeting the needs of natural helpers calls for a variety of skills from the church leader. In order to identify the natural helpers, the church leader may need the skills of an anthropologist, approaching the congregation as if it were an African tribe or a Norwegian fishing village. Through observing participants, he or she can discover the helping networks and the characteristic styles of giving and receiving help. Then, depending on the particular situation, the church leader may be called upon for counsel regarding mental or physical problems, interpersonal relations, life-stage issues or crisis intervention. Additionally, the church leader may need to make referrals, suggest program development, and use group process skills if a more organized program is called for.

Few of us are likely to be able to perform all of these tasks well. Since we do not want to disappoint the natural helpers, we can feel somewhat anxious about being able to meet the needs of the helpers. A good way to alleviate this anxiety is through a team approach, if possible. In a project in Chicago, professional and paraprofessional workers from a settlement house developed services for natural helpers in a previously unserved neighborhood. Meeting regularly as a group, the workers could support each other in this new enterprise on unfamiliar territory as well as critique each other's work (Morales, Friedlander, and Andrews, n.d.). If it is not possible for church leaders who are assisting the natural helpers to work as part of a team, they should at least arrange to have access to someone with whom they can talk over the work.

Church leaders do not need to feel that they must meet all the needs personally. One of their most important functions is to serve as a link between natural helpers and other parts of the formal service network. This linkage models the usefulness of referral for the natural helper's own network.

Confidentiality and Liability

Two other issues are usually raised when the possibility of offering assistance to natural helpers is first discussed: confidentiality and liability. These issues usually turn out to be much less important in practice than is initially anticipated.

As was mentioned earlier, natural helpers are very sensitive about keeping confidences within their networks. They usually have a fine-tuned sense of who should know what. They will be less sure about what they should tell a church leader and will need some help sorting out what is or is not appropriate. If the church leader learns something from a natural helper that seems serious enough to require professional intervention, it is usually possible to explain that to the natural helper and to take action in a way that does not damage the relationships involved. The issues for the church leader should be similar to those that arise in professional counseling relationships or in other aspects of church life. Again, it is helpful for the church leader to have someone with whom such problems can be discussed.

Legal liability has become a major issue for many forms of professional intervention and has also affected many volunteer activities. Any specific concerns should be discussed with appropriate legal counsel. In general, the more organized the informal helping is, the more it can be seen to be under the sponsorship of the church. The sort of ad hoc assistance to natural helpers that we have been discussing is less likely to raise issues of liability. In any case, the best way to deal with the issue is to have a full discussion of it and to ask for a legal opinion as to the potential implications of any specific activity.

Conclusion

It is paramount for those who work in churches to realize the rich resources for caring that exist within congregations. In particular, natural helpers are the "heavy hitters" in the congregation who act upon their Christian convictions in their daily lives by providing extensive help to members of their networks. The basic teachings of the church provide ample recognition of the value of their activities, but day-to-day practice in the church setting may take these natural helpers for granted and fail to perceive that they have needs for support and enhancement.

The general philosophy of this chapter has been "if it ain't broke, don't fix it." Natural helpers have been validated by their peers as effective helpers. They have a good feeling about what they do and a time-tested appreciation of their limitations. Little is to be gained from attempting to change what they do unless they ask for new ideas. They cannot be expected to meet all the needs of the congregation or even to continue to act as natural helpers if their life circumstances change. We need to know more about how to support them effectively and about how helping patterns differ in different settings. But we need not be too cautious about interacting with natural helpers. They are robust and skillful and will welcome our interest.

References

Beattie, M. 1987. *Codependent no more*. San Francisco: Harper and Row.

Collins, A. H., and D. L. Pancoast. 1976 *Natural helping networks*. New York: National Association of Social Workers.

Froland, C. et al. 1981. *Helping networks and human services*. Beverly Hills: Sage.

Guay, J. 1984. *L'intervenant professionnel face a l'aide naturelle*. Chicoutimi, Quebec: Gaetan Morin Editeur.

Gottlieb, B. H. 1983. *Social support strategies: Guidelines for mental health practice*. Beverly Hills: Sage.

Kelley, P., and V. R. Kelley. 1985. Supporting natural helpers: A cross-cultural study. *Social Casework* (June):358–66.

Kenkel, M. B. 1986. Stress-coping-support in rural communities: A model for primary prevention. *American Journal of Community Psychology* 14(5):457–77.

Morales, J., W. Friedlander, and E. Andrews. n.d. *Neighborhood self-help: A guidebook*. Chicago: Taylor Institute for Policy Studies.

Norton, D., J. Morales, and E. Andrews. 1980. The neighborhood self-help project. Occasional Paper No. 9. Chicago: University of Chicago, School of Social Service Administration.

Patterson, S. L. 1984. The characteristics and helping patterns of older rural natural helpers in the Midwest and in New England (Ph.D. diss., University of Wisconsin-Madison). *Dissertation Abstracts International* 46: (1)A.

Pilisuk, M., and S. H. Parks. 1986. *The healing web: Social networks and human survival*. Hanover, N.H.: University of New England Press.

Todd, D. M., and D. Armstrong. 1984. Support systems of elders in rural communities. *International Journal of Family Therapy* 6(2):82–92.

Whittaker, J. K., and J. Garbarino. 1983. *Social support networks: Informal helping in the human services*. New York: Aldine.

Wolf, J. H. 1985. "Professionalizing" volunteer work in a black neighborhood. *Social Service Review* (September):423–34.

14

Living with Contradictions: Training Natural Helpers for Lay Ministry

Ted Bowman

Lay ministry goes with the territory. That is, the act of choosing to be a member of a church is also a choice for lay ministry. From Paul's image of the church as the body of Christ to affirmations made when joining a church to be a part of that community, expectations abound that church membership involves lay ministry. Beyond that general expectation, however, are many presumptions about the nature of lay ministry. What is required of and what will be offered to lay ministers varies greatly.

Many churches, for example, operate by the principle of naturalism (Vincent 1973), which is a belief that the skills for lay ministry come naturally. These churches require very little or no training for board and committee members, offer no orientation for ushers or greeters, and let people teach in church school without an interview or in-service training. They are relieved and glad just to get somebody to do the job. Furthermore, dedicated people, according to the naturalism principle, naturally do well in their assigned roles or tasks. In most churches, the only consistent exception to the principle of naturalism is the choir. A rehearsal or practice is scheduled each week in order for choir members to be prepared to perform their ministry of music during upcoming worship services. Even for choir, however, a typical attitude is "if you miss the rehearsal, come and sing anyway."

Other churches do require training, especially for specialized lay ministry. Examples include visitation, befriending, family clusters, marriage or family enrichment, parent education, and intergenerational activities. Many churches make training programs available to their members, often providing ongoing support and education for such ministries. These churches operate by the

TED W. BOWMAN, M.Div., is associate director of community care resources of the Amherst H. Wilder Foundation in St. Paul, Minnesota. Additionally, he is a special instructor in home economics education at the University of Minnesota and adjunct faculty member at United Theological Seminary.

principle that laypeople need to be well equipped in order to effectively perform their ministry.

The principle of naturalism and the principle of equipping form a continuum of expectations for lay ministry. In this chapter we will:

- explore the tension inherent in this continuum;
- look carefully at the risks in under-preparation as well as requirements which may inadvertently transform laypersons into paraprofessionals or more;
- present the case that it is prudent to train and supervise those who provide a variety of forms of family ministry; and
- bring examples from training and supervision which show that these supports can be provided in ways that reinforce the natural tools of the helper.

Howard Stone has written that training of laypeople can, "highlight, bless, and strengthen the care already being offered by the laity. Second, it will increase the confidence of those laypeople who desire to care for others but feel themselves lacking in skills or ability" (Stone 1983, viii). He goes on to write that the priesthood of all believers can be put into effective practice by such training.

Lay ministry is clearly not professional ministry. Laypersons are peers to those with whom they minister. As Janice Harris points out, "Sharing from one's own background and experience with others may be a unique dimension of intimacy exhibited by 'lay helpers'" (Harris 1985, 168), and indeed a special bond is formed when someone in transition or stress is befriended by someone "who has been there." Phyllis Silverman suggests that support groups have emerged because of people's need to find others like themselves who have experienced a similar problem (Silverman 1985). The term *mutual help* describes this process, conveying the sense of reciprocity that occurs but also stating clearly the mutuality of the helping that occurs between peers. Lay ministry is peer ministry inasmuch as one or more of the priesthood of believers befriends in some way another of God's priests. But, lay ministry is also something more. "When dedicated laypeople become informal pastors to their neighbors, associates, and . . . church members, they become the church—the body of Christ serving those in need" (Clinebell 1966, 284).

Principles for Training and Supervision

Imagine that you have been asked by your minister to stop by and visit Lori and her children. Lori and her husband, David, have recently separated after a lengthy period of tension, some of which spilled over into the church at times. You recall a coffee hour incident in which Lori and David openly argued about how many cookies one of the children had had. You wanted to do something then but didn't know what to say or do and so did nothing, as did everyone else. Now, you are faced with a request to befriend Lori and the children as she struggles with marital separation and its ripple of emotions and issues.

In order to get someone to volunteer to visit Lori, is an offer of training required? Is training needed? If training is provided, what form should it take? What are some of the underpinnings for quality training of lay ministry volunteers? In the pages that follow, these questions will be addressed by discussing several principles utilized when training and supervising family ministry volunteers:

1. The volunteer's natural helping capacity and skills need to be respected.
2. Empowerment of the layperson is essential.
3. Volunteers are seen as only one of many potential resources in a family's life. Complementary efforts among family/household, formal, and informal helpers are in the best interests of people being helped and of helpers also. It is important for helpers to keep their helping in perspective.
4. Family ministry is best done in a setting where the helper receives ongoing support, consultation, and supervision. Without reinforcement and support, the quality of helping diminishes.
5. Experiential training is the best kind of training. Volunteers should have opportunities to practice their craft.
6. Lay ministry is a mutual helping process; those being helped are not the only beneficiaries. The rewards of volunteering can include gaining insight, receiving support, and other forms of help.
7. The role of the professional is one of supporting, facilitating, advocating, and linking of resources in behalf of or with volunteers.

Examination and elaboration of each of these principles show that living with contradictions—the paradox of training natural helpers—can be a desirable condition. Indeed, it is preferred over all other options. A healthy state of tension between too little and too much training is advisable as a constant reminder to volunteers and volunteer trainers alike.

Respect for Natural Helping

Social work has traditionally employed the principle of starting where the person is. That same approach is a wise and healthy attitude to take when training for lay ministry. The concept of natural helping includes a presumption that those engaged in lay ministry possess helping resources—experiences, attitudes, tools—useful for lay ministry. That, then, is the starting place. Some volunteers may be unaware of their resources, others may be uncertain or ambivalent about applying the ways they do things with friends or family to a client, and still others may be all too eager to "generalize" the use of their methods. The task of the trainer becomes affirming existing resources, discovering hidden resources, and helping refine these resources toward appropriate application. For all these goals, the starting place rests with the volunteer.

Such a perspective is quite in contrast to many training programs which prescribe, manipulate, or mold the volunteer to fit a vision of what helping and the helper is. A training program that employs respect for natural helping will be one that builds on familiar, habitual ways of functioning informally (Collins and Pancoast 1976). This implies that a variety of ways of peer helping or leading a group will be acceptable and expected. Furthermore, the training process will be participant-centered rather than leader-centered. Practicing what is being preached, trainees will build upon their natural abilities rather than simply assimilate input and directives from the leader. This is consistent also with adult education principles of self-direction (Knowles 1975) which assume that adults learn best when they are free to create their own responses to situations, that they learn in their own ways, and that they can learn from one another (Auerbach 1968). Lay ministry can also include children and adolescents; when that is the case, these assumptions will require review for age-appropriate expectations. But most lay ministry is performed by adults. And adult lay ministry is the focus of this chapter. Trainers must look not only at training goals and objectives but also at the audience being trained. An example from training may clarify the point.

Picture a group of people being trained to lead parent support groups. In the midst of the training, someone asks the trainer how to deal with a parent coping with multiple stressors, a parent so overwhelmed that she or he could easily dominate the group. Operating by the intention to affirm existing tools and perspectives, the skilled trainer might turn to the trainees and ask, "What do you think?" In addition, the trainer might aid the group in getting into the shoes of the stressed parent, using role play, for example, for the purpose of examining preferred responses from the participant perspective. Still another way of reinforcing natural helping talent would be to guide a process in which participants start from their past experiences of being overwhelmed, or stressed, using those memories to help them examine choices for this situation. What worked for them then and there? Might that experience be applicable here? If additional information is needed and is not forthcoming through these or other means, then, and only then, would it be offered by the trainer. Support for the natural helping skills of volunteers means that the starting place is with their wisdom and experience, not the leader's.

Empowerment of Laypersons

Empowerment seems to be one of those words whose time has come. Words that get transformed into jargon or are simply overused can lose their vitality and meaning. They become trite. Hopefully, that will not be the case with empowerment. Discretionary use of the word, even efforts to find substitutes, may be in order; but the concept itself needs to be central in working with volunteers. One goal of training is for trainees to feel greater confidence in performing their service after training. The combination of support and affirmation for their own resources and the addition of new information or tools emboldens and empowers the layperson to do his or her task.

While virtually all trainers agree that empowering is crucial, they differ in the integration of the empowering principle into the training process. Many trainers impart information, teach people skills and tools, and provide solid role models. By doing so, they believe that they are empowering those in training, and they are. However, a golden opportunity for further empowerment is missed when the training itself does not embody empowerment. Laypeople frequently leave traditional training wanting to mimic the trainer, only to become disillusioned later because they are unable to match the trainer's skills. Even if volunteers have been advised to add their own unique stamp to their ministry, they will have missed the experience of trying it out in advance of the actual ministry. Self-confidence grows best when practice and feedback are available— personal, specific feedback.

The old adage, *catch somebody doing something right*, certainly applies when training for lay ministry. Many people begin a training experience questioning their ability or their fit for the task awaiting them. If the training experience does not exude empowering affirmation, something very significant will be missing. Yet, while affirmations can be made and have immense power as a caring perspective from another person, affirmation by itself will not empower.

"Empowerment is not something that can be given; it must be taken. What those who have it and want to share it can do is to provide the conditions and the language and belief that make it possible to be taken by those who need it" (Rappaport 1985, 18). The trainer must create opportunities during training in which participants can discover their own power to be helpful, and their abilities to be present with someone at a time of pain or stress, to balance individual needs and group needs as a group facilitator, and to blend their own resources with those of the group in a climate of support and growth. Such empowerment will most likely happen when experiential educational methods are used that allow for self-discovery, the taking of empowerment.

All other forms of empowerment suggest arrogance. When empowerment means only that I have something to bestow upon you or give you, then the mutual is taken out of mutual help. I have become the helper and you the helped. Power rests with me. The presumption on the other hand, that persons have resources no matter how troubled, (see Karpel 1986) unskilled, or new to what they are doing is an empowering affirmation. We start with their natural skills and create opportunities for empowering self-discovery and growth. "People can be empowered without diminishing the power of others" (Swift and Levin 1987, 76). Rather, mutual help involves a transformation of power in which none of the parties loses and some, if not all, gain.

Volunteers and Families in Context:
The Importance of Multiplying Resources

Resourcefulness in leading marriage enrichment groups, befriending a person with a chronic condition, or any other form of family ministry requires more than on-the-spot skills. Indeed, one of the most important services offered may be aiding someone in enhancing his or her support system, in drawing upon community resources, or better utilizing one's own personal resources (Bowman 1988).

Expanded resources should be a goal of virtually all ministry. Better care can be provided by creating links with the rest of society rather than by separating people and care into special compartments. Yet, there is a magnetic pull to think of the support group as *my group*, the person befriended as *my befriendee*, or the workshop participants as *mine* to train or prepare. Such an independent, isolationist spirit ignores several realities, including the helping match.

Matchmaking between participant and provider is a delicate, difficult-to-achieve process. An unfortunate development in some churches occurs when someone gets the idea that "what this congregation needs is support groups" and mistakenly thinks that one group will fit everyone (McMakin and Navy 1988). Registrants to a marriage or family enrichment event, for instance, may want more or less structure than provided, more or less sharing among participants, and more or less homogeneity of participants than is present. Furthermore, the perceived desire and readiness for a particular kind of event may be unrealistic. Couples preoccupied with immediate marital stresses are often unable to pay attention to skills and, hence, are not good "matches" for a couples communication program. They will need to defuse some of the conflict before attempting mastery of skills.

Similarly, one-to-one helpers may not relate easily to all persons. Specific information on informational or promotional brochures about what is and is not being offered will eliminate some mismatches. Nevertheless, referral to a better match may be in order. Lay ministry providers need not possess diagnostic skills in order to do this. Rather, their task is to ascertain the fit of a person for the service/program they are providing. If a mismatch is discovered, other communities, a mental health center, or a minister can aid in finding the appropriate referral place. "Ministry empowerment is served when congregations have a variety of options available to members, including referral" (McMakin and Navy 1988, 10).

Consideration of context requires looking at the family as well as community resources. *Family systems* is the term used by family therapists and others to describe the important interrelationships between a person and his or her family. *Person in situation* and *circles of care* also refer to the social support resources. While in many cases lay ministry is performed with one member of a household or family, many others need to be considered.

Marriage enrichment programs, for example, have traditionally focused attention on the couple relationship. This concentration on one role or relationship parallels personal growth, parent education, and other enrichment programs with their singular audiences. A strong case can be made for maintaining such specialization, but marriage enrichment must take into account the family dimension. A couple relationship does not occur in a vacuum. Marriage is not just to another person; it is into a family. William Oglesby, Jr., writes of pastoral work that takes into account a family context even when working with only one or two of the household or family. "I am constantly aware that those persons (family) are 'in the room'" (Oglesby 1980, 144).

Lay ministry should also consider support systems, those "attachments among individuals or between individuals and groups that serve to improve adaptive competence in dealing with short-term crises and life transitions as well as long-term challenges, stresses and privations" (Caplan 1974, 2). When one has only a limited support system, the tools of the lay minister change significantly. Consider the following training example.

Picture a trainee beginning to feel overwhelmed, imagining many examples of people dealing with stress. "What if . . ." questions are voiced. Others share the concern and ask for assistance in how to and when to refer persons to community resources.

In response, most trainers would probably, then or later, provide information about referral—to the minister or to church-related or community resources—as a way of responding to these expressions. A different response which heightens awareness of a wide range of resources builds on trainee experiences, and provides a teaching opportunity that might go on as follows:

The trainer asks trainees to name possible reasons for referral. The group begins to create a list. In the process, trainees get to name some of their fears and discover that they are not alone. They also become aware of additional situations for which other resources might be beneficial. Then the trainer asks participants to name some of their feelings, should one of these situations occur to them. Marital stress to the point of separation might be an example. Feelings are expressed and discussed. Then the trainees are encouraged to think of resources, personal and otherwise, which they might utilize at such a time. A predictable response would include family members, prayer, special friends, crying, and talking to someone.

The point of such a process is to help trainees expand their ideas of resources beyond themselves or professionals. It helps trainees become aware of the variety of resources that people have, especially one's family and friends. Drawing on their own personal experiences and those of other trainees, they will then be better prepared to think of people and their contexts of care or lack thereof when considering referral.

Resources for families and volunteers are at the heart of under- or overpreparation of volunteers. Training must emphasize the importance of families in context and referral to other resources. On the other hand, there is a danger of providing more information and training than is necessary, thereby professionalizing the volunteer. What has been suggested is a way of highlighting the delicate balance of contextual resources in lay ministry.

Support and Supervision Follows Training

If there is a danger of professionalizing natural helpers by training them, there is an even greater danger after training. In all too many programs, persons are trained well, but then left to their own resources in sustaining their ministry. Without a support group or program coordinator to guide the volunteer, there can be a magnetic pull to the professional side of the continuum of helping. Most of the visible models of helping available for comparison will be professionals. Zeal to be competent in providing service can lead to greater and greater demands for preparation and resources to meet ever-increasing standards.

Support or consultation after training is not there for the sole purpose of continuing education; it is also provided as a time and place of affirmation and support, and of checking to see if the limits and boundaries are still clear. As Frank Wright put it, the agent of healing "isn't to be in the analysis business, to pretend to a professionalism which is superfluous, or to concentrate so much on the wound that the wound becomes the person, and the healer sees a problem and not a person" (Wright 1982, 24). The job description of the lay volunteer is to be a lay volunteer, bringing his or her peer resources to another person. Without some form of continuing support, natural helpers can lose their naturalness.

Training should be provided for lay ministry volunteers, followed by ongoing consultation for the purpose of keeping them clear about their roles. Whether intended for people leading a structured parent-education group or serving as a befriender, the job description at its core is the same—to be a volunteer. However, the same motivation that propels people to be engaged in lay ministry can pull them beyond the scope of the original ministry. Trainees frequently speak of the difficulty of listening before responding; of constraining their desire to change a situation so as not to take over or "fix it"; and of not imposing their own timing for change rather than honoring the timing of the person being helped. This side of helping is rarely discussed. All helpers, professional and lay, need to be alerted to the reality that, "one person's emotional and material investments in the outcome of another's coping efforts can lead to a miscarried helping process" (Coyne, Wortman, and Lehman 1988, 328). "Even when . . . help is solicited and comes with the best of human motives, it may have an unplanned detrimental effect on the helpee" (Brammer 1988, 5). This possibility, more than anything else, makes the case for training and supervising natural helpers.

Family ministry volunteers deserve the back-up support of minister and peers, knowing that they can regularly check in about the ministry they are providing. In many churches, the pastor serves as the sole superviser. While his or her role is critical, the maintenance of the "peer-helping" philosophy suggests that peers carry major responsibility for monitoring each other's work. Shared ownership for the program, rather than only "my part" of it, frequently results when peer supervision is utilized.

Regular meetings of the family ministry volunteers are recommended. In order to maintain the confidentiality of those participating, the focus of the sessions should be on the volunteer and his or her work, not the recipients of the services. In most cases, names or identifying information need not be used. Rather, volunteers discuss their ministries, possible issues or questions, and the help desired from the group. For example:

Picture a supervisory group for family ministry volunteers. The opening and announcements have been completed. The coordinator turns to the group and invites each to give a preview of the issue on which work is wanted in the session. You might hear the following:

"There's a parent in my group who is so opinionated that she dominates the group. I try to interrupt her and encourage other opinions. I've even tried avoiding her. I'm getting frustrated and so is the group. I need your help with this situation."

"I'm befriending an older member of the church who increasingly is unable to take adequate care of herself. I'm finding dirty dishes piled up more often than before. She seems less clean herself. The refrigerator seems emptier. When I have offered to come more often or do more she has put me off. I don't want to step on her pride. Shall I call the Department of Human Services?"

"I'm concerned about the tension that one of the couples in the marriage group exhibiting. They are coming regularly and participating like everyone else. But when they work there is so much tension. The group has tried to support each of them, but the tension is still there. Should we confront them more directly?"

The examples demonstrate how family-ministry volunteers can request help for themselves without identifying participants in a group. Furthermore, the examples demonstrate that the attention is on the volunteer, not the person being helped. Supervision need not include detailed stories about fellow church members or persons from the community. Doing family ministry supervision effectively can require that volunteers daringly examine their ministries, involve themselves in each other's pain, wrestle with their own feelings, and struggle with theological issues (Detwiler-Zapp and Dixon 1982), all for the purpose of retaining their lay ministry role.

The Professional Role

"Professional human service agencies and mutual help groups often have a tense and competitive relationship" (Silverman 1985, 5). The same has been the case for many ministers with respect to laypeople's active involvement in personal and family ministries. "Most pastors see themselves as shepherds who are there to do whatever is needed for their flocks. It follows that, in their minds, they are the ones to do the serving, rather than the ones to train others to serve" (Stone 1983, 7). Such attitudes and behavior, as Detwiler-Zapp and Dixon point out, can be counterproductive. By jumping in, "the pastor can unintentionally inhibit those in crisis from using personal resources, prevent them from calling on available support from family or friends, and increase their feelings of inadequacy. The result is an exhausted helper and a discouraged, dependent person ill-equipped to meet the next crisis. The inclination and ability to act quickly could prevent a pastor from recognizing an opportunity to use the talents, life experiences, and caregiving skills of many church members" (Detwiler-Zapp and Dixon 1982, 10–11). Similarly, if a pastor is unwilling to give up leadership of support groups, retreats, and enrichment events, overload and burnout can result.

The purpose of this section is not to make a case for lay ministry or to describe the resistance of some clergy to active lay ministry. Rather, knowledge of these realities is necessary to adequately discuss the professional role in relation to the training of lay ministers. If lay ministry is to reach its potential, pastors and other professionals must be clear about their roles and responsibilities. And the primary role is one of enhancing and supporting the natural-helping tendencies of laypeople. Even for the church member leading a structured parent-education group— one that utilizes a step-by-step curriculum—the ministry is still a peer ministry. Substantial differences are inherent between peer leadership and leadership provided by a professional family educator, not necessarily in quality, but in the tone that is added by peer leadership. The professional role of the consultant to peer-led services is to affirm and sustain that dimension in the training and ongoing support of the volunteer. The resulting partnership can be beneficial to pastors, volunteers, and recipients of or participants in the services provided. Each brings his or her strengths to the process. As Gottlieb points out, professionals have special expertise that can enhance the helping process (Gottlieb 1988). Matched with the abilities of lay members, a broader, deeper family ministry program can be offered.

There are many vantage points for looking at families and churches. This book gives evidence to those varied perspectives. In this chapter, we have examined one of the points at which we translate our information, experiences, and theology into action. We have seen that training can enhance the quality of family ministries and that it can be done in ways that reinforce the peer dimension of lay ministry. Sophistication in the provision of family ministries need not mean that a very special, personal, peer dimension is lost. Rather, through effective training, lay ministry can be strengthened. The richness of formal and informal services, professional and lay leadership, is a combination that offers much to families and churches. Let both continue in abundance and in quality.

References

Auerbach, A. B. 1968. *Parents learn through discussion*. New York: John Wiley and Sons.

Bowman, T. W. 1988. Musings about group leadership: Referral out of a group. *Family Resource Coalition Report* 3:19.

Brammer, L. M. 1988. *The helping relationship: Process and skills*. Englewood Cliffs, N.J.: Prentice-Hall.

Caplan, G. 1974. *Support system and community mental health*. New York: Behavioral Publications.

Clinebell, H. J. 1966. *Basic types of pastoral counseling*. Nashville: Abingdon.

Collins, A. H., and D. L. Pancoast. 1976. *Natural helping networks: a strategy for prevention*. Washington: National Association of Social Workers, Inc.

Coyne, J. C., C. B. Wortman, and D. R. Lehman. 1988. The other side of support: Emotional overinvolvement and miscarried helping. In *Marshaling Social Support*, ed. B. H. Gottlieb. Newbury Park, Calif.: Sage.

Detwiler-Zapp, D., and W. C. Dixon. 1982. *Lay caregiving*. Philadelphia: Fortress.

Gottlieb, B. H. 1988. Marshaling social support: The state of the art in research and practice. In *Marshaling Social Support*, ed. B. H. Gottlieb. Newbury Park, Calif.: Sage.

Harris, J. 1985. Non-professionals as effective helpers for pastoral counselors. *The Journal of Pastoral Care* 39:165–72.

Karpel, M. A. 1986. *Family resources*. New York: The Guilford Press.

Knowles, M. 1975. *Self-directed learning*. New York: Association Press.

McMakin, J., and R. Navy. 1988. Empowering the ministries of the laity. *Action Information* 14:7–10.

Oglesby, W. B., Jr. 1980. *Biblical themes for pastoral care.* Nashville: Abingdon.

Rappaport, J. 1985. The power of empowerment language. *Social Policy* 16: 15–21.

Silverman, P. 1985. Mutual help groups. *The Harvard Medical School Mental Health Letter* 1:4–6.

Stone, H. W. 1983. *The caring church.* San Francisco: Harper and Row.

Swift, C., and A. Levin. 1987. Empowerment: An emerging mental health technology. *Journal of Primary Prevention* 8:71–94.

Vincent, C. 1973. *Sexual and marital health.* New York: McGraw-Hill.

Wright, F. 1982. *Pastoral care for lay people.* London: SCM Press.

15

Issues for the Future

Diane L. Pancoast and Diana S. Richmond Garland

We have offered this book as a first resource. We were inspired by the exciting programs we saw being developed in churches around the country, encouraged by the response of the participants in the Louisville Conference, and spurred on by the tremendous needs we saw for support, services, and linkages that churches could provide to individuals and families. Even though we knew that better theoretical formulations and better programmatic models certainly lie ahead, we pressed ahead. Some of the ideas put forth in these pages will be new and strange to the readers. Writing for Christians and with an appreciation of Christian values and traditions, we have tried to be ecumenical, not adopting the particular doctrines of any denomination while respecting the efforts of each to provide moral guideposts to their congregations. Many of the perspectives and ideas offered in these pages, we think, will be useful to those in other religious traditions.

Redefining the Family

We have devoted a considerable portion of this book to making the case for a broader definition of the family. The basis of our reconceptualization has been the *ecological family*, a family system defined by shared commitment, obligation, and love developed through ongoing, face-to-face contact with a limited number of significant others, a family system that goes beyond the sociological definition of the nuclear family and blood kinship. This model needs a great deal of further development. Like newly discovered land, there are relationships to be identified, named, measured, and observed over time. We hope that our idea of ecological families is firmly rooted in (1) family forms that have proved their validity by their staying power and (2) a theology that reflects, with little distortion, God's intention for the family as we understand it from Scripture.

We think the church can be a powerful ally to this form of family life. In a way, family relationships *are* the church. If the church is the body of Christ, the human relationships within the congregation and between congregants and others in the community are the circulatory and nervous systems. The way to know God's love is through relationships with others, so family ministry must be central to the mission of the church. If we cannot get that right, we will not be able to perform any of the other missions expected of us. The Good News itself is that God offers to be our parent, and Jesus promises to be our brother if we follow him. When we do, we find ourselves entering a whole new family of brothers and sisters and parents. Even evangelism cannot take place, then, unless persons are embraced in relationships which mirror the family-like love of God through which the spirit of God can work.

Defining Family Ministry

As the notion of the ecological family expands our ideas about meaningful relationships, it can also expand our ideas about programs and activities in family ministry. We have made the point that all members of the congregation are ministers and hence have a role to play in family ministry. It is not the exclusive province of pastors, family life education specialists, or social workers. We have tried to provide many examples of important work that can be done by laypeople, sometimes with some training and guidance from "experts" and sometimes in the course of their daily lives. We have argued that the focus of family ministry should be on affirming and strengthening family relationships—in ecological as well as nuclear families.

Family ministry also has a place at the edges of people's personal social networks, at the boundaries of families and groups. Ecological families can be enriched by reaching out to incorporate new members—elderly persons whose kin may be too far away or too busy to play a role in their daily lives, widows who are searching for new definitions of their roles and responsibilities, children for whom parents are the only meaningful adults. Intergenerational matches can be made, to the enrichment of all participants. Troubled young families can be included in the life of the church. Lonely and isolated people with mental illness can be encouraged to find in the church the sanctuary and caring relationships that will support them in their struggle to live in the community.

Issues for the Future

Preliminary as these ideas are, we are aware that they already raise questions and problems as well as offering answers and solutions. Undoubtedly, other issues will arise as these ideas are developed further and acted upon. For now, the following are some of the concerns that occur to us.

1. Developing ecological families, although perhaps appealing as a concept, is an attempt to swim upstream against a powerful current. Cultural norms about who can constitute a family are strong. We live with a strong myth that friends cannot be family, that blood is thicker than water. "Your friends are always 'other'; your

family is who you are. Friends, in that most demeaning of phrases, are 'just friends'" (Lindsey 1981, 9). Believing this, whether true or not, makes it true and consequently difficult to create family relationships that extend beyond kinship.

Indeed, it may be that people are prone to outgrow their ecological families over time, or at least grow in different directions, finding that they don't have anything in common anymore. However, this also happens in the nuclear family. Some marital relationships become empty and devoid of meaning, and conflicts between parents and their children or between siblings may lead to cut-offs. Even so, parents and siblings, and even exmarital partners (Garland and Garland 1989), continue to be family to one another, to influence one another and shape one another's lives. They are like plants growing in a pot intertwined with one another, continuing to bear one another's shapes long after they have been repotted in separate containers.

Can ecological families ever reach the same depth of involvement, commitment, and influence for their members as we know occurs in the nuclear family? For example, will ecological family members continue to have this lasting impact on one another, even when relationships seem to have been severed? Obviously, we think the answer is yes, but research into these questions is still in the future.

2. Finding ways to encompass ecological families in the life of the church may require changes in doctrines, rituals, procedures, and programs. Change is always difficult. Many people turn to the church for the comfort they find in longstanding beliefs and practices. As many a pastor can testify, any attempt to create even minor changes—a changed format in the bulletin or an altered order of worship—can be fuel for disagreement among church members. An ecological definition of the family, therefore, may not only create difficult tasks; it also may lead to heated conflict within some church communities.

3. Those who feel a strong loyalty to nuclear-family concepts may see the ideas in this volume as a further weakening of the family. We, of course, feel that an ecological perspective builds and strengthens families, including nuclear families. Others may feel, however, that our notion provides an excuse for lightweight commitments or that it equates relationships that are really very different. Although ecological families have existed throughout history, they have often not been named as *family* or been seen as a form just as viable as the nuclear family. They were therefore not an open threat to the nuclear family. The concepts in this book may be construed as such a threat, because we have named these relationships "family" and called for the church to recognize them.

4. If there is a danger that the concept of the ecological family might be repellent, there is also a danger that it might be too attractive. It might encourage congregants to focus exclusively on immediate, interpersonal relationships and pull away from other concerns such as issues of world peace or poverty, personal journeys of faith, or involvement in the maintenance of the church as a community and as an organization. As central as family ministry needs to be in the church, it is not sufficient to serve as a single focus for the work of the church. It is not everything that the church should be about, even though it is a necessary part.

5. Our model asks people to be very tolerant of lifestyles that are different from the ones they choose, to accept diversity, and, perhaps, to extend their own networks. There are probably limits to this tolerance, even with the best of intentions.

6. Not all relationships are enriching; not all networks are supportive. Ecological families, just like nuclear families, can be the source of problems just as they can be beneficial. They can foster autocratic power, the sacrifice of individual perspectives and gifts to a false sense of harmony and uniformity, dangerous dependency and crippling ideologies, isolation from a supportive network of nonfamily relationships, and loneliness in the midst of relationships that are supposed to provide empathy and support.

Simply encouraging the formation and development of ecological family relationships does not ensure that they will be nurturing, supportive, and challenging environments for family members, relationships that mirror well God's nurture, support, and challenge to the family of believers. Ecological family members need to know how to create positive relationships and to value these relationships as means of living out their covenants with God. They also need to have the relational skills to put these values and knowledge into practice. Some families cannot overcome the problems that they create for their members, and ties may need to be severed. This is often very difficult to do in a church community, as many will testify who have experienced marital divorce and have tried to continue to be involved in and receive support from their church communities. In short, ecological families are not a shortcut around the often difficult tasks of family living.

7. Redefining the family from the ecological perspective pushes the church toward a position of advocacy with the myriad of social institutions of our culture, advocacy in behalf of families that are not defined by marriage or blood kinship. Legal barriers have to be confronted. Some communities have legal ordinances restricting the numbers of people who can live together who are not related by legal ties. Some hospitals restrict visiting in intensive care and other wards to those who are "immediate family," meaning nuclear family relations. Often, only parents are able to obtain medical care for their children in nonlife-threatening situations, with varying policies and procedures by which other adults can be authorized to obtain such care. Tax laws specify who can be considered dependents. Of course, not every congregation can or should attempt to tackle the legal and tax structures of our society, but, nevertheless, these issues indicate the significant prophetic role implicit in advocating for an ecological definition of the family. Legal definitions of family relationships, based on legal marriage and blood relatedness, are foundations to our culture. In many respects, an ecological definition of the family is countercultural.

It is our hope that the readers of this book will prod and poke at the ideas offered here, hold them up against the lives and programs they see around them to check for fit, and be inspired to change and expand them. We expect that, ten years from now, this book will seem outdated. We have just begun to be aware of the discrepancy between what the statistics tell us about family living patterns and the models we continue to uphold as ideal or typical. We are groping for new forms of relatedness and expressions of concern that can be developed to fill this emptiness, experimenting with institutional changes and structures that can support new forms of community. The church should be at the vanguard of these efforts, and it is our hope that this book will challenge and stimulate church leaders to contribute to strengthening and enriching family life.

References

Garland, D. S. R., and David E. Garland, 1989. *Marriage for better or for worse*. Nashville: Broadman.

Lindsey, Karen. 1981. *Friends as family*. Boston: Beacon Press.

Appendix 1

Empowering Parent Networks:
A Selected Annotated Bibliography

Boukydis, C. F. Z., ed. 1986. *Support for parents and infants*. New York: Routledge & Kegan Paul.

> Describes how to organize and maintain a parent's support group, their advantages and risks, and how to use parent-professional collaboration. Groups are designed for parents of preterm infants, seriously ill children, and fathers of newborns. Principles can be applied to a broader range of parent groups and networks.

The Children's Defense Fund. 1983. *In celebration of children: An interfaith religious action kit*. Children's Defense Fund, 122 C Street, N.W., Washington, D.C. 20001.

> Provides resources for celebrating children's sabbath, including sermons, children's lessons, and litany. Includes resources for celebrating children in the family, and describes ways to motivate and include the entire faith community in advocacy in behalf of children.

The Children's Defense Fund. 1982. *It's time to stand up for your children: A parent's guide to child advocacy*. Children's Defense Fund, 122 C Street, N.W., Washington, D.C. 20001.

> Describes ways parents can advocate for the needs of children. The CDF also has publications to help parents who are concerned about teen-age pregnancy, adequate child care, and handicapped children.

Family Resource Coalition Report. A report published yearly by the Family Resource Coalition, 230 N. Michigan Ave., Suite 1625, Chicago, IL 60601.

> The Coalition is a national federation of individuals and organizations promoting the development of prevention-oriented, community-based programs to strengthen families, with a particular focus on parents and children. In addition to the *Report*, the Coalition publishes the *FRC Connection* bimonthly; promotes research on family resource programs; operates a national

240

clearinghouse for parenting programs; offers technical assistance on program development; publishes books, reports, and directories; offers a national parent referral service; and advocates in behalf of families. The 1984 issue (No. 2) of the *Report* deals specifically with religious groups and family support.

Cochran, Moncrieff, et al. n.d. *Empowering families: Home visiting and building clusters.* Distribution Center, 7 Research Park, Cornell University, Ithaca, NY 14850.

Describes a model for training personnel (paraprofessionals or volunteer home visitors) to build parent clusters, with the purposes of empowering parents and improving communication between families and people in community organizations who share their care for children. The strength of this program is its working definition of empowerment.

Crane, Jessie. 1986. *A parent guide: About making it through the teen years.* Family Enhancement Program, 605 Spruce Street, Madison, WI 53715.

Describes the Parent Haven program, which provides information and support to parents of teen-agers. The parent guide includes the guidelines of the program and action steps parents can use to help their teen-agers. It also includes information for parents on the topics of truancy, running away, low self-esteem, teen-age sexuality, alcohol and other drugs, legal issues, emotional health, and family violence.

Garland, D. S. R., K. C. Chapman, and J. Pounds. 1990. *Parenting by grace: Self-esteem.* Nashville: The Sunday School Board of the Southern Baptist Convention.

A thirteen-session parent education program for use with a group of parents in a local church. Based on biblical principles of Christian living. Emphasis is communicating with and disciplining children in ways that encourage the development of healthy self-esteem. Two lessons focus on importance of and skills for developing parent networks.

Houghton, E. W. 1986. *Organizing parents into an effective prevention network.* Deerfield, Illinois: Informed Networks Inc., 200 Ramsey Rd., Deerfield, IL 60015.

Describes how to organize and maintain a parents' network to prevent common problems such as alcohol and drug abuse. Is developed for use in schools, but could be adapted to churches and church agencies.

Intensive Care Unlimited, 910 Bent Lane, Philadelphia, PA 19118.

A newsletter for parent support organizations to share information and resources with parents who have children who are premature, high-risk, or have special problems, who are experiencing a high-risk pregnancy, or who have lost a child. A counselor training manual is also available.

Johns, Mary Lee. 1988. *Developing church programs to prevent child abuse.* Austin: Texas Conference of Churches.

Describes four model projects implemented in churches to provide caring ministries to abusive or potentially abusive parents and their children using trained volunteers. The projects include: (1) a parents' warmline, providing phone-in support, parenting information, referral, and lay counseling; (2) a visitation program for parents of newborns, offering support, information and modeling, assistance in locating needed services, and infant-care modeling; (3) an after-school care program for elementary school children of working parents; and (4) a family support program, in which a team of trained volunteers from a church is linked with a family in crisis to provide emotional support, modeling, information, and assistance in securing other needed services. Useful descriptions of program design, development, and evaluation are provided.

Kelker, Katharin A. 1987. *Making the system work: An advocacy workshop for parents*. Families as Allies Project. Regional Research Institute for Human Services. Portland State University, Portland, OR 97207-0751.

A one-day workshop for parents of children with emotional handicaps. The goal of the workshop is to identify the characteristics and skills of an effective advocate for children and youth with emotional handicaps. Excellent role-play situations are provided so that parents can learn and practice advocacy skills.

Levine, Carole, ed. 1988. *Programs to strengthen families: A resource guide*. Chicago: Family Resource Coalition.

Describes seventy-two prevention-oriented, community-based programs designed to strengthen families. Each program's goals, community, services, clients, and outcomes are described, along with suggestions for those developing similar programs. Includes a variety of parent-to-parent approaches, educational plans, and programs designed to link parents with information and resources.

McGinnis, James, ed. 1984. *Partners in peacemaking: Family workshop models. Guidebook for leaders*. Institute for Peace and Justice, 4144 Lindell Blvd. #400, St. Louis, MO 63108.

Provides models for cross-generational learning experiences on the topics of peace and justice. It includes programs for family camps, family weekend seminars in a church facility, a day-long program in a school, afternoon or evening events in a community center, and a series of Sunday potluck programs. Programs for preschoolers are also described.

McGinnis, Kathleen, and James McGinnis, 1981. *Parenting for peace and justice*. Institute for Peace and Justice, 4144 Lindell Blvd. #400, St. Louis, MO 63108.

A description of a group of thirteen families working to make peace and justice an integral part of family life. They describe how they have deepened their own family community in their efforts as Christians to make a difference in the world. A videotape program and other guides are available. The

Parenting for Peace and Justice Network helps parents start and maintain local support groups.

Nickel, Phyllis, and Holly Delany. 1985. *Working with teen parents: A survey of promising approaches.* Chicago: Family Resource Coalition.

Describes drop-in centers, home-centered programs, and pregnancy-prevention programs designed to address the issues and consequences of teen pregnancy. It provides detailed suggestions for professionals wanting to develop and direct such an activity. Appendices provide resources and a directory of services currently available to pregnant and parenting teens and programs designed to prevent teen pregnancy.

Pancoast, Diane L. 1980. Finding and enlisting neighbors to support families. In *Protecting children from abuse and neglect,* eds. Garbarino and Socking, 109–32. San Francisco: Jossey-Bass.

Describes how to locate and consult with natural helpers or central figures who help identify and support families at risk for child maltreatment.

Porter, Fran. n.d. *A design for developing a program for parents of handicapped children.* Omaha: Greater Omaha Association for Retarded Citizens, 3610 Dodge Street, Omaha, NE 68131.

The manual for the Pilot Parent program, this is for parents of children with mental retardation, cerebral palsy, epilepsy, autism, or other developmental disabilities. Trains parents who have successfully coped with their own child's handicaps to reach out to parents whose child has been diagnosed with a similar handicap, offering friendship, understanding of the complex emotions and family dynamics that are created by the handicap, and help in locating and advocating for needed services for the child. Describes the philosophy of the program, how to establish a local group, and how to recruit, train, and match parents.

Sawin, M. M. 1979. *Family enrichment with family clusters.* Valley Forge: Judson.

Describes ways to organize family clusters across generations in a local church. The goal of these groups is to provide mutual support and sharing.

Stepfamily Association of America. 28 Allegheny Ave., Suite 1307, Baltimore, MD 21204.

A national organization with local chapters designed to provide support, education, and social activities for stepfamilies. Available from the Association is a manual for group leaders entitled *Learning to step together: A course for stepfamily adults,* written by Cecile Currier.

York, Phyllis, David York, and Ted Wachtel. 1984. *Toughlove solutions.* Garden City, NY: Doubleday & Co.

Manual for a Toughlove group. Toughlove groups are designed to help parents cope with children, especially adolescents, who are acting in unacceptable ways—using drugs, running away, sexually acting out, abusing others verbally or physically, etc. The groups are self-help in nature; parents help one another develop solutions. Parents may provide alternative shelter for each other's children during family crisis and provide one another with other kinds of back-up support in dealing with one another's children. Concerned relatives are also encouraged to get involved. The goal of Toughlove is to stop hurtful and abusive children from destroying themselves and their families.

Appendix 2

National Organizations for the Widowed: A Selected Annotated Bibliography

The Society of Military Widows (SMW) and *National Association for Uniformed Services* (NAUS). 5535 Hempstead Way, Springfield, VA 22151-4094, (703) 750-1342.

> An independent nonprofit organization that operates for the benefit of widows and widowers of members of all uniformed services of the United States. Their services include legislation, social support through local chapter organizations, membership, political education, special counseling services, medical assistance information, and public relations. They have chapters in Arizona, California, Colorado, District of Columbia, Florida, Hawaii, Kansas, Maryland, New York, Oklahoma, South Carolina, Texas, and Washington. Military widows are needed in other states to form chapters.

Survivors of Suicide, Suicide Prevention Center, Inc. P.O. Box 1393, Dayton, OH 45401-1393, (513) 223-9096.

> This center has developed a variety of educational print, visual, and audio resources for suicide prevention and families of suicide victims, including an excellent booklet entitled, *The Care of the Suicide Survivor: A Guide for Professionals.*

Stephen Ministries. 1325 Boland, St. Louis, MO 63117, (314) 645-5511.

> The Stephen Series is a complete system of training and organizing laypersons for caring ministry in and around their congregations. Although its training is much broader than ministering to widowed persons, there is specific help for ministering to the widowed population. The Stephen Series is proven, organized, adaptable, transdenominational, easy to understand (but in-depth), effective, complete, and distinctively Christian.

Widowed Persons Service (WPS). 1909 K St., N.W., Washington, DC 20049, (202) 872-4700.

Sponsored by the American Association of Retired Persons, WPS is designed to provide support to widows and widowers of all ages. A coalition of community groups offers a variety of services that include telephone contact, referral service discussion groups, and community education. No fees are charged for the service.

Appendix 3
Additional Resources for Cross-Age Programs

INFORMATION CLEARINGHOUSES

Several centers have been founded in the past few years to disseminate information about cross-age programing. They publish newsletters, maintain collections of audio- and videotapes and other program materials, and help to connect persons interested in developing programs.

Children of Aging Parents. 2761 Trenton Road, Levittown, PA 19056.
The CAPSule **(newsletter).**

> CAPS is a national organization that helps develop support groups for children of aging parents. It provides published materials and other media as well as information and referral services. *The CAPSule* newsletter contains articles that "address concerns of caregivers, financial information, emotional issues, national resources, support groups."

Generations Together. University Center for Social and Urban Research. University of Pittsburgh, 811 William Pitt Union, Pittsburgh, PA 15260. *Exchange* **(newsletter).**

> "A newsletter exchanging information on intergenerational programs." It contains articles on social issues such as the older worker, intergenerational child care; legislative updates, book reviews, ongoing intergenerational programs, and research update.

RSVP of Dane County, Inc., 540 W. Olin Avenue, Madison, WI 53715. Intergenerational Clearinghouse Newsletter.

> This newsletter which is published by the Retired Senior Volunteer Program of Dane County, Inc., has a wide circulation on a national scale. Readers are invited to submit articles and/or information on their intergenerational programs. Each issue is full of inspiring ideas for programs of all sizes, in all places. Some examples include: RSVP volunteers receiving training to use an alcohol substance-abuse prevention program with young

children in preschools, and an apprenticeship program linking seniors and seventh graders in an opportunity for hands-on learning and intergenerational interaction.

PROGRAM GUIDES

Some excellent guides to intergenerational programs have been published by national organizations for the elderly.

The Beverly Foundation. 1984. *A Time and Place for Sharing: A Practical Guide for Developing Intergenerational Programs*. The Beverly Foundation, 99 South Oakland Ave., Suite 227, Pasadena, CA 91101.

This book is designed for nursing home and senior center activity directors, classroom teachers, scouting and other youth leaders, civic and religious group leaders, and other interested persons. It presents an outline with explanation on how to organize cross-age programs in a variety of settings. The appendix contains a lengthy annotated bibliography of children's books dealing with an intergenerational theme. In addition, there is an equally lengthy reference section of books for adults about aging as well as audiovisual resources. Sample lesson plans and ideas for cross-age activities are also included.

Ventura-Merkel, C. and L. Lidoff. 1983. *Program Innovations in Aging: Volume VIII, Community Planning for Intergenerational Programming*. National Council on the Aging, Inc., 600 Maryland Ave. S.W., West Wing 100, Washington, DC 20024.

This is a clear-cut "how to" book. The contents include: an introduction to their model and its use; planning steps; organizing steps; implementation steps; words of advice from the experts; resources on intergenerational programming and general references on program development and funding. This would be a good resource for a church or organization planning to apply for funding through grants.

MODEL PROGRAMS

Several programs have described their activities in sufficient detail to serve as handbooks for anyone who might want to start a similar program.

Allen, J. 1988. "Roots 'n' Shoots." *National Gardening* 11:58–60.

The Roots 'n' Shoots project paired senior volunteers with third graders with the stated purpose "to create a project that would involve all age groups and give older and younger generations more access to one another." The project received a grant and an award from the National Gardening Association. The students were paired up with garden grandparents at a ratio of about 1:2 or 3 for a one-and-a-half-hour lesson in gardening. They planted and harvested all year, and in December they had a class harvest party featuring foods from the garden. The gardens were cared for in the summer by the seniors. The pumpkins planted in the spring by the outgoing class were the first things harvested by the incoming class. The seniors received training for this program, and the activities were carefully planned and sequenced. At a typical session, seniors might read a garden story to the children, describe the history of a particular vegetable, or discuss botanical topics, like the parts of a plant.

American Association of Retired Persons. 1909 K Street N.W., Washington, DC 20049. *Books About Aging Are Time Machines: AARP Book Purchase Project.*

The Book Purchase Project, in existence since 1977, ". . . selects books with a meaningful message about old age and buys them for local secondary school and community libraries. Working with high school students, librarians, teachers, and others in the community, [AARP members] can make another important contribution, . . . sparking activities to encourage teenagers and others to read the books—and travel the generations."

Kaplan, B. H., M. D., et al. n.d. PROJECT LINC: *A Model for Building Intergenerational Neighborhood-based Networks.* PROJECT LINC, 5000 Colfax, N. Hollywood, CA 91601.

This manual describes Project LINC which is designed to help older people and their caregivers by organizing neighbors of all ages into helping networks and linking these networks to community agencies for access to additional resources. In this project, there were over 450 participants, ranging in age from 20 years to 93 years who exchanged services in excess of 2,045 times in the implementation phase of the project. "Evaluation of the project revealed that older persons were provided with needed services, acted as volunteers, developed new friendships, participated in more social activities, and increased their life satisfaction as a result of their involvement. Younger persons reached out to the frail elderly in their neighborhoods, and in the process, better met their own needs for specific services and a sense of 'belonging.'"

Murphy, M. B. 1984. *A Guide to Intergenerational Programs.* National Association of State Units on Aging, 600 Maryland Ave. S.W., West Wing, #208, Washington, DC 20024.

This project, which compiles information on the content, impact, and characteristics of intergenerational programs in place across America, is a source of ideas, models of sound practice, sources, and resources. The categories of programs include: child care; elementary and secondary education; higher education; vulnerable youth; political action and community planning; arts, humanities, and enrichment; home sharing; grandparenting; chore services and employment; and informal family and community supports. Each category is treated with an overview, description of programs, and sources and resources.

Struntz, K. A., and S. Reville, eds. 1985. *Growing Together: An Intergenerational Sourcebook*. Washington, D.C.: American Association of Retired Persons, and Palm Springs, Calif.: the Elvirita Lewis Foundation.

This book is a rich blend of research, commentaries, program descriptions, resource lists, and bibliographies. A church or other organization that is considering developing cross-generational programs would find this book extremely helpful in the brainstorming and data-gathering stages of planning. Some of the titles of the articles are: "Survey Research as the Initial Step in Developing Intergenerational Projects"; "The Impact of Intergenerational Programs on Children's Growth and Older Persons' Life Satisfaction"; "Becoming a Better Grandparent"; and "New Home for Our Family: Building an Intergenerational Day Care Center."

OTHER MATERIALS

HOST-Hands of Shared Time, 3438 Olney-Laytonsville Road, Olney, MD 20832.

This interfaith, intergenerational volunteer project is designed to provide supportive services for isolated older adults in their homes or in nursing homes. Provides some information about volunteer intergenerational programs.

Institute for Health and Aging, University of California, Resource Center, Room N531, San Francisco, CA 94143-0612. "Selected Publications of the Institute Faculty and Staff" and "Books and Monographs."

The institute is an organized, multidisciplinary, research unit of the University, whose faculty conduct research on issues of aging and health. Their publications are designed to provide the knowledge and understanding basic to improving the health and social conditions of an aging population.

Kaplan, R. J. 1965. Brooklyn School Program. In *First National Conference of Senior Centers*, ed. E. Lindey. New York: The National Council on the Aging.

This program was done through the Council Center for Senior Citizens, a project of the Brooklyn Section of the National Council of Jewish Women. Senior citizens became involved in the neighborhood elementary school, doing such things as the maintenance and repair of library books, publication of the school newspaper, gardening and telling personal histories to the sixth-grade class in a project called "Living History."

Kingson, E. R., B. A. Hirshorn, and L. K. Harootyan. n.d. *The Common Stake: The Interdependence of Generations: A Policy Framework for an Aging Society*. The Gerontological Society of America, 1411 K Street NW, Washington, DC 20005.

This paper summarizes two major approaches to an aging society. One is based on misunderstandings about competition and conflict between young and old over the distribution of scarce resources. The other approach "recognizes that the reciprocity of giving and receiving among individuals and generations over time is critical to social progress. Finding the aging of the population both a success and a challenge, it asks how generations can work together to meet the needs of people across the life course."

Mayer, Hans. 1966. Intergenerational Programming. In *Third National Conference of Senior Centers*, ed. R. Eckstein. New York: The National Council on Aging.

The St. Louis Jewish Community Centers Association began to work with seniors to develop intergenerational programming so the younger participants could "clearly identify the role of the older person in a wholesome, productive, and natural fashion. . . ." The Association wanted to establish "meaningful communications between the generations, whether that be via dialogue, active participation, or by creating opportunities for a positive awareness." One of the activities started was a four-generation Chanukah Party.

ONE TO ONE: The Generation Connection. Terra Nova Films, Inc. 9848 S. Winchester Ave., Chicago, IL 60643. Video (24 minutes).

This film is an exploration of face-to-face intergenerational contact between a group of sixteen- to eighteen-year-olds and a group of seventy- to eighty-year-olds. They explore issues such as the generation gap, self-esteem, goal setting, family issues, death, and the aging process. "The video enables us to see the wisdom and individuality of older adults, and also reveals the perceptions, fears, and potential of young adults." The video, which won a 1988 National Educational Film Festival award, comes with a fifteen-page viewer's guide.

Pratt, Fran. 1984. Teaching Today's Kids—Tomorrow's Elders. *Aging* 346:19–26.

Pratt describes intergenerational programming that is combined with new curricula on aging. The purposes for designing curricula to accompany cross-age programs include: to dismantle myths about aging, counter misinformation, and fight the problems of ageism and gerontophobia (fear of aging and the aged). Older volunteers are recruited for service in classrooms as teacher aids, tutors, colearners, demonstrators of crafts, oral history resources, and guest speakers. Numerous organizations run these programs, such as: Foster Grandparents, Retired Senior Volunteer Program (R.S.V.P.), A.A.R.P., and National Retired Teachers Association.

Thune, J. M. 1967. "Adding Dimensions to Practice: Older Adults and Children—A Service Oriented Relationship." In *Fourth National Conference of Senior Centers*, ed. R. Eckstein. New York: The National Council on the Aging.

This article describes some early attempts at intergenerational programing, including the precursor to the Foster Grandparents Program. It gives some examples of simple programs that had positive results and showed that the natural combination of a grandparent and a child is a winning combination in the field of community services.

Walls, N. 1987. "Three Generations of Love." *Aging* **355:2–5.**

This article describes three in-school teen parenting programs utilizing fifteen foster grandparents. Each is assigned to two children who need special attention. Their presence, dependability, and reliability created a good role model for the teens and created a sense of family.

Index